MAPPING

Michel Serres

Studies in Literature and Science
published in association with the
Society for Literature and Science

Editorial Board

Titles in the series

MAPPING
Michel Serres

Edited by Niran Abbas

THE UNIVERSITY OF MICHIGAN PRESS
Ann Arbor

Copyright © by the University of Michigan 2005
All rights reserved
Published in the United States of America by
The University of Michigan Press
Manufactured in the United States of America
⊗ Printed on acid-free paper

2008   2007   2006   2005   4   3   2   1

A CIP catalog record for this book is available from the British Library.

Library of Congress Cataloging-in-Publication Data

Mapping Michel Serres / edited by Niran Abbas.
    p.   cm.
  Includes index.
    ISBN 0-472-11438-7 (cloth : alk. paper) — ISBN 0-472-03059-0
(pbk. : alk.   paper)
    1. Science—Philosophy.   2. Serres, Michel.
I. Abbas, Niran, 1969–   II. Title.

Q175.M347   2005
501—dc22   2004020270

ACKNOWLEDGMENTS

First and foremost I would like to thank Steven Connor for his expertise and invaluable help on this project and for his idea for the conference on Michel Serres from which many of the essays in this volume originated. Thanks also to Ana Parejo Vadillo for co-organizing the event.

I would like to thank all the contributors for their support and enthusiasm. Special thanks to Marcel Hénaff, René Girard, and Marjorie Perloff and to their publishers for allowing me to reprint their essays in this collection: "Of Stones, Angels, and Humans: Michel Serres and the Global City," by Marcel Hénaff, *SubStance* 83, Vol. 26, No. 2. © 1997. Reprinted by permission of the University of Wisconsin Press. "From Ritual to Science," by René Girard. *Configurations* 8:2 (2000), 171–85. © The Johns Hopkins University Press and Society for Literature and Science. Reprinted with permission of The Johns Hopkins University Press. "'Multiple Pleats': Some Applications of Michel Serres's Poetics," by Marjorie Perloff. *Configurations* 8:2 (2000), 187–200. © The Johns Hopkins University Press and Society for Literature and Science. Reprinted with permission of The Johns Hopkins University Press.

Thanks go to LeAnn Fields, Allison Liefer, Marcia LaBrenz, and the editorial team at the University of Michigan Press. And finally I would like to thank my friends and family for their encouragement and support.

CONTENTS

ABBREVIATIONS

A   *Atlas*. Paris Éditions Juillard, 1994.

AM   *Angels: A Modern Myth*. Trans. Francis Cowper. Paris: Flammarion, 1994.

B   *The Birth of Physics*. Ed. David Webb. Trans. Jack Hawkes. Manchester: Clinamen Press, 2000.

C   With Bruno Latour. *Conversations on Science, Culture, and Time*. Trans. Roxanne Lapidus. Ann Arbor: University of Michigan Press, 1995.

CS   *Les Cinq Sens*. Paris: Grasset et Fasquelle, 1985.

E   *Éclaircissements: Entretiens avec Bruno Latour*. Paris: Éditions François Bourin, 1992.

EF   *Eloge de la philosophie en langue française*, Paris: Fayard, 1996.

G   *Genesis*. Trans. Geneviève James and James Nielson. Ann Arbor: University of Michigan Press, 1995.

H   *Hermes: Literature, Science, Philosophy*. Ed. Josué V. Harari and David Bell. Baltimore: Johns Hopkins University Press, 1982.

J   *Jouvences sur Jules Verne*. Paris: Minuit, 1974.

LC   *Hermès I: La Communication*. Paris: Minuit, 1969.

LD   *Hermès IV: La Distribution*. Paris: Minuit, 1977.

LH   *L'Hermaphrodite: Sarrasine sculpteur*. Paris: Flammarion, 1987.

LI   *Hermès II: L'Interférence*. Paris: Minuit, 1972.

LT   *Hermès III: La Traduction*. Paris: Minuit, 1974.

N   *La Naissance de la physique dans le texte de Lucrèce: Fleuves et turbulences*. Paris: Minuit, 1977.

NC   *The Natural Contract*. Trans. Elizabeth MacArthur and William Paulson. Ann Arbor: University of Michigan Press, 1995.

P   *The Parasite*. Trans. Lawrence R. Schehr. Baltimore: Johns Hopkins University Press, 1982.

R   *Rome: Le livre des fondations*. Paris: Grasset, 1983.

TK   *The Troubadour of Knowledge.* Trans. Sheila Faria Glaser with William
      Paulson. Ann Arbor: University of Michigan Press, 1997.
Z   *Feux et signaux de brume: Zola.* Paris: Grasset, 1975.

INTRODUCTION

NIRAN ABBAS

> *When one looks at a certain object only as representing another, the idea one has of it is a sign.*
>
> —*Antoine Arnauld,*
> Logique de Port-Royal, 1872

To map is to take the measure of a world in such a way that the measure may be communicated between people, places, or times. The measure of mapping is not restricted to the mathematical; it may equally be spiritual, political, or moral. Acts of mapping are creative, sometimes anxious, moments in coming to knowledge of the world, and the map is both the spatial embodiment of knowledge and a stimulus to further cognitive engagements. This is how I read the philosopher and writer Michel Serres, as a nomadic, exploratory mapmaker and storyteller who engages with what remains hidden. Mapping is neither secondary nor representational, but doubly operative: digging, finding, and exposing on the one hand, and relating, connecting, and structuring on the other. For Michel Serres, the philosopher's role is not to develop an ontology or epistemology. Knowledge is not about *something;* rather it is *how* ideas and concepts interact.[1]

The surface of the map functions like an operating table, a staging ground or a theater of operations upon which the mapper collects, combines, connects, marks, masks, relates, and generally explores. The analogous-abstract character of the map surface means that it is doubly projective; it both captures the projected elements off the ground and projects back a variety of effects through use.

The essays in this book embrace the concept of mapping as an active agent in Serres's work. The contributors underline the various processes and effects of what mapping *means,* but also what mapping *does.* The concept of mapping's most productive effects provide a finding that is also a founding; its agency lies in neither reproduction nor imposition but rather in uncovering realities previously unseen or unimagined. William Paulson asks, "Do speakers strive to put prelinguistic ideas in words, or do ideas arise out of words in the mind?"[2] Mapping, like the prelinguistic, *unfolds* potential; it remakes territory with new and diverse consequences each time. Steven Connor observes in this collection that Serres rewrites the map of inner and outer, self and not-self on the surface of our skins, invoking a gymnastic condition (i.e., a condition of being active, in constant motion). *The senses are like countries on a map, a topography that is tactile.* The senses become a Serresean *quasiobject,* not entirely an *object* nor a relational phenomenon, but indicates of possibility.[3]

> This quasi-object that is a marker of the subject is an astonishing constructer of intersubjectivity. We know, through it, how and when we are subjects and when and how we are no longer subjects. "We": what does that we mean? We are precisely the fluctuating moving back and forth of the "I." The "I" in the game is a token exchanged. And this passing, this network of passes, these vicariances of subjects weave the collection. (*P*, 227)

As Steven D. Brown points out, "We become subjects through the way in which we are caught up in the circulation of that which will make us 'it'— the moving back and forth of the 'I.'" Humans, Serres claims, are distinctive because they make things into objects that act as stabilizers of social relations (e.g., the plate stabilizes eating arrangements, the weapon formalizes conflict). We owe our present sociality to this invention of the object:

> Our relationships, social bonds, would be as airy as clouds were there only contracts between subjects. In fact, the object, specific to Hominidae, stabilizes our relationships, it slows down the time of our revolutions. For an unstable bond of baboons, social changes are flaring up every minute. One could characterize their history as unbound, insanely so. The object makes our history slow. (*G*, 87)

Michel Serres's storytelling of history takes us back to ancient Rome, Maupassant's tales, Turner's landscapes, and Hiroshima in various guises—"Hermes," "Parasite," "Harlequin," "Multiple," among others. Storytelling is a form of recollection and a way of reconciling ourselves to the past—a way of knowing who and what we are in relation to the world. Hence story and history imbricate each other. The world we understand is a written world—a plurality, a multiplicity of narratives. Between the particularly of one's natality and the plurality of the world lies the story: the mastering of a moment of the past, for a moment. In Lacanian language, the storyteller becomes *le sujet suppose savoir,* the subject (who is) supposed to know—only for the duration of the story.

Serres tells his stories through channels, or what he calls passages, that connect motifs. "The global wandering, the mythical adventure or target of discourse were only to connect, or as if the junction, the relation, constituted the route by which the first discourse passes" (*H,* 49). The "nomadic theorist" appellation that Paul Harris applies to Serres produces theoretical itineraries, in the triple sense of the word: a route, a record of a journey, and a guidebook. He seeks through these itineraries to weave the fabric of knowledge into a "pattern that connects humans and the world."[4]

Maps fall between the virtual and the real. Maps permit an excavation (downward) and extension (outward) to expose, reveal, and construct latent possibilities within a greater milieu. The map "gathers" and "shows" things presently (and always) invisible, things that may appear incongruous or untimely but that may also harbor potential for the unfolding of alternative events.

Topology is the discourse or means that Serres provides us with which to map out a generalized space of relationships. Serres likes to draw a contrast between topology, "the science of nearness and rifts," and metrical geometry, "the science of stable and well-defined distances" (*C,* 60). "Topology thus provides a kind of syntax and vocabulary for figuring abstract relationships between terms in the nodes and passages of the 'inter-information network.'"[5] The difference, as Hanjo Berressem discusses, is between an attempt to dominate and efface space and the careful exploration of tangled relationships that exist between specific locales that are continually within a Lucretian meditation of laminar flux and Brownian melee—a place that Maria Assad in her essays aligns with feminine silence and exclusion.

This fluidity creates passages within Serres's texts that lead to a progression based on iteration: Acting as narrative background, the metaphoric chains form a feedback mechanism by which an insight once attained becomes a metaphoric input for the next argument, which, in turn, deploys its metaphoric power to produce yet another insight, and so on. This may sound like the worst kind of postmodern carnivalesque, but Serres's border crossings are always structured. Serres's writing, according to Bruno Latour's apt metaphor, enacts "a *crossover,* in attributes of another origin."[6] In a typical crossover—or, as Andrew Gibson discusses, where the moment of crisis and decision takes place—Serres treats Lucretius's poem as a physics treatise that announces a "creative science of change and circumstance," which in turn "breaks the chains of violence, interrupts the reign of the same" that characterizes the ethos of modern science (*H,* 100). Serres suggests that what happens *between* rather than *at* points is the source of complexity. Lucretius provides at the first step in relation to nature and science that human knowledge makes man the other of nature, and science becomes a matter of inventing and deploying strategies for winning; in the second, our knowledge is knowledge of our sameness, of the intimate involvement (biological, intellectual, social, and political) of the human in a world of flow, clinamen (Lucretius's swerve of atoms that brings the world into being), and turbulence; and the relationship with nature involves the social contract of which Lucretius speaks.

Crossroads are charged spaces. Crossroads create what the anthropologist Victor Turner calls "liminal zones," ambiguous but potent spaces of transformation and threat at the edge of cultural maps.[7] "Through Hermes," the mythographer Karl Kerényi writes, "every house becomes an opening and a point of departure to the paths that come from far off and lead away into the distance."[8] In his study *Hermes the Thief,* Norman O. Brown points out that the liminal quality of the crossroads also derives from the more mundane traffic of trade. The exchange of goods often took place at crossroads and village borders; these swaps were fraught with ambiguity, for they blurred the distinction between gift, barter, magic, and theft. As commercial networks of the Greek city-states developed, this economic border zone eventually shifted from the wild edges of the village into the more organized markets at the heart of the new urban centers. The outside was swallowed within. Hermes became *agorios,* "he of the agora," the patron saint of merchants, middlemen, while the god's epithet *tricky* came to mean "good for securing profit."[9]

Within Serres's work the concept of crossroads has never been that of a simple geometrically defined "parcel of land," but a much larger and more active milieu.[10] Marcel Hénaff notes in his essay that power in ancient civilizations was concentrated in one spot, and thus the idea of monumentality has become obsolete. "It does not matter where the storage sites are since our networks connect them; they might as well be just as much dispersed as the stations that exchange information" (*A,* 152–53). Milieu has neither beginning nor end, but is surrounded by other middles, in a field of connections, relationships, extensions, and potentials. In this sense, then, a grounded site invokes a host of "other" places. A "site" today is a multiplicitous and complex affair, comprising a potentially boundless field of phenomena, some palpable and some imaginary. Connor's essay observes that "the body is the site of the nonsite: a teeming plurality that overruns and overrules every vicious and narrow dichotomy . . . Serres celebrates the unraveling and reknitting of the body." In making visible what is otherwise hidden and inaccessible, the contributors to this volume provide a map, a working table for identifying and reworking polyvalent conditions; their analogous-abstract surfaces enable accumulation, organization, and restructuring of the strata that comprise an ever-emerging milieu.

A particularly important aspect of mapping in this regard is the acknowledgment of the maker's own participation and engagement with the cartographic process. The situationist theorist Guy Debord made a series of maps, or "psycho-geographic guides," of Paris. These were constructed after Debord had walked aimlessly around the streets and alleys of the city. Recording these wanderings, Debord cut up and reconfigured a standard Paris map as a series of turns and detours. The resultant map reflected subjective, street-level desires and perceptions rather than a synoptic totality of the city's fabric. A form of cognitive mapping rather than a mimetic description of the cityscape, Debord's maps located his own play and representation within the recessive nooks and crannies of everyday life. Such activity became known later as the *dérive,* the dreamlike drifting through the rifts of the city, mapping alternative itineraries and subverting dominant readings and authoritarian regimes.[11]

What is interesting about the *dérive* is the way in which the contigent, the ephemeral, the vague, fugitive eventfulness of spatial experience becomes foregrounded in place of the dominant, ocular gaze. Marcel Hénaff's essay remarks on Serres's wonder at

> the Paris of Balzac or Zola, the furnace-city imbued with the representations of thermodynamics, Musil's Vienna, which is contemporary with Boltzman, the city of the Brownian movement of characters and events; finally, all the cities visited by angels, those ancient and modern figures of messages and relations that outline a virtual space as the global site of our experience. This is precisely what interests Serres, and not what he ironically calls a return to "farm ontologies."

As Hénaff notes, something is happening on multiple levels in Serres's work. The mapping precedes the map, to the degree that it cannot properly anticipate its final form. Arthur Robinson and Barbara Petchenik claim that "in mapping, one objective is to discover (by seeing) meaningful physical and intellectual shape organizations in the *milieu,* structures that are likely to remain hidden until they have been mapped . . . plotting out or mapping is a method for searching for such meaningful designs."[12] In other words, some phenomena can achieve visibility only through representation, not through direct experience. Furthermore, mapping engenders new and meaningful relationships among otherwise disparate parts. The resultant relational structure is not something already "out there," but rather something constructed, bodied forth through the act of mapping. The philosopher Brand Blanshard observes that "space is simply a relation of systematized outsideness, but itself neither sensible nor imaginable";[13] it is *created* in the process of mapping.

Serres maps with what Harris points out are "operators" (tropes or characters) that are extracted from one discourse and used to labor in other fields. Serres's interest is not fixed identities, but possible transformations. According to Paulson, these are the figures that help Michel Serres think.

> I have at my disposal operators taken from naïve symbols, operators at work upon something unspoken (at least by philosophy), namely the accidents or catastrophes of space, and at work upon the multiplicity of spatial varieties. What is closed? What is open? What is a connective path? What is a tear? What are the continuous and the discontinuous? What is a threshold, a limit? The elementary program of topology. (*H*, 44)

Multilayered articulations of concept and connotation run through his choice of words and the structure of his sentences. Every place in the text is truly a place. What matters most is not a single line of argument running through a book (though strong and coherent argument there is) but rather the connections made through continuous interwoven "digressions" that turn out to be the very texture of the writing and thought.[14]

When these separate layers are overlaid, a stratified amalgam of relationships among parts appears. The resulting structure is a complex fabric, without center, hierarchy, or single organizing principle. The composite field is instead one of multiple elements, cohesive at one layer but disjunct in relation to others. This produces, as Philipp Schweighauser's essays points out, a mosaic of multiple interpretations, transformations, and open-ended rhizomatic orders that confound any sense of unity.

Serres speaks about the spaces of communication sparked by rediscoveries of previous discoveries. According to René Girard, "an endless wheel of deaths and resurrections" plunges mathematics like the wisdom of the *ouroboros* into its own past, from which it reemerges when old discoveries are reformulated to become new theoretical configurations. Serres's work fits perfectly with a Dymaxion mapping structure[15] that can be folded and reoriented in any number of different ways, depending on the thematics of one's point of view. The polyhedral geometry provides a remarkably flexible and adaptive system wherein different locations and regions can be placed into significantly different sets of relationship. Precisely where the map is cut and folded determines how the parts are seen in relationship to each other. Each arrangement possesses efficacy with regard to certain sociopolitical, strategic, and imaginative possibilities.

Unlike the scientific objectivism that guides most modern cartographers, artists have been conscious of the essentially fictional status of maps and the power they possess for construing and constructing worlds. The Dymaxion map is perhaps one of the few modern instances where singular orientation is not a prerequisite. Maps of this sort are still legible and "correct" in their depiction of spatial relationship, but the reader must first learn the relevant mapping codes and conventions.

Thus we can identify three essential operations in mapping out Serres's work; first, the creation of a field, the setting of rules, and the establishment of a system (the foundation); second, the extraction, isolation, or "deterritorialization" of parts and data (multiplicities); and third, the plotting, drawing out, setting up of relationships, or the "reterritorialization" of parts, local and global.

One does not read Michel Serres for answers, for certainties, or for conclusions, but perhaps for questions and suggestions. His manner has parataxis at its heart. As Denis Cosgrove states, maps are intensely familiar, naturalized but not natural, "objects working within a modern society of high if uneven cartographic literacy. They are also troubling."[16] Their apparent stability and their aesthetics of closure and finality dissolve with a little reflection on their partiality and provisionality, their embodiment of intention, their imaginative and creative capacities, their mythical qualities, their appeal to reverie, their ability to record and stimulate anxiety, their silences and their powers of deception. At the same time their spaces of representation can appear liberating, their dimensionality freeing the Serresean reader from the controlling linearity of narrative description.

Yet the poetic universe of Michel Serres, as Marjorie Perloff shows, is not a world without order; but in it order is the product of more or less accidental "eddies" occurring in the disorderly flow of cosmic energy, never-ceasing interaction of entropy and negentropy, information and noise. A text by Serres is just such an "eddy of words, a small informational island formed by order but undermined by a prevailing disorder that tugs at its structure, so that in its relative cohesion and relative evanescence it is like the proverbial cookie that crumbles, it has the texture of a cloud" (*H*)

Attempting to impose an order to Serres, some conception of what the "essential" Serres is about, one becomes aware of what his work teaches us to expect: that ordering is a falsification of the real, which has disorder as its fundamental and prevailing feature, and that, consequently, there is no ordering without violence, exclusion, injustice, and sacrifice. The residue—what ordering excludes as inessential, peripheral (or, in Isabella Winkler's formulation, a parasitic "thermal exciter," that is, as disorder and "noise")—proves to be what Serres is in fact "all about." By excluding the "inessential," one misses the essential. In short, the truth his writing embodies by suggesting what it does not state and including its own residue, is what the anthologizing, selecting, and ordering act perforce obscures.

"All perceiving is also thinking, all reasoning is also intuition, all observation is also invention," wrote Rudolf Arnheim.[17] In this intersubjective and active sense, mappings are not transparent, neutral, or passive devices of spatial measurement observations in the world. Mappings are neither depictions nor representations but mental constructs that enable and effect change. In describing and visualizing otherwise hidden facts, maps set the stage for future work. Mapping, like poetry, is always a project in the making.

Shelley said that poets are the unacknowledged legislators of the world.[18] Poets and imaginative prose writers are prophets, not in the sense of foretelling things, but of generating forceful visions. They express not just feelings, but crucial ideas in a direct, concentrated form that precedes and makes possible their articulations in our actions.

This book considers ways in which literature and science may be mapped and embraced in the same discourse, ways in which they have been held together by rethinking "the complex nature of historical process, the troubled relationship between the disciplines" (Stephen Clucas, in this volume) and the relationship between its many scientific and literary interlocutors (William Johnsen, also in this volume). Literature and science are modes of discourse, neither of which is privileged except by the conventions of the cultures in which they are embedded. The essays in this volume discuss mapping points of convergence, the spatialities of connectivity, networked linkage, marginality and liminality, and the transgression of linear boundaries and hermetic categories, that is, spatial flow. If the discourses converge, it is important to consider precisely how they do so, why they do so, whether the convergence is fortuitous, whether it can lead to important illuminations, to something like real dialogue, to genuine "influence." The contributors in this volume are concerned with the nature of the relations that have always existed between science and literature, and the usefulness of understanding them.

NOTES

1. For a detailed discussion, see *Mappings,* ed. Denis Cosgrove (London: Reaktion Books, 1999), especially James Corner, "The Agency of Mapping: Speculation, Critique, and Invention," 213–52, and Armand Mattelart, "Mapping Modernity: Utopia and Communication Networks," 169–92.

2. William Paulson, "Writing That Matters," *SubStance* 83 (1997): 32.

3. For insightful discussion on science and myth, see Steven D. Brown, "Michel Serres: Myth, Mediation, and the Logic of the Parasite," http://www.devpsy .lboro.ac.uk/psygroup/sb/Serres.htm, accessed July 28, 2004.

4. Paul A. Harris, "The Itinerant Theorist: Nature and Knowledge/Ecology and Topology in Michel Serres," *SubStance* 83 (1997): 37.

5. Ibid., 44.

6. Burno Latour, "The Enlightenment without the Critique: A Word on Michel Serres's Philosophy," in *Contemporary French Philosophy,* ed. A. Phillips Griffiths (Cambridge: Cambridge University Press, 1987), 90–91.

7. Erik Davis, *Techgnosis* (New York: Harmony Books, 1998), 16. The Greeks

marked crossroads, village borders, and household doorways with the *herm,* a rectangular pillar surmounted by the head of Hermes (a common operator in Serres's work).

8. Karl Kerényi, *Hermes: Guide of Souls,* trans. Murray Stein (Dallas: Spring Publications, 1976), 84.

9. Norman O. Brown, *Hermes the Thief* (Great Barrington, Mass.: Lindisfarne, 1990), 39.

10. In French the term *milieu* means "surroundings," "medium," and "middle."

11. In 1950 Debord began his association with the Lettrist International, which was being led by Isidore Isou at the time. The Lettrists were attempting to fuse poetry and music and were interested in transforming the urban landscape. In 1953 they mapped out what they called the "psychogeography" of Paris by walking through the city in a free-associative manner, or "drifts." Texts on this activity were first published in *Naked Lips* in 1955 and 1956, in essays titled "Detournement: How to Use" and "Theory of the Dérive."

12. Arthur H. Robinson and Barbara Bartz Petchenik, *The Nature of Maps: Essays toward Understanding Maps and Mapping* (Chicago: University of Chicago Press, 1976), 74.

13. Brand Blanshard, *The Nature of Thought* (London: Allen and Unwin, 1939), 525.

14. Paulson, "Writing That Matters," 30–31.

15. The Dymaxion map is a projection of a global map onto the surface of a three-dimensional regular solid that can be unfolded in many different ways and flattened to form a two-dimensional map that retains most of the relative proportional integrity of the spherical globe map. It was created by Buckminster Fuller and patented in 1946.

16. Cosgrove, *Mappings,* 2.

17. Rudolf Arnheirn, *Art and Visual Perception* (Berkeley and Los Angeles: University of California Press, 1964), viii.

18. P. B. Shelley, *The Defence of Poetry* in *Political Tracts of Wordsworth, Coleridge, and Shelley,* ed. R. J. White (Cambridge: Cambridge University Press, 1953), concluding sentence.

FROM RITUAL TO SCIENCE

RENÉ GIRARD

"Contrary to what is always said, science does not cancel out nonscience.
. . . Myth remains dense in knowledge, and vice versa" (*Z, 32, 49*). Thus,
we must not believe in the dogma of the "two cultures," almost foreign to
one another—the first vigorous, utilitarian, but "deprived of imagination,"
the second useless, imaginary, gratuitous, always free to go where it likes.

There is something disconcerting in this, first of all for the scientists
who want science to be taken seriously. It is in an antiscientific spirit, until
now, that attention has been called to the proximity of science and myth,
in order to cancel out science in the preliminary nullity of mythology. Of
course, there is no question of doing this. The growing efficiency of scientific models is not denied, but, between the most recent state of knowledge and all that precedes it, the famous "epistemological break" is always
there. That is to say that it is never there, and that it is a part of myth in the
most ordinary sense. Scientific ideology sees fecundity only in rupture
with the past. It is from continuity, on the contrary, that science draws
constantly renewed forces, but this continuity also renews the literatures
and other cultural artifacts that are often at the same level of elaboration as
science. There are also time lags, but not always in the interest of the scientists. We cannot count on the inevitable lateness of literature under the
pretext that literature is necessarily impressionistic and regressive.

It is literary people's turn to be worried. More than anything else,
they do not want literature to be taken seriously. For a century, they
have wanted as prophets only people who say to them: art and literature,
that's zero. Sudden menace to the derisory autonomy of the zero. "Literariness" and "scientificity" vacillate together. Serres disturbs. It is better not to listen.

In Zola, the point of contact between science, literature, and myth should not escape notice because it is everywhere. It is the essence of the oeuvre, and Serres brings this out well. However, the authors of theses on "Zola and science" have never seen it. They think according to epistemological breaks, or rather they let themselves be thought by them. They have been taught that the literary person and the scientist can meet only in a conscious reprise and repetition of certain results already perceived as "scientific." The scientific and the novelistic are opposed to and repel one another—while in Serres, they are one; beauty would serve as proof if only those who make a profession of the latter could see the former. To say of the novel that it functions here as a machine is to tell the strict truth in terms of aesthetic effect as well as scientific rigor. To make this unity other than an abstract truth we must rediscover, with Serres, the grand principles of thermodynamics. If Zola's novel invokes the locomotive, it is not for superficial reasons that belong above all to modernist demagoguery. Before any allusion to the railroad, Zola's text already operates like a steam engine:

> The practice of the stoker, of the locomotive engineer, puts them in close contact with Carnot's great principle. We know that a steam engine could not function if it did not have at its disposal, simultaneously, a hot source, here the firebox-boiler complex, and a cold source, here the condenser or the outside atmosphere. Their *difference,* experienced as an *opposition,* modeled as a *fall,* from a reservoir in general to its consumption, *produces* work and thus movement. Zola's beasts are plunged into this difference, men, women, locomotives, objects, world. And it is this difference that produces the narrative, that develops it. Globally speaking, everything functions like the steam engine: the novel, its loves, and its crimes. (Z, 1 3 1)

If we observe the thermodynamic function in part of Zola's oeuvre and in many other writers, philosophers, and so forth, we find a relation to myth and above all, I think, to rite. Far from opposing rite to myth, as is done today, we must bring them together as was always done before. We must recognize in the rite the operation of mythological speech, but without seeking to make the latter the original of the former, or vice versa. The original is elsewhere.

In rites, as in Zola, the work of difference presents itself as an opposition, and even as a conflict between participants. But the conflict itself tends to suppress differences and to efface them in the symmetry and the reciprocity of all confrontation. In the initial stages of rites, to summarize, as in the thermodynamic machine, differences wear out and exhaust themselves. This exhaustion should tend toward complete immobility, the pure and simple absence of energy, the irreducible inertia of the second law. And this is indeed what happens, I repeat, in part of Zola's oeuvre. In another part, on the contrary, difference undoes itself and dies in work and conflict, only to be reborn and to remake itself at once more lively and more different than ever. Everything works as though indifferentiation, far from bringing itself back to a simple energetic zero, constituted a sort of spring, more and more tense and capable, on its own, of setting off the differentiating process all over again.

There is in this a principle of revival, inexhaustible because it is linked to the very exhaustion of the system. If we imagine it in the direct prolongation of the religious, this principle of revival is suddenly suspect. It is one—this is evident—with the religious fecundity of death itself for resurrection. It looks too much like everything that not only precedes supernatural ascensions and assumptions but determines them and sets them off under the name of "descent into the underworld" or "initiation ordeal."

In a thermodynamic context, this perpetual motion is conceivable only in a system that recharges itself automatically from the very fact that it exhausts itself—one thinks of a sort of thermostat—by an inexhaustible source of energy: the sun, naturally, which nearly always shines a discreet ray on resurrections. This thermodynamics of the eternal return is a final solar culture and must extinguish itself along with our confidence in the eternity of the stars, a little like those burning asters that accompany the Hugolian Satan in his fall. But in Hugo, as in Zola, suns may die without interrupting, elsewhere (or even here), the cycle of resurrections:

The sun was there, dying in the chasm.
Coal of an extinguished world, torch blown out by God![1]

The God who blows out suns can relight other ones. This is still the old fecundity of death for life, and of disorder for putting back in order. Our ex-metaphysicians employ an incredible zeal in chasing away, everywhere, the traces of this guilty metaphysics. For centuries, it has been thought to be simply the product of a childish belief, a primitive tendency, well rooted in man, to take his desires for realities. Panicked fear of death would be sufficient to forge the myths capable of exorcising it. Serres does not always directly oppose this old formula, but all his works, it seems to me, call it into question.

In a perspective that gives priority to order and difference—that of thermodynamics without solar eternity—Zolaesque resurrections appear as an unjustifiable religious relic. Everything changes in the perspective of the other great scientific model, that which gives priority to disorder. On Michel Serres, I think, and perhaps also on Zola, this model exerts an attraction even stronger than does the first. It has its own fecundity, and it does not cease to reappear, alternating with the other model, especially in our time, against the positivism that is perpetuated among us thanks to the linguistic and differential taboo of a certain structuralism: "How could order come from disorder?" Lévi-Strauss asks rhetorically at the end of *L'Homme nu.*[2] It is understood that the answer can only be negative. Ridiculous, indeed, in the context of an order that always has priority, which is that of a science outdated today; the question becomes legitimate again in a more current context, that of *La Distribution,* or of Prigogine's research:

> Order is a rare island; it is an archipelago. Disorder is the common ocean from which these islands emerge. The undertow erodes the banks; the soil, worn, little by little loses its order and collapses. Elsewhere, a new archipelago will emerge from the waters. Disorder is the end of systems, and their beginning. Everything always goes toward chaos, and, sometimes, everything comes from it. *(LD)*

Even if everything only recommences "elsewhere," the endless alternation of disorder and order is no stranger to the mythico-ritual play of the "undifferentiated" always prior and posterior to each differentiation. The endless wheel of deaths and resurrections is simply a particular translation of this play, and it too can demand the "elsewhere" through metempsychosis.

The proximity of all these types of play had to lead Michel Serres to *De rerum natura.* More than any other, Lucretius's text is born of the "spaces of communication" between several cultural varieties. We exhaust ourselves in vain in distinguishing what might prefigure science, in this text, from what still belongs to myth. Gaining access to the scientific model means gaining access to the structure of myth, and vice versa.

Everything begins, ends, and begins again in the atoms that drop in an ever-freer fall, vertical and parallel, undoing what exists and preventing any new junction of atoms. Circulation becomes "laminar," and this must be so in order for the clinamen, somewhere, to come forth—the first departure from equilibrium, and the first difference that permits atoms to agglutinate. A new world constitutes itself, destined to end as the previous one did, and so on. The obvious absurdity of the clinamen comes from the fact that it has always been imagined in the framework of a solid mechanics. In the framework of a fluid mechanics, Serres shows, "the declination is the germ of a vortex in a hydraulic flow" *(N)*.

What is important here is not only disorder's anteriority to order, but also its genetic function. There is no new clinamen without the prior destruction of all that the previous clinamen has sustained as to both world and existence. This genetic function of disorder dominates the ritual, and we are mistaken about the nature of the latter from overlooking the former. In so-called seasonal rites, for example, the disquieting modifications of natural order set the religious process in motion. When the weather "goes bad" *(se gate)* or "is rotten" *(pourn),* as we have been saying for the past few years, one might believe that nature itself is decomposing. Far from working against the forces of corruption, the rites hold out their hand to them, one might say, and collaborate in the subversive work. This strange paradox must be accepted: the community actively participates in the disorder that it dreads. We bustle about in all directions, we break laws, we mix what, according to the rules, should be differentiated. Observing this vain commotion, the ethnology of pure difference concludes from it, quite falsely, that the rite "takes pleasure in the undifferentiated" (*N,* 124). Rites never have any other goal than difference and order, but they always take place as though the (re)generative principle of order were found in disorder itself. To assure the best possible, the most vigorous, order, disorder must first be overactivated. A paroxysm of disorder must take place.

Rites of initiation work by the same principle as seasonal rites. The initiation ordeal is a loss of difference, a veritable immersion in conflictual disorder, and it must be as prolonged, as painfully as possible, to ensure an adequate metamorphosis, one that corresponds to the status sought by the postulant.

Our examples, up to this point, are not of a nature to modify the universal conception of the religious as superstition. This conception has not changed since the eighteenth century. Saying "phantasmatic superstructure" is but a more complicated way of repeating "superstition." Neither rites of initiation nor, above all, seasonal rites really cut into the real. To achieve its cycle, nature has no need of these men who absurdly gesticulate. Serres affirms, let me repeat, that *myth—rite—remains dense in knowledge, and vice versa.* It is the first part of this proposition that is always illustrated in the superior regions of science, those we visit with Michel Serres, as tourists often frightened, always marveling. The inferior regions do not have the same prestige, but it is to them that we must look, in order to illustrate the second part of the proposition, the *and vice versa.* Where does the reciprocal complicity between knowledge and the mythico-ritual begin? Serres's oeuvre suggests, it seems to me, that it is already there at the most rustic and most archaic level. For Serres to be completely correct, knowledge would have to be consubstantial with ritual. But we will not show this, I repeat, with the examples of rites *that come* to *mind,* even if we read them with the extreme goodwill of a Malinowski or, more recently, of a Victor Turner.

This is the case because the behaviors officially recognized and labeled as religious are preselected by virtue of their very absurdity. Always prior to all analysis, the definition of the religious as superstition or superstructure requires, unbeknownst to us, the partitioning of cultural data. We only recognize as essentially ritual, in other words, the conducts that have not led (and can never lead) to a technique we perceive as useful, to a knowledge that would truly be knowledge. In archaic societies, for example, the grape harvests and the making of wine almost always have a ritual character, but we immediately separate the technical aspect of the affair from its religious aspect. The latter thus always seems as useless, adventitious, and superfluous to us as in the example of the seasonal rites. Precisely because they are useful, technical gestures seem to us necessarily motivated by this utility—foreign, by the same token, to the religious; yet, on the contrary, only the religious can furnish the motivation and the type of behavior capable of leading to the discovery of these techniques.

In the invention of foodstuffs such as wine, bread, or cheese, chance must have played a part. Chance sometimes does things well, but spirits prepared to take advantage of it are still needed. Contrary to appearances, the ritual framework is the only one that makes this thinkable. The categories of the pure and the impure have always dominated the religious mentality. The spontaneous alterations of animal and vegetable secretions, like milk or fruit juice, must have struck humans as an impure phenomenon. They must have seen there something analogous to all that falls under rigorous interdiction: rotting corpses, gangrenous wounds, excrement, and so on. They must have reacted, at first, with mistrust and avoidance.

Behaviors of avoidance, relative to the impure, can degenerate into veritable religious phobias, and this is the case of the Nietzsche of the *Antichrist,* as of a certain Christianity. Serres quite justly opposes to these opposed but analogous puritanisms the scientific truth of caseation, foreign to the sinister image it has been given. One must see, however, that the religious is equally distanced, in its principle, from the puritanism stigmatized by Serres and from the delirium of innovation that also characterizes us, and that doubtless constitutes the other side, symmetrical and inverse, of our religious decomposition.

The religious spirit never goes without terrified repugnance toward the impure, but, in its balanced forms, it gives man the audacity to overcome this initial reaction and to intervene in the process of corruption—not at all in order to work against it, but in order to accelerate it. Noticing, or believing it notices, a loss of differences, the beginning of baneful confusion between things that should remain distinct, the rite overexcites the crisis and precipitates the mixtures in order to bring about a favorable resolution.

In order to regenerate order, in sum, disorder must be made to give all that it can give in the order of disorder (one might say). In the case of natural alterations, like those of milk or of flour, ritual intervention will doubtless strive to further alter the substances. It will perhaps multiply the unnatural mixtures. It will push us, in sum, toward experimentation on the rotten, the spoiled, the fermented; it alone has this power, for above the disorder whose accomplice it never truly is, religious vision holds out the shining hope for an order as good as or better than the original order. The manipulations and the mixtures suggested by the religious are not always hollow mimicries in the sense of the old "imitative magic." They are oriented toward a result about which everything is unknown except that it might be favorable—and that is precisely what is needed to awaken the spirit of discovery. Metamorphoses are dreaded; almost all of them are monstrous, but there often exists at least one good one, and in order to guide the sacred fermentation toward this one, it is enough to discover the appropriate rites, under the aegis of the divinity. Wherever possibilities of useful transformation are real, rite ends up taking them over with conse-quences so decisive, even in our desacralized culture, that they blind us to the ritual origin of bread, of wine, of cheese, and so forth. We admit the centrality of rite only where its technique remains unproductive, without noticing that there is no fundamental difference here between productive procedures and unproductive ones. In order to understand this, the com-parisons must be multiplied. We must establish a connection between the behaviors whose ritual nature seems doubtful to us, because they lead to true techniques and to veritable knowledge, and the behaviors whose rit-ual nature seems indubitable to us, because they lead to nothing. This is what I tried to do in *Des choses cachées depuis la fondation du monde.*[3] We do not wish to recognize, in the religious conduct of the Ainu toward their bears, a behavior analogous to that which visibly led to the domestication of certain animal species by the pastoral population. Results that are too positive hide the ritual origin of our butchered meat from us.

In the case of cheese, or of fermented foodstuffs, in order to reinforce the probability of a ritual origin, one could turn to certain funerary rites that include two quite distinct stages. The first begins with death and lasts as long as the decomposition of the corpse; it may require manipulations of more or less decomposed flesh, and altogether repugnant daubings. The second cycle, with a more serene tonality, is centered on the bones of the deceased, carefully bleached, polished, and scoured. Reading Robert Hertz leaves no doubt, I think, as to the meaning of these double funeral rites.[4] The death and decay of the corpse are perceived as a crisis of differ-ences, an invasion by disorder. Ritual intervention has the same meaning here as everywhere else: it aims to encourage and to overactivate the process, in order to lead as rapidly as possible to "good" differential stabi-lization—and it is this stabilization that it believes it recognizes in the metamorphosis of the corpse into bones. The dried-out skeleton presents, indeed, all the characters of the structuralist ideal finally realized. It is truly the return to order, and also to that solid mechanics which traditional commentators instinctively adopt when faced with the Lucretian model.

The only difference between these manipulations of more or less decomposed corpses and cheese making lies in the illusory character of the first operation and the real character of the second. In the first case, the faithful believe they direct a metamorphosis that, in reality, would be accomplished without them (as in the case of seasonal rites); while in the second, they really do direct it. This is indeed what fools us and makes us believe in two behaviors of different natures, entirely foreign to one another, while in reality they are one and the same. It is still the illusion of the "epistemological break" that dominates our way of thinking, the illusion that Michel Serres denounces, and it is very difficult to uproot because it plays an essential role, at all levels, in the flattering, aseptic image that we create for ourselves of our history and of our origins.

The funerary practices that I have just evoked inspire a distaste in us that gains in intensity when we compare such practices with cheese and its fabrication. We must reflect on this distaste, which visibly perpetuates in us the separation of the pure and the impure. We vomit out the sudden proximity of an evidence that should elude us: evidence of a ritual origin common to institutions and customs that we wish to think of as incompatible.

Georges Bataille was not insensitive to this relation between cheese and funeral rites. In his preface to *Les Larmes d'Éros,* J.-M. Lo Duca describes to us Bataille's ecstatic hesitation before a particularly strong-smelling piece of cheese: "His eyes bright with admiration, he murmured: 'It's almost a tomb.'"[5] What remains, in Bataille, in the state of aesthetic intuition, of Baudelairean correspondence, is not impenetrable. The time has come for ethnology to put it to use *(d'en faire son fromage).* The puritanism of difference recoils, horrified.

Certain peoples manipulate their corpses; others bury them; still others "pass them through the fire"—always in order to put them back into order, or to resuscitate them (which comes down to the same thing). Similarly, there are peoples who manipulate milk, others who bury seeds, still others who pass flour through the fire—and this is also in order to put these substances back into order or, what comes down to the same thing, in order to provoke the astonishing "resurrections" that are called cheese, bread, wine, germination, and so forth.

To complete the analogy between funerary techniques and all that the English language designates as *food processing,* we must also think of the attitude that is the opposite of the one that occupies us here and that also figures in religious behaviors—as much in funerary rites, where it results in mummification, as in the alimentary sector, where one speaks of processes of preservation. The insectlike stubbornness with which men often carry out their ineffective practices reveals a prodigious source of energy without which the perfection of effective techniques—those which make us what we are—cannot even be conceived of. It is in ritual that the origin of work must be sought, and not in slavery, as Georges Bataille, fooled (on this point as on so many others) by a Hegelianism that sterilized his best intuitions, believed.

The ritual source, however, cannot be primary. Without truly being subordinate to what appears to us as the rationality of its ends, neither is the rite foreign to what we call reason. Behind all human activity, there must exist a unique model, always hidden from view by our furious appetite for absolute differentiation between the rational and the irrational. There is no question of effacing these differences (as a certain mysticism and a certain philosophism still do): they must be kept in mind in order to notice that men apply, at length, a single ritual technique to the most heterogeneous domains, without at first paying the slightest attention to what determines, in our eyes, the technical character of an activity, the rationality of the end and of the means. Depending on the domains of application, the ritual activity has revealed itself to be more or less fecund—but it has continued for a long time, with tenacity, even in the domains where it is (or seems to us to be) sterile, the only ones whose ritual character we admit today. The "epistemological break" permits us not to recognize in the rite our educator of all times, the initial and fundamental mode of exploration and transformation of the real.

As a unique model of ritual action, I have proposed the mimetic play of human relations, functioning in a regime much more intense than our own, and by definition unobservable in the societies that produce as well as in those that do not produce religions. The conflictual phase of this play—rooted in the mimetic character of the appropriation—would go, in its collective paroxysm, all the way to hallucinatory frenzy, easily detectable in the staging of numerous rites. This paroxysm would detach the mimesis from the disputed objects and attach it to the antagonists—but in an unstable manner, subject to substitutions and thus to unanimous polarization against any victim, due to the very nature of this mimesis that is contagious, cumulative, transferential.

This character explains and justifies the "disorderly" character of ritual action, sometimes so striking that it causes the desire for order, always present in ritual, to be underrated. If a spontaneous mechanism of autoregulation exists in unsettled communities, people will wish to reproduce it each time something around them becomes unsettled or seems to become unsettled. We understand this without difficulty, and we also understand their desire to reproduce the phenomenal sequence in all its exactitude, in order to give it back its effectiveness. It is true that the regulatory mechanism only sets itself off at the paroxysm of unsettledness, but people have no need to know why. In order to regenerate, differences must first be effaced. In order to set off the unifying, restructuring mechanism, the community must first be destructured in mimetic hysteria. Sacrificial substitutions require this destructuration. People conform to this principle without knowing it because they have the spontaneous model of all ritual action before their eyes. This model is very strongly imprinted upon our memory because it brings into play the very existence of the community.

In the domain of human relations, and of the mimesis that governs them, disorder is really instrumental to all (re)placing in order. Ultimately, terms like *paradox* should not be pronounced, and the antinomy of end and means should not be spoken of. To speak in this way is still to perpetuate the misunderstanding of the representations sustained by the mechanism of victimization itself, the sacred representations that push people toward effective action by inciting them to reproduce the original sequence very scrupulously, but hide the rationality of this conduct from them. Precisely because it reconciles the community, the mechanism makes the victim, in reality powerless and passive, appear as the supremely active agent of the mimetic metamorphosis, the incarnation of a mysterious power, by turns malevolent and benevolent, destructuring and restructuring. At all stages of animality, mimesis tends to produce differences as well as to efface them, to make signs appear and make them disappear. When we interpret, for example, what we call the mimesis of certain insects now as "intimidation," now as "camouflage," it is in all appearances to this double property that our interpretation returns.

In the domain of human relations, there is a paradox only for a *doxa* still incapable of identifying the true model of the ritual and the role of paroxystic disorder in cultural organization. This *doxa* is visibly a tributary of the religious, which it denies in an abstract fashion in order to consolidate, as does the religious, the differences that come from the mechanism of victimization. This is the rationalist, positivist, or structuralist model, which thinks exclusively in terms of differences and sees in attention to "the undifferentiated" only "dubious mysticism" and more or less camouflaged religious nostalgia. In reality, it will become possible to articulate rationally the alternation of undifferentiated and of undifferentiation in all sorts of domains, beginning with that of human relations and of the mythicoritual model that flows directly from them. This is indeed what mimetic theory does. Far from succumbing to mysticism and to the irrational, it constitutes the first veritable attempt at formalization in the two domains.

If we return to the funeral rites, we will see the indices of what I have put forth multiply. Aside from the phenomena already mentioned, these rites often include disorders and violences inside the group directly affected by the death of one of its members. We must not be too quick to see outrageous expressions of the pain caused by this death or theatrical manifestations of mourning in these conducts, even (and especially) if all that appears appropriate to us as mourning and susceptible of translating its suffering is ultimately rooted in this type of behavior. The slightest comparison reveals that mimetic rivalries, as always, are in question there—

that is to say, the agitation and the destructuration indispensable to the triggering of the mechanism of victimization. Funerals are only one adaptation among others of the fundamental ritual and sacrificial process. If we resort to this process on the occasion of death as on so many other occasions, it is because death is clearly one of the disquieting phenomena that justify resorting to ritual. We know from experience that the decomposition of the community and the decomposition of the human body must go together.

The universal principle of organizing disorder governs the banal phenomenon of collective commotion in rites, funerary or other, as well as the apparently stranger phenomenon of the manipulations destined to accelerate the decay of the corpse. The different usages of the word *perturbation* cover the same sectors as do ritual practices and may help us to comprehend their proximity. Perturbation, from *turba,* the crowd, is quite literally collective agitation, but it is also atmospheric disturbance, which brings us back to the seasonal rites, and it is equally the alteration of any substance. The manipulations of the corpse strive to actualize the fundamental perturbation, which is that of the community, at the level of these easily perturbed substances which are cadaverous flesh, milk, fruit juices, flours, and so forth. This must not be dramatized by seeking particular explanations for ritual conducts that, in reality, are only distinguished by the apparent incongruity of their objects. Before the funerary rites that disconcert him, the contemporary *homo psychanalyticus* reacts a little like a belated Aristotelian. He pompously pronounces "phantasm of necrophilia" or something analogous, sincerely believing that he contributes an element of comprehension—while in reality he reinforces, by cloaking it in a pedantic label, the illusory singularity of the phenomenon, its belated and misleading differentiation, which must on the contrary be dissolved in order to arrive at a true understanding.

If we renounce illusory singularities, we notice that we are always dealing in rites with a single behavior; but this unique behavior differentiates itself, little by little, into effective techniques and ineffective ritual relics. It is always a question of bringing the already perturbed back to calm and stability by way of a greater perturbation. From *turbare* comes as well, it seems, our *trouver* (to find) in French.

It is Michel Serres, in his book on Lucretius, who draws our attention to the revelatory character of the term *perturbation.* In the Lucretian model, the laminar circulation of atoms corresponds exactly to the indifferentiation of the social group under the effect of mimetic rivalries. This is indeed why this laminar circulation is associated with the *plague,* whose role in the mythological translations of these rivalries is well known. The same correspondence is found between the mechanism of victimization and the clinamen, that first difference born from the destruction of all difference. The scientific model is no less mythical—more mythical, in truth—than many myths, since it makes a clean sweep of everything that could conjure up the victim. Lucretius himself believes in the innocence of a scientific activity that he opposes to the sacrificial violence of the religious. Lucretius is mistaken, and Serres shows us his mistake. The traces of the foundational victim are better hidden here than in the myths and the rites where the old lynching shows through, but they have not entirely disappeared: they are buried in the language, and in order to detect them the mimetic and religious signification of the atomic vocabulary must be brought up to date. It is the *perlurbatio* that makes the declination. And in his reflection on the void and the atom—that is to say, on the elementary discrimination between something and nothing—it is not the sacrificial nature of science alone that Serres deciphers, but of all that can be called "perception," initial constitution of the object:

> The void, *inane,* has its root in the Greek verb *inein,* which means to purge, to expel, or, in the passive, to be chased by a purge. The void is part of chaos but is also a catharsis. . . . But the first object is a purge; *it is only the physical concept* of *catharsis.* The second object, the atom. The sacred solution begins with a division and separation of space. The temple is a dichotomized space; the word itself tells us so. Inside is the religious; outside is the profane. A two-valued logic, a two-valued geometry, a two-valued ontology, inside, outside; sacred, profane; matter, void. *The word temple is* of *the same family as atom.* The atom is the last or the first temple, and the void is the last or the first purge. The two objects are, in the balance, the physical concepts of catharsis and temple. . . . Nature is still another sacrificial substitute. Violence is still—and always—in physics. . . . It is not politics or sociology that is projected on nature, but the sacred. Beneath the sacred, there is violence. Beneath the object, relations reappear. (*N,* 1 6 5–66)

This is the same foundational violence, it seems to me, that the comparison of the genesis of mathematics and the Platonic dialogue already brought forth, in *La Communication:*

> Mathematics provides the example of a nearly perfect communication, of an information that is univocal upon both emission and reception. This is so true that it is not forbidden to think that its very origin resides in a dialogue in which the two interlocutors talk together against the powers of noise, that mathematics is established from the moment when victory is theirs. It is thus natural that Platonism presents at once a philosophy of the pure mathematon and a dialectics. . . . I have tried to show this above, by defining the role of a third man, or of a third party scrambling the dialogue, whose exclusion the entire Platonic

effort tries to put into practice. . . . This exclusion . . . would be a condition of pure thought, in a transcendental intersubjectivity. Let no one enter here who is not a geometrist. *(LC, 95)*

In the Platonic model, the difference between noise and message is given; it is a priori. Why is there always noise? Why is there always someone to make noise? The two good desires to communicate suppose a third, bad one that must be reduced to silence. And what if noise were only the way in which the desire of others to communicate is communicated to each person? And what if all the desires were the same? In order to decide the difference between message and noise, an alliance of two against one would always be needed—perfectly arbitrary this time, but incapable of maintaining itself as such because the designation of the third as uniquely at fault for the noise constitutes the first successful communication. And this communication proves the truth of the division. It was indeed the excluded third who scrambled the messages, since excluding him was enough to begin to understand one another.

The foundational narrative always presents itself in the same way, except for a few variations. The correct understanding of messages rests, everywhere, on the same misunderstanding. Neither the scientific text, nor the philosophical text, nor the mythical text ever enunciates, by definition, the misunderstanding that structures them. The hypothesis of this misunderstanding figures in none of the texts that we see as authoritative. It is thus thought possible to set it aside with a simple shrug of the shoulders. Authority is at one with the fundamental misunderstanding. The hypothesis is, however, far from being undemonstrable; it is even *only* demonstrable, indirectly and by as many structural crosschecks as one would like—that is to say, perfectly demonstrable, but nothing other than demonstrable.

Between the Platonic outline, for example, and foundational myths, the continuity is visible. Myths as such distinguish themselves only by the greater extension and, one might say, the perfection of the misunderstanding that makes the excluded third responsible not only for the impeded communication but also for restored or instituted communication. The sacred vision is this more total misunderstanding, perhaps still *intact,* but not without justice, since it makes this excluded third party who assures the clarity of the message, by its very exclusion, responsible for the intelligible at the same time as the unintelligible. There is communication thanks only to the incommunicable.

Translated by Trina Marmarelli and Matthew Tiews

NOTES

1. Victor Hugo, *La Fin de Satan* (Paris: Gallimard, 1984), 43.

2. Claude Lévi-Strauss, *L'Homme nu* (Paris: Librarie Plon, 1971); in English: *The Naked Man,* trans. John Wrightman and Doreen Wrightman (New York: Harper and Row, 1981), 562.

3. René Girard, *Des choses cachées depuis la fondation du monde* (Paris: Grasset et Fasquelle, 1978); in English: *Things Hidden since the Foundation of the World,* trans. Stephen Bann and Michael Metter, with revisions by the author (Stanford: Stanford University Press, 1987).

4. See Robert Hertz, *Sociologie religieuse et folklore* (Paris: PUF, 1970).

5. Georges Bataille, *Les Larmes d'Éros* (Paris: Jacques Pauvert, 1961); in English: *The Tears of Eros,* trans. Peter Connor (San Francisco: City Lights Books, 1989), 3.

SWIMMING THE CHANNEL

WILLIAM PAULSON

> *The real passage occurs in the middle. What-*
> *ever direction determined by the swim, the*
> *ground lies dozens or hundreds of yards below*
> *the belly or miles behind and ahead. The voy-*
> *ager is alone. One must cross in order to know*
> *solitude, which is signaled by the disappear-*
> *ance of all reference points.*
> —The Troubadour of Knowledge

Michel Serres's parable of learning as swimming locates the most decisive experiences of education in the body, in the somatic encounter with a turbulent, physical world. But the reference to the miles that lie ahead or behind suggest the feat of swimming the English Channel, a possibility reinforced a few lines later by a reference to Calais and Dover as starting and end points of a passage from one state to another.[1] France to England: crossing the channel can serve, among other things, as a figure for translating Serres into the language of what the French call the Anglo-Saxon world.

In large part, my qualification for contributing a chapter on the subject of "swimming the channel" in Serres's language and thought is that, having had a hand in translating two of his books and an article, I have worked at bringing his writings across the narrow but sometimes treacherous divide separating French and English. To be Serres's translator, moreover, is at least a respectable role, whereas to be his commentator, or to use him as a theorist in the humanities, has proven more controversial. People have often asked me, in effect, "How can you justify using Serres's work when he's said so many times that he doesn't want to have any disciples?" The role of follower or disciple, hardly a glorious one in any case—although very common in the humanities, and indeed throughout the academy— seems to be particularly stigmatized when the "master thinker" in question has protested against playing this part. The ethics of this reproach, however, strike me as shaky, somewhat akin to the immoralism of sociobiology: it's fine, so it seems, to have followers and influence as long as you think there's nothing wrong with this, but if you question the mechanisms of discipleship, then in order for you to be consistent, your ideas deserve to die out for lack of adherents. In this kind of game, scruples about intellectual self-replication are headed for well-deserved extinction in the cultural selection of ideas. Still, the reproach of unauthorized discipleship poses intriguing challenges—not only to me, but to other contributors to this volume and ultimately to its readers. What are we up to when we write or speak about Michel Serres, or when we make use of his ideas and texts? Does his work resist appropriation or reproduction, and, if so, how? If so, is it incoherent of us to draw on it, circulate it, put it to work? In what manner can or should his thought live outside of him and his books, if not via disciples?

These are some of the questions to which I will offer at least provisional answers in these pages, taking the experience of translation as my point of departure. Putting Serres into English is not just a matter of translating philosophical concepts: from the outset, my cotranslators and I felt obliged to contend with, and try to carry across, the materiality of his language, the specificity of signifiers, his wordplay and etymologies, intertextuality, the music and even the prosody, at times, of his sentences. In *Le Tiers-instruit* (which, with Serres's blessing, we rebaptized *The Troubadour of Knowledge*), he says that a person learning a new language, or undergoing any truly transforming educational experience, "passes unceasingly through the fold of the dictionary" (*TK*, 6). Surely this describes Serres's translators, but also his readers, who know that the most striking surface feature of his writing is its difficult and unconventional vocabulary. This is not a matter of jargon or philosophical technicity, but simply of a thousand and one rarely frequented entries in the dictionary.

There can be few readers familiar with all the words found in Serres's writings. His philosophical idiom is always rich and most often highly concrete. Richness and concreteness go hand in hand, for it is in avoiding conventional generalities and abstract words that Serres uses so many local, archaic, or concrete ones. He writes, as it were, not of fish, but of salmon, mackerel, and tuna; not of artisans, but of joiners, wheelwrights, and coopers. In so doing, he has often remarked, he considers himself to be fulfilling Victor Hugo's goal of putting the Revolution's red cap on the dictionary, because he is using the language of the people, the idioms of specific crafts and places, rather than the abstract, citified idiom of politicians, experts, or the news media. In a 1980 interview, he quoted Hugo's "J'ai mis un bonnet rouge au vieux dictionnaire" and commented: "That means that I'm going to use the vocabulary of carpenters, of lute-makers, of sailors, I'm going to use popular language."[2] To be sure, this may now seem an archaic version of "popular language," one with which most people, whether tradesmen or university professors, have lost touch. As Serres himself writes in *The Natural Contract,* today's city dwellers and consumers of cultural spectacle can barely recognize or distinguish the tools of such fundamental trades as farming and seafaring. The vocabulary of artisans may now be a basis for "popular" language that is utopian in the negative sense, existing nowhere. (It's also, at least in an English-speaking context, a paradoxical claim to the legacy of the French Revolution in that it identifies the Revolution with concreteness, locality, and specificity— traits more characteristic of English antirevolutionary thought than of the Revolutionist claim to universality.) But it is certainly not the language of experts, opinion makers, and theoreticians.

At the same time, however, Serres's preference for concrete words by no means excludes the abstractions of conceptual thought. But he does not equate the abstract concept with the abstract word. His general concepts often emerge from a series of more specific terms, whose commonality may form an abstraction in his mind and eventually in that of the reader, but which retain their specificity and differences in his texts. Consider the case of a series of nouns at the beginning of *The Natural Contract: belligerents* (*parties* to a declaration of war), *competitors (adversaries* in the economic sphere), *duelists* (rivals in single combat), enemies, *fighters, opponents* . . . (*NC,* 1–8). When our editors at the University of Michigan Press saw this riot of near-synonyms, they suggested that we choose one word as a standard term and stick to it! Which of course drew a strong and eventually successful protest from Elizabeth MacArthur and myself. For not only do these words contribute their nuances to the shifting contexts in which they occur, even within a space of a few pages, they also offer their diverse forms, histories, and roots. You cannot take away the linguistic concreteness and specificity and still call the result the writing of Michel Serres, or even a translation thereof.

And yet, we also realized, we could not content ourselves with translating so as to produce equivalent signifiers, either, or so as to be faithful to some French literary quality or stylistic idiosyncrasies: the concepts are too important and must be put across with clarity. The attention Serres lavishes on his language is only incidentally poetic, in the sense of a "set toward the message itself":[3] even the most poetic or ornamented passages in Serres do not suggest that his works should be read as poetry. More important, Serres's attention to language does not constitute the kind of reflexivity or foregrounding that aims to suspend or denounce naive belief in language's powers of representation. Serres is certainly not naive about the subtleties and limits of language, but he spends no time accusing others of naïveté so that he may correct them. Serres's language is that of philosophical invention and not of poetry or cultural critique. After all, he first became known as a kind of mathematical structuralist, a scholar who tenaciously revealed abstract models and formal invariants in places where no one would have expected to find them, and this mathematical bent for homology, isomorphism, proof, and generalization remains a strong impulse even in his most recent writings. In translating *The Natural Contract,* we wound up spending far more time and effort on conceptual clarity than on stylistic fidelity. Conveying the arguments and ideas in English always came first. We then concerned ourselves with preservation of signifiers, syntax, and style whenever concepts and arguments were at stake in them—in other words, most of the time.

Instead of saying, as I almost did a moment ago, that Serres's language does not move consistently toward the philosophical concept, it is more accurate to suggest that he gets concepts out of many levels of language: signifiers, etymons, intertexts, concrete meanings of abstract words and abstract meanings of concrete words. In his prose, then, words are much more than discrete units of meaning ready to be organized into larger units of signification through the syntactic chunking of sentence, paragraph, chapter, and book. While not neglecting such organization, Serres repeatedly delves inside words, bouncing arguments off their inner syllables, their roots, and their etymological kin. A contract *draws together (con-tra-here)* and is thus understood to be a matter of cords and bonds, wires and cables, of oxen yoked to draw a plough, and so the text evokes and articulates the concept of a contract through stories of roped mountaineering parties, tethered goats, and ships' hawsers. An accord or contract is thus akin to *treaties, traités,* fellow derivatives of *trahere,* as is the French *trait,* which—like the English *draft*—designates both a mark written on paper and the pulling of a load by harnessed animals (*NC,* 103–11). Thus glossed by its etymology, a contract is already more than an agreement among subjects in society; its signifiers point to human beings bound to the stuff of the world before Serres argues that a natural contract must be added to the social one. What might at first seem to resemble punning, etymological play, or a window dressing of erudition in fact propels Serres's writing to the relations between contracts, the agricultural practices of tethering and harnessing animals, of measuring, enclosing, and plowing land, the collective security against omnipresent danger offered by the roping together of mountain-climbing parties, the new social bonds of communications networks.

Arguments based on etymology, of course, are not universally admired. In his classic essay, "Alain ou la preuve par l'étymologie," Jean Paulhan argued that attempts to elucidate the true meaning of words via their etymologies were linguistically misleading or trivial: "The etymology of a word usually remains unknown to us; if it's known, it's uninformative; if it informs us of some detail, it's misleading; if it's right, its truth is just that of an anecdote."[4] But Serres is generally concerned not with the origins but with the displacements of words; the anecdotal character of etymological knowledge is precisely what makes it productive in his works. Paulhan remarks with some disdain that certain etymological details would be of interest only in the history of cooking, small landholding, or vegetable growing.[5] But it is precisely the interest of such extralinguistic domains that Serres makes part of his arguments via etymology.

Serres, in other words, draws concrete images, figures, comparisons, and stories out of the inner resources of language, exploiting the multiple concepts opened up by the seemingly preconceptual, concrete origins of abstract words. His work with signifiers connects language to the stories and places of the world. Style, for Serres, is a means not of adorning but of *inventing* and *finding*. His choice of words and the structure of his sentences produce multilayered articulations of concepts, connotations, and multiple referents.

Serres's language thus seems to lead in all directions, whether in turn or all at once. His writing is neither strictly conceptual, nor metalingual, nor poetic, nor affective, nor expressive, nor referential, but rather all of these in quick and sometimes dizzying succession. Meaning in his texts does not flow in a linear, laminar fashion, whether downstream toward unproblematic concepts and referents or back upstream toward the conditions of its production via a reflexivity determined to question the illusion of representation. Instead, its movement is omnidirectional, akin to the turbulence evoked by Serres in *Le Tiers-instruit* in an extended metaphor for the process of learning, or of crossing from one language, culture, or world to another. His vehicle, as I noted at the outset, is that of swimming through the turbulent middle of a river or channel:

> In crossing the river, in delivering itself completely naked to belonging to the opposite shore, it has just learned a third thing. The other side, new customs, a new language, certainly. But above all, it has just discovered learning in this blank middle that has no direction [change "directions" to "direction"] from which to find all directions. . . . Universal means what is unique yet versed in all directions. Infinity enters the body of the one who, for a long time, crosses a rather dangerous and large river in order to know those regions where, as on the high seas, whatever direction one adopts or decides, reference points lie equally far. From then on, the solitary soul, wandering without belonging, can receive and integrate everything: all directions are equal. Did he traverse the totality of the concrete to enter abstraction? (*TK,* 7)

Serres's translators, I would say, dive into their task only to discover that they knew his work—and French, and indeed their own native languages—less well than they thought, and who must undergo a sudden "sink or swim" education if they are to proceed. Yet my comparison of this passage to the omnidirectional flow of meaning in his texts is motivated not only by my own judgment as a translator but by the figures Serres uses elsewhere in the same book to describe the experience of pursuing knowledge through the totality of language:

> The thinker must begin by learning everything, but because he thinks in his language, he must also become a writer and in order to do so traverse its capacity in every *direction. . . . Patient* work, that of the writer who *navigates the long course of his entire language and who, fearing no waters, writes his language, describes it up to its furthest shores, and tries to exhaust its capacities.* (*TK,* 72–73; emphasis added).

Language is a long and turbulent body of water—perhaps a river, perhaps a channel, perhaps the high seas. Only by throwing yourself into language, Serres seems to say, by pursuing and undergoing its multiple meanings and directions, its multiply directed meanings, can you create something new or reach beyond language to evoke what lies outside it.

But can one ever use language to reach what lies beyond it? Serres insists several times, in the passage on learning as swimming the channel, on the loss of reference, by which he seems to designate some stable link to either the near or far shore. This insistence is intriguing, since—as I've tried to suggest—he is no debunker of linguistic reference or representation. Evoking the risks of a scholastic nominalism that came with the very real methodological successes of structuralism, Serres wrote that knowledge always requires a "direct and reciprocal, productive, almost homeostatic relation between a discourse and a subset, which it indicates, of what is not itself" (*LD,* 279). The loss of reference does not imply the loss of the nondiscursive world. It is crucial, I think, to understand Serres's texts and their possibilities of reference as occupying and growing out from what he describes as a middle space. Reference, in Serres, is neither given nor refused; it is something that happens, that is worked toward, that is an event. The constantly worked-on relation between discourse and its outside, evoked above, is itself fluid, subjected to "fluctuations of phase" (*LD,* 279; cf. 288–89). "The discursive is plunged in the intuitive; it is an archipelago in the sea" (*LD,* 282).

Without actually leaving this problem of reference, I'd like to make a slight detour at this point via the younger French philosopher Bruno Latour, a reader of and sometime collaborator with Serres whose increasingly prominent work centers on the implications of anthropological studies of science for philosophy. Latour's book of interviews with Serres, *Eclaircissements* (in English, *Conversations on Science, Culture, and Time*) is a skillfully conducted duet in which, to mix musical metaphors, Serres may be the featured soloist but Latour is clearly the conductor. I suspect, by the way, that Latour's work, with its more Anglo-American tonality, its more pointed sense of oppositions, and above all its forthright proposal of an alternative to dominant philosophical and methodological dualisms, is headed for a much wider reception, at least in the English-speaking world, than that of Serres. Whereas until now many people, like myself, have come to Latour via Serres, many more may in the future come to Serres via Latour. (Latour, it's worth noting, has actually practiced the bilingual crossover that Serres praises but never tries in writing himself; some of Latour's most important books—including his latest, *Pandora's Hope*—are written in English, with acknowledged correction from colleagues and editors.)

In an uncollected article published in 1988, "The Politics of Explanation: An Alternative," Latour defines explanation as establishing some sort of relation between two lists, one comprising an inventory of elements to be explained (B) and the other a repertoire of elements to provide the explanation (A).

> [A]n explanation is said to be provided only when more *than* one element in list B is related to one element of list A. . . . The corollary of this "holding of" several elements by one is a general feeling of strength, economy, and aesthetic satisfaction. . . . This simple definition enables us to measure the power of an explanation. An explanation becomes more powerful by relating more elements of B to a single element of A.[6]

A continuous scale of explanatory power can thus be defined, its "weak" pole constituted by description or narrative, its middle involving various forms of correlation, its "strong" pole including algorithms and deductions. Explanation, especially in its stronger forms, serves as a means of control, of performing action at a distance (one acts on elements of B by acting on those of A).

If we think in this light of the modes of explanation at work in Serres's texts, it is immediately obvious that he deploys the full range, from story and description to algebraic invariance and geometric deduction. Serres consistently refuses to make his texts into instruments of reduction or universal tools; he avoids offering a concise set of verbal formulae or conceptual methods that can be taken over and that work every time. Yet he is always including moments of synthesis and generalization, and unlike many postmodernists he chooses not to stand only on the side of the local. "It is not worth entering philosophy as a youth if one does not have the hope, project, or dream of one day attempting synthesis. . . . Doubtless this is the only risk adventure to be had, here and today, in a space held by uniform powers, so as to escape them, only this risk to be run, so as to see open air."[7] Yet this synthetic vocation does not entail the desire for (or the practice of) abstract or disembodied knowledge.

It is certainly possible to pull out abstract structures and operators from Serres and use them—many years ago, for example, I produced a straightforward Serresean reading of *Le Cousin Pons* by applying the central concepts of *Le Parasite* to Balzac's poor relation.[8] It would even be possible, I think, to create an abstract, conceptual handbook from Serres, a kind of dogmatic, synthetic textbook of "Serresean philosophy," with an emphasis on the invariant models and the philosophical translations of scientific concepts. Yet although such a handbook strikes me as a real possibility, it is one, I suspect, that no one really devoted to his work could quite want to do. Serres's books are notoriously resistant to summary, mainly because they are saturated with multiple levels of image, metaphor, concept, story, and argument. What matters is less an overarching argument running through a book (though strong and coherent argument there is), but rather the connections being made through continuous interwoven "digressions" that turn out to be the very texture of the writing and thought. This resistance to summary or to abstract representation poses a problem to anyone who would use his writings by gleaning nuggets that can be taken away and carried over into one's own work. By undermining the "Serres handbook" option, the rich concreteness of his writing thus serves to prevent his texts from becoming instruments of power and control—with all the dangers for loss of intellectual influence that this stance implies.

The form of Serres's writing, in other words, helps to keep his texts from functioning as models for powerful, repeatable explanations, and to stave off imitative or reductive appropriation. Not for him the rationality produced by unambiguous and thus instrumentally effective communication. There is, of course, plenty of reason and logical argument in his writing, and there would be still be serious and worthwhile messages in it without most of its stylistic idiosyncrasy or its archaic or unusual vocabulary. Were that the case, however, more people might start repeating his phrases in their head, or dropping them on political talk shows or making them the clichés of a generation of academic books. The difficulty of his writing, never fully graspable on a given reading, prevents his ideas from spreading epidemically through his readers' brains, or from becoming the tools of a well-disciplined intellectual faction. It also enables his work to last and not be used up, allowing readers to keep coming back to it and learning new things from a page of it years after they thought they knew quite well what it meant and what it had to offer.

What actually does go on in Serres's texts, then? What is their status, what do they refer to? Here another detour via Latour will be in order, one that will return us to the question of reference and that of "what goes on in Serres." In *Pandora's Hope,* Latour offers a pragmatic, process-oriented account of the referentiality of science.[9] Narrating—with accompanying photographs—a scientific expedition to the edge of the Amazon forest in which he was a participant-observer, he describes the many small and controlled steps through which the material world is inscribed into samples, charts, data, and finally into discursive accounts such as published articles. His central point is that instead of a single great gap between language and the world that must be bridged by the difficult or mysterious operation of reference, there is a chain involving dozens of small gaps and local operators by which translations from matter to form are accomplished. Each step is both a displacement and an inscription. Scientists find their way into the territory with the help of maps and aerial photographs. They turn a forest into a proto-laboratory by placing numerical markers on trees at regular intervals so as to be able to move in Amazonia as if in a system of Cartesian coordinates. They extract plant specimens and soil samples, and then label, classify, and organize them. A box holding a two-dimensional array of soil samples, a pedocomparator, enables information about soil characteristics to pass into a diagram or chart. A book of color charts similar to those of paint stores enables the soil color to be coded and thus transmitted to distant laboratories. The written, published account of the expedition is accompanied by the diagrams and charts, so that its language does not have to refer directly to the world but to knowledge of it already extracted and inscribed. For Latour, the many referential steps of the expedition show that the problem of reference between words and world is not to be grasped as a leap from one endpoint to another but from the middle outward, as a series of small mediating steps, each of them involving a gap in the passage from matter to form, but a small and potentially reversible gap.

Serres's texts, I would argue, resemble this expedition (and, to a certain extent, Latour's multilayered account of it) much more than they resemble a scientific paper, or a disciplined work of philosophy, or—for that matter—any disciplinary discourse. He displays a series of steps in his thought: the passages between concrete and abstract, the way etymology overlaps or seconds a concrete or technical process. He treats *governance* and *cybernetics* not as prestigious or dangerous master-words but as practices whose workings and implications can be better understood if we understand the real-time work of the helmsman, the *kubernetes*. Serres's texts are of course not the world, nor are they science, nor are they *Science in Action,* to borrow one of Latour's titles, but they mime the whole context and process of knowing rather than simply reporting knowledge. As Latour put it in the 1988 article cited above, they "display the knower and the known" and all the processes of connection and mediation that connect them.[10] They are, perhaps, *Writing in Action* or *Language in Action.* Serres includes not only the abstractions and reductions, the general statements that gain in universality and portability over their referents, but also many of the steps and processes by which one reaches them, and a strong sense of the locality and materiality to which they are connected and without which they would have no reason to exist. His texts, in other words, mimic science in the making, philosophy in the making, even while they include and present settled statements of both scientists and philosophers. Of course in one sense this is simply good argumentative rhetoric: Serres convinces readers by enabling them to follow and assent to the steps he takes. Its particularity is not simply that it is rhetoric (and often narrative, and sometimes poetic) but that it is undisciplined rhetoric, in that Serres rarely presupposes the world already mapped and repertoried and conceptually cut up so that a discipline can apply its knowledge to it at well-defined levels, in an orderly direction. In this respect Serres's texts exemplify Latour's suggestion, in "The Politics of Explanation," that what's needed in the making and communication of knowledge are not theoretical or methodological protocols and precautions, but many forms of explanation, "the many genres and styles of narration invented by novelists, journalists, artists, cartoonists, scientists, and philosophers."[11]

Serres's particular medium of communication is writing, and this is the obvious and not incorrect answer to the question of why language and story are so important to him. But it is too easy to say the obvious, and in fact there are more specific reasons, supported by both Serres's practices as a writer and his discussions of language, for contending that language and the narrative knowledge that accompanies it are central to his thought and work.

These reasons, however, are very different from those that have put language at or near the center of much critical work for generation or two, ever since the first flourishing of structuralism. The insight that society, forms of behavior, self, and the unconscious are ordered by language and language-like structures made the analysis of language and culture into a crucial activity for those who wished to lay claim to an understanding of, or a capacity for action in, the humanly ordered world. The sense that discourse powerfully shapes and constrains perception, thought, habit, and action made exposing and, if necessary, denouncing the workings of discourse a seeming royal road to social change, or at least to the cultural work that seemed so important to social change.[12] The commonplace that reality, or at least much of it, is linguistically (or culturally or socially) constructed, so that interventions in discourse remake reality, has become for many a central legitimization of scholarship in the humanities. This language-centered paradigm, Serres wrote in 1977, offers worthwhile results but risks becoming blind to what is outside its own scope: "It cannot see, by virtue of its hypothesis, that things are in a space and transform one another even when we are not there to write or speak about them" (*LD*, 280).

Serres's project, by contrast, is to use words so as best to evoke what is outside them. This gap between his project for using language and the agenda of many people in the humanities may account for much of the resistance or indifference to his work. Serres's writings don't correspond to what by now are the standard expectations of the "postmodern" or "cultural constructivist" humanities community. They don't directly provide justification or material for the task of cultural critique. Instead of offering exhortations or techniques useful in denouncing conventional language and culture as manipulative or oppressive (or in praising emergent, avant-garde productions for carrying out such denunciation), Serres continually renews his attempts to show that the writer's task is not only to deploy words but to reach the world, to convey something of its extrahuman beauty and structure to the minds of its readers so that they can think in new ways and through new words about the times and places in which they live.

The most crucial reason for Serres's emphasis on language and story, I believe, is that he regards them as central to human understanding; or, in other words, that he locates them at or near the middle of the stages of human cognitive development. One could compare Serres's observations on this point, found most obviously in *Genesis, Les Cinq Sens,* and *The Troubadour of Knowledge,* to an account offered by the Canadian educational philosopher Kieran Egan. In his 1997 book, *The Educated Mind: How Cognitive Tools Shape Our Understanding,*[13] Egan argues that individual education recapitulates the developmental series of modes of knowing that have unfolded over the course of human prehistory and history. He calls these forms somatic, mythic, romantic, philosophic, and ironic understanding; they correspond, very roughly, to the prelinguistic body (somatic), the stories and practices of oral culture (mythic), the additional forms of memory and narrative made possible by writing (romantic), the more fixed and abstracted modes of language use fostered by print (philosophic), and finally what one might call the postprint synthesis and interference of all the preceding modes (ironic). Language, from its oral through its printed forms, is clearly at the heart of this sequence: the crucial technology for the long middle of human cultural evolution and individual education.

Serres, for his part, uses a similar framework in arguing that forms of perception and knowledge are not autonomous or isolated, that disciplines and discourses are not self-contained or self-validating. He hears speakers of language saying, "In the beginning was the word," scientists announcing that truth is in science, and he declines to accept these self-authentifying claims. Each level of knowledge and discourse production, he argues, arises out of a more fundamental level to which it retains connections, without which it could not have come into being, and whose knowledge is vaster and in some ways closer to the materiality and local specificity of its objects in the world. The user of language inhabits a sensory and kinesthetic body, the novelist draws on the accretions of language, the philosopher follows repertoires of stories and tales, the scientist draws on the whole cultural reservoir. "In the beginning is not the word. The word comes where it is expected. one writes initially through a wave of music, a groundswell that comes from the background noise, from the whole body, maybe" (*G,* 138). The honor of philosophy, in some ways too removed from what matters, lies in articulating this general principle of knowledge: that abstract and general knowledge is neither fundamental nor superior. "But only philosophy can go deep enough to show that literature goes still deeper than philosophy" (*TK,* 65). Serres is a philosopher arguing that stories are more fundamental than arguments, a writer telling the story that in the beginning was not the word.[14]

Language and story, then, would be central for Serres not because the linguistic construction of reality is foundational or because myths are primordial, but because language and the forms of knowledge most dependent on it occupy such a large middle in the developmentally layered forms of human knowledge. He locates speech as, in effect, the first major technology added to the body and its five senses, and then as the platform or environment for such further techniques as writing-based philosophical reasoning and instrumentally and mathematically based science.

Serres's desire not to have disciples corresponds to his conviction that the matrices of theoretical language are poor and repetitive beside the rich fluctuations of natural languages in their concreteness, and that human language in general owes what variety and rhythm it has to being produced by complex, warm-blooded creatures in a variegated world, formed in material processes of becoming far longer and deeper than anything we human latecomers can imagine. Intellectual alignment takes place indoors, or at least in policed spaces: on-line, in the seminar room or amphitheater, at best in the public square of the city. The experiences and words that matter most, for Serres, that have the power to reshape minds, bodies, and live, are those that take place or lead outside the academy and the polis. The swimmer's body must adapt to the turbulence of the channel, just as the translators must invent new ways of using both their languages so as to pass between them.

Just as there is both sound and inscription in language, Serres writes in *Nouvelles du monde,* the sea both makes the music of its waves and writes the traces of its ebb and flow on beaches and banks. The roar and traces are natural signs of the sea's complex and powerful movements. But humans can only understand this nonhuman language if they throw themselves into it, risking their all, swimming naked or piloting a small and vulnerable craft. Those who stay on the surface, whether as cruise passengers on deck or even surfers encased in rubber suits, will be unable to translate the sea. Likewise for language: "He who surfs on the work forgets what the body can do and know when it puts its faith, madly, in the adventure of writing."[15] Human writing and language join an already articulated world and must complement it by offering comparable complexities, comparable risks of becoming.

How, then, should one react to Serres's writing except by being *influenced*—buffeted and shaped by its flow? His texts are an invitation that is also an expulsion, a challenge to use the powers of language and mind in an outdoor, embodied way. No disciples, then, but translators swimming the channels of communication; no followers on the same path, but a thousand readers and writers whose own paths changed course when they wandered into the mountains, gorges, beaches, and waters of his texts.

NOTES

1. Note also the initial description of the body of water in question: "a large and tempestuous river or a rough strait, an arm of the sea" (*TK,* 4).

2. "Voyages extraordinaires au pays des parasites," *Libération,* March 8–9, 1980, 14.

3. Roman Jakobson, "Closing Statement: Linguistics and Poetics," in *Style and Language,* ed. Thomas Sebeok (Cambridge: MIT Press, 1960), 356.

4. Jean Paulhan, "Alain ou la preuve par l'étymologie," in *Oeuvres completes* (Paris: Cercle du livre précieux, 1966), 3:275.

5. Ibid., 276.

6. Bruno Latour, "The Politics of Explanation: An Alternative," in *Knowledge and Reflexivity: New Frontiers in the Sociology of Knowledge,* ed. Steve Woolgar (London: Sage, 1988), 157–58.

7. Michel Serres, *Le Passage du nord-ouest. Hermès* V (Paris: Minuit, 1980), 24.

8. William Paulson, "Le Cousin Parasite: Balzac, Serres et le démon de Maxwell," *Stanford French Review* 9 (1985): 397–414.

9. Bruno Latour, *Pandora's Hope: Essays on the Reality of Science Studies* (Cambridge: Harvard University Press, 1999), 24–79.

10. Latour, "The Politics of Explanation," 172.

11. Ibid., 173.

12. Paul de Man can be said to have provided the canonical formulation of this argument: "[M]ore than any other mode of inquiry, including economics, the linguistics of literariness is a powerful and indispensable tool in the unmasking of ideological aberrations." "The Resistance to Theory," *Yale French Studies* 63 (1982): 11.

13. Kieran Egan, *The Educated Mind: How Cognitive Tools Shape Our Understanding* (Chicago: University of Chicago Press, 1997).

14. I develop the preceding point at greater length in William Paulson, "Writing That Matters," *SubStance,* no. 83 (1997): 25–27.

15. Michel Serres, *Nouvelles du monde* (Paris: Editions J'ai Lu, 1999), 119 (vv. 112–19).

FRÈRES AMIS, NOT ENEMIES

Serres between Prigogine and Girard

WILLIAM JOHNSEN

Before anything else, an inaugurating memory from the Stanford Conference on Disorder and Order in the Human Sciences in 1981, an all-world collection of Nobel Prize winners and luminaries organized principally by René Girard and Jean Pierre Dupuy, but bearing the unmistakable stamp of Michel Serres's aspirations for passages between the sciences.[1] Ilya Prigogine had just finished lecturing on turbulence theory and dissipative structures. Serres reminded the audience that turbulence was rooted etymologically in *turba,* linking the activity of crowd and molecular behavior, which levitated Girard and half a dozen others into a torrent of spirited exchange.

In addition to his strategic interventions throughout, Serres's paper "Dream" was the last word of the conference. It is worth noting that the delegates Serres tied into a communicative knot were themselves voyagers between disciplines. To link up Girard and Prigogine is to connect work that is already ambitious of connections across the sciences, but in the case of Prigogine and Girard, it is work not already interconnected. And it is here that we can identify Serres's ambitiousness: no one else could risk his itinerary, no one else could achieve his level of success at bridging the sciences. If we were to go further into the dynamics of conferencing, we might identify Serres's human effectiveness in working with others (despite his avowed abhorrence of "debate"), but it would be better to underline his success in injecting that bold comradeliness in his writing.

Intellectuals as independent as Henri Atlan, Francisco Varela, Edgar Morin, Paul Watzlawick, Cornelius Castoriadis, Heinz Von Foerster, and Kenneth Arrow were not likely to become mere ephebes of the Girardian or any other paradigm. (Nor has discipleship for anyone ever been part of

Serres's mission.) But an appropriate measure for Serres's effectiveness at the conference and his travels between the sciences is the idea of a *hypothesis* common to his work and Girard's: not a theory already finished, not a proof that repeats the already known, a hypothesis is a proposal of some likeliness that negotiates the greatest possible risk of failure with the greatest possible gain.[2] What hypothesis was Serres proposing?

Serres's interventions at Stanford can stand for his writing, given over to his readers with the stylistic freshness of the engineer's inspired invention of special tools unique to the task that any *bricoleur* can only dream about. Yet it would be wrong to suggest that Serres had just cooked up the connection in *turba* between Girard's model for disorder breeding order and turbulence theory in the physical sciences, for it is written into his work of the late seventies. Further, it is just what is needed to connect up (at least) Prigogine and Girard from the same period. As a way of surveying Serres's work at the conference and his lifelong travels between the sciences, it may be appropriate to reinvoke that historical moment in the work of Serres and Girard.

Leading up to the conference in 1981, Serres had published *La Naissance de la physique dans le texte de Lucrèce. Fleuves et turbulences* (1977), *Hermes IV. La distribution* (1977), *Hèrmes V. Le passage du Nord-Ouest* (1980), *Le Parasite* (1980); *Genèse* (1982) and *Rome* (1983) would soon follow. A special issue of *Critique* in 1979 was devoted to Michel Serres, where both Girard and Ilya Prigogine and Isabelle Stengers place Serres's work.[3] Further, Johns Hopkins University Press brought out *Hermes: Literature, Science, and Philosophy* (selections from his work) and *The Parasite* in 1982.

Girard had published *Des choses cachées depuis la fondation du monde* in 1978, which expanded *La Violence et la sacré* (1972) as prodigiously as *La Violence* had expanded the remarkable book on the novel, *Mensonge romantique et vérité romanesque* (1963). Girard would spend the next twenty years elaborating and detailing this summa, but this process would begin with *Le Bouc émissaire* in 1982, after the conference.

Ilya Prigogine's Nobel Prize in chemistry in 1977 was awarded for his work on dissipative structures. Prigogine has tirelessly spoken up on the global implications for science and technology, yet it is *La Nouvelle Alliance,* coauthored with Isabelle Stengers in 1979, that articulated for a generation the fundamental changes in scientific knowledge and method.

As we review Serres's titles for this period, we see the important shift in method and style that has divided his readers, a division that Bruno Latour usefully characterizes as commentary and creation. Serres explained to Latour that he was himself transformed by the modern transformation of scientific knowledge and method that he encountered early in his academic studies. His earliest work follows a common paradigm. Art (and language itself, by means of etymology, which links the earliest conceptualizations in language with the latest, especially in French) is given a new credit and a new distinction by suggesting the way some works anticipate and participate in this new scientific knowledge.

Serres is not exercising any fashionable structuralist neoprimitivism, insisting that everything we know is already in Lucretius—his reasoning here, at least, is simple. Art sees, hears, feels. The greatest masters of the human sensorium cannot help but observe beyond and beside the conventions of knowledge, the pieties of their own time. Their care in recording what they found to be true has a quasi-theoretical potential. Lucretius, La Fontaine, Zola, Turner, Verlaine are delivered from two opposed camps who agree solely in the way they trivialize cultural knowledge. Within these two camps, either these artists are irrelevant because they are trapped in an outmoded world view of reality, or, worse still, they are encased by their admirers in a false transcendence that frees them from ever commenting on a mundane reality.

The strength or answerability of this earliest period in Serres's writing is that (as he himself argues) even the old-fashioned explication de texte will verify that his hypothesis for Lucretius or Leibniz is stronger because it accounts for more of their work, in detail and in general.

However, when we come to *The Parasite,* we see the results of a development already signaled in the *Hermes* series. The balance has shifted from the more comfortable world of philosophy as textual commentary and textual verification (the purification of error) to philosophy as poetic creation. There are no doubt many reasons for this shift; no single reason could ever account for it. Yet a more careful consideration of this work around the time of the Stanford conference may give us another way of estimating this fundamental shift in Serres's writing.

In *La Naissance de la physique dans le texte de Lucrèce* (1977), Serres had already deployed the etymology of *turba* to stand for the chaotic and unassimilable quality of reality irreducible to cause and effect, and *turbo* to represent the apparently random Brownian motions. *Turba* and *turbo* can be conceptualized twice, in the strict figures of Lucretius's poetic language, and in the advanced physics of dissipative structures.[4] A theory of turbulence is what Lucretius shares with contemporary physics, and Serres ultimately plots out from the poem as well a radically different science and social order.

Serres gives the reader a global reading of Lucretius that unites his science and religion, superior to the readings that outmode him by tying him to a dismissable science and pagan religion, and gives the reader as well the expansive delight of feeling one more intelligent and subtle writer has been added to one's intellectual life. The whole demonstration in *La naissance de la physique* still gives pleasure by its elegance, briefness, and verifiability.

Across the book Serres develops Lucretius's distinction between a science of Mars and a science of Venus, into a distinction between a violent and nonviolent social order, the disabling or enabling social context in which all knowledge resides. In the section entitled "Conditions culterelles. Violence et contrat: Science et religion" Serres argues that Lucretius's poem calls the change between these two social orders that propose two different knowledges or sciences, the *foedus* or *foedera fati* and a new *foedera naturae*.

> This is the *foedus fati,* what physics understands as a law; things are that way. It is also the legal statute in the sense of dominant legislation: they wish things to be that way. Mars chose this sort of physics, the science of the fall and of silence. And here again is the plague. It is always the same sequence of events: an epidemic becomes pandemic in proportions, if not to say a pandemonium; violence never stops, streaming the length of the thalweg; the atoms fall endlessly; reason repeats indefinitely. Buboes, weapons, miasmas, causes: it is always the same law, in which the effect repeats the cause in exactly the same way. (*H,* 100)

The new *foedera naturae* breaks this chain of plague and causality.

> The angle of inclination cures the plague, breaks the chain of violence, interrupts the reign of the same, invents the new reason and the new law, *foedera naturae,* gives birth to nature as it really is. The minimal angle of turbulence produces the first spirals here and there. It is literally revolution. Or it is the first evolution toward something else other than the same. Turbulence perturbs the chain, troubling the flow of the identical as Venus had troubled Mars. *(H,* 100)

In the natural world, successive marshaled waves are always broken sooner or later by rock or eddy, spawning a turbulence and a new order that Lucretius's poem can reverence and contemporary physics theorize, but the starkness of the choice between the "Heracleitan physics of war" and "the physics of vortices, of sweetness, and of smiling voluptuousness" (*H,* 100) means it is not a question of what physics anyone would choose, but how to make the choice possible.

For Serres, the promise in Lucretius's physics was put aside in classical science. Serres reminds us that Bacon felt that man should serve nature, but Descartes would rather master it. The *foedera* or contract with nature was redefined as the relation of master to slave. The role for science that society determines cannot change scientific truth, but it conditions the manner in which science is learned and deployed. "The presence of Mars or Venus determines the shape of the realm of knowledge" (*H,* 107).

Yet the theorizing of that loss is forecast in Lucretius as well. The *foed-*

era fati, the "blood contract" (*H,* 109), is embodied in the sacrifice of Iphigenia that opens *De rerum natura.* Sacrifice temporarily solves the immediate problem of internal disorder and conflict in the community by polarizing everyone against one, but itself becomes another problem.

> The problem at hand consists in stemming a series of murders without another assassination. For that solution is only temporary until a new crisis, a new squall, or a new epidemic erupts and the whole process is repeated. Nothing is new under the bloodied sun of history. The plague reappears in an Athens bestrewn with cadavers. The scapegoats too must be saved by putting a stop to the series of sacrifices. From this comes the reversal: he who speaks and thereby gives rise to a new history does not place the sins of the world on the shoulders of another; of his own volition, he takes upon himself the thunderous roars of the heavens, the fire that has been set at the world's gates, the wrath of Jupiter. Spontaneously, he accepts the dangerous position that is determined by his knowledge of the laws of the universe and of human mechanisms. Faced with these horrible menaces, he goes forward unarmed. . . . To take on oneself alone the fire of the heavens and not to foist unleashed violence on the first passerby, the virgin Iphigenia, to go forward unarmed, straight ahead, lucidly deciphering what is happening, is to proceed in a fashion opposed to the world's religions and contrary to the terrifying constitution of the sacred. But this conduct can only be practiced if one knows the laws of constitution and if one is a master of justice. Epicurus is a god outside of all the gods, the new god of another history who has examined all the archaic traditions and turned against them. He abolishes the sacred by fulfilling it. The atheistic Epicureans were not wrong to venerate the founder of this science as a god. And through his courageous gesture, heroic above the call of heroism, Epicurus lets Venus be born above the troubled waters. That is to say, the *foedus,* love, and friendship; the contract of nature, *foedera naturae.* It is finally definitive, and the gods are no longer in the world, since an end to the ancient repetition of the sacrificial crisis has intervened, a cessation which is the basis of Epicurean wisdom. (*H,* 109–10)

In a kind of sidebar to his own construing, Serres concludes this long and eloquent paragraph: "This is, I believe, the solution that René Girard would have given to the whole question, a solution parallel to my own" [C'est la solution qu'aurait, je croix, donnée René Girard à l'ensemble de la question. Elle est parallèle à la mienne] (*N,* 163).[5] Serres brings in Girard suddenly in a manner so remarkable that it is worth discussing at length.

Once we have been alerted to Girard's sympathetic presence, we can see him just off the page throughout *La Naissance de la physique.* In theory it is not difficult to isolate the Girardian model. *Mensonge romantique et vérité romanesque* (1963) proposed that certain novels tell the truth of human behavior: desire is mediated, copied from others. Copying the desire of another (while pretending not to) leads to conflict between subject and model, often exacerbated to a point where a mutual fascination-obsession of subject and model excludes the contested object of desire.

La Violence et la sacré (1972) found this mimetic rivalry covertly everywhere in myth and ritual, and Girard expanded the theory to provide a genetic model for all cultural forms. Primitive myth and ritual address everything that affects humans that they cannot control but above all, violence. The scapegoat mechanism, which is behind every ritual, is the formalization of the wearing out of spontaneous violence. In the undifferentiated melee of breakaway violence, everyone is fighting with everyone else. But whoever wins or survives the immediate conflict must "take sides" with an adjoining conflict, or become the object of someone else's decision. This line of development produces eventually, and at great cost, a final solution: everyone left against the last antagonist.

Beyond the primitive bonds well explained by ethological models of dominance patterns in herds and packs, the size of the group depends on its ability to recall this solution with the least number of casualties. The best score is all against one. Humans have no doubt made other attempts at social cohesion, but the near universal presence of sacrificial rite and prohibition in every human culture suggests that scapegoat effects alone have been the only effective form of cultural survival.

The victim is sacred because s/he is blamed for everything that has gone wrong, but also, once the scapegoat is expelled, s/he is credited with the peace that follows. Rite and prohibition resemble each other all over the world because scapegoat effects seem to have been the only successful solution to the problem of human conflict. Rite and prohibition are nevertheless somewhat different all over the world because human groups interpret, or rather, *misinterpret* the scapegoat mechanism. (In fact, if they interpret it correctly, recognizing the arbitrary nature of the scapegoat, they lose it.) Societies think out, rationalize what they believe, what they must do to keep the peace. Some societies emphasize the beneficial effect of their victim. (Girard boldly derives the kingship system from this effect.) Other societies emphasize the malignant nature of the scapegoat. Necessarily, the mechanism deteriorates into crisis over time. Societies that cannot agree on whom to blame, that find themselves disunited despite rite and prohibition, multiply their victims in search of the right (efficacious) one. They find a new unity or disintegration.

After 1972, beginning in interviews,[6] Girard began considering the relation of "texts of persecution" to *l'écriture judéo-chrétienne*. Medieval texts of persecution that blamed witches or Jews for everything that went wrong were unknowingly driven by a scapegoat mechanism invisible to the author, but a text (above all, the Gospels) that consciously sided with victims, elaborated the truth of scapegoating. Over time, the Christian revelation of a perfectly innocent victim has marked all the other persecuted as not uniquely guilty of what they are accused. The revelation of scapegoating as a principle divests humanity of the only method it has devised up until now to control human violence (through violence). Humans are left with only one solution to the problem: make peace without any violence or destroy themselves.

Serres's emphasis on Lucretius's veneration of Epicurus as innocent, and tying Lucretius to the possibility of a new science, shows that Serres has followed out Girard's development of the model in the journals in the early seventies, before its elaboration in *Des choses cachées depuis la fondation du monde* in 1978. But where does Girard's "solution" begin in *La Naissance de la physique*? Where did Serres's solution disappear? Are they somehow both present, in parallel position? Serres has written up his thinking in such a comradely way that it's not possible to "decide," to surgically separate these twins, no matter how carefully the reader walks back from this place in the text. It is probably better to invoke the troubadour custom of including a friend's poem among your own, best to follow out Serres by securing our hold on the problem to which this is a solution.

Serres has been situating science as unconditional but conditioned: entropy will always increase in a closed system, but individual societies will deploy their science according to different values.

> Lucretius speaks of eponymous heroes; Descartes and Bacon speak in abstract principles, but these principles sparkle with metaphors; we speak as historians. The question, however, remains the same in all three languages, bearing on the very conditions of possibility of science. What can be said about nature: is she an enemy or a slave, an adversary or partner in a contract that Lucretius would have made with Venus? (*H*, 105)

To prepare ourselves for Girard's response in their theoretical *renga*,[7] we can identify the cultural variables or languages as myth (the term we use for what others believe or say), and the unconditional as the truth of human knowledge and behavior no matter where and how it is said.

In "Rite, travail, science" published in the issue of *Critique* devoted to Michel Serres, Girard begins with Serres's idea from *Feux et signaux de brume: Zola* that myth and knowledge are intermixed in science, that knowledge is present in myth.

> Serres affirme, répétons-le, que *le myth—le rite—reste dense dans le savoir, et reciproquement*. C'est la première partie de cette proposition qui

est toujours illustrée dans les régions supérieures de la science, celles
que nous visitons avec Michel Serres, touristes souvent effarés, toujours
émerveillés. Les régions inférieures n'ont pas les mêmes prestiges mais
c'est vers elles qu'il faut se porter pour illustrer la seconde partie de la
proposition, le *et réciproquement*. Où commence la complicité
réciproque entre le savoir et le mythico-rituel? . . .

Il en est ainsi parce que les comportements officiellement reconnus et
étiquetés comme religieux sont pré-sélectionnés en vertu de leur
inefficacité même. Toujours préalable à toute analyse, le définition du
religieux comme superstition ou superstructuelle commande à notre
insu le découpage des données culturelles. Nous ne reconnaissions
comme essentiellement rituelles, en d'autres termes; que les conduites
qui n'ont pas abouti et ne peuvent jamais aboutir à une technique perçue
par nous comme utile, à un savoir qui serait véritablement savoir.[8]

Girard humorously acknowledges the extent to which Serres's command
of scientific knowledge exceeds his own, but still manages to address Serres's special subject, the "two cultures" problem, from the common side:
the common negligence of myth's capacity for generating knowledge.
Moderns recognize rite solely in the ritualistic, by which we mean empty,
repetitive, compulsive. Seasonal and funerary rites cannot change anything, of course, but tell us a good deal about ritual itself. All forms of
change in primitive society are monitored by ritual and prohibition. Anything that resembles the decomposition of the social order is seen as a
sacred sign of an impending crisis.

Thus Girard brings the discussion back to the central problem of cultural crisis. Ritual would restore order through disorder by pushing
through disorder as quickly and completely as possible. The decomposition of the dead is pushed through by fire or interment. Girard strictly
satisfies the series indicated in his title ("Rite, travail, science") by linking
the ritual processing of the dead to food processing. Lingering rituals sur-
rounding the sciences of fermentation (wine, cheese, bread), which we
ignore because these practices embody real knowledge, suggest that such
homely industries (like the more well-established vocations of hunting and
smithwork) are brought to fruition by the ritual process.

Il faut rapprocher les comportements dont la nature rituelle nous sem-
ble douteuse, parce qu'ils aboutissent à de vrais techniques et à un véri-
table savoir, des comportements dont la nature rituelle nous paraît
indubitable; parce qu'ils ne mènent à rien. C'est ce que j'ai essayé de
faire dans *Des choses cachées depuis la fondation du monde*. Nous ne voulons
pas reconnaître dans la conduite religieuse des Aïnous; à l'égard de leurs
ours, un comportement analogue à celui qui a visiblement entraîné,
chez peuples de pasteurs, la domestication de certaines espèces ani-

males. Les résultats trop positifs nous dissimulent l'origine rituelle de notre viande de boucherie.[9]

There can be only one logical choice between the idea that primitive groups bred and trained sheep, cattle, dogs, fowl knowing that their efforts would bear fruit hundreds of years later, or that these animals were subjects of ritual practice whose management ultimately produced as a fortunate by-product domesticated animals useful for labor or food (and produced as well the knowledge that some sacrificial animals, like bears, couldn't be domesticated).

Thus, reading Serres has allowed Girard to elaborate further a position he initially established at Lévi-Strauss's expense in *La Violence,* that myth can sometimes produce knowledge. Girard upended Lévi-Strauss's statement that sometimes myths "take the biological facts into account"[10] by suggesting that myth is usually prior to such a biological "fact" as paternity. In fact, prohibitions regulating sexual relations alone are capable of creating the conditions that limit sexual behavior sufficiently to make the observation of these "facts" possible.

Girard's self-deprecating modesty as he imagines himself a tourist in Serres's native habitat of scientific theory perhaps marks a difficult problem for Serres's agenda for voyaging between the sciences of nature and man. The great majority of his readers are closer to Girard in their modest knowledge of scientific theory than to Serres. And who is listening on the other side?

In "La Dynamique, de Leibniz à Lucrèce,"[11] Ilya Prigogine and Isabelle Stengers address with irreversible clarity the issue of style in scientific theory, which becomes their means of focusing on Serres's contribution to the understanding of science as it is practiced in society.

Serres is credited with disturbing the easy and too-familiar dismissal of "classical" physics by the moderns. Prigogine and Stengers locate the ultimate model of one recurring style in the history of science in Leibniz's monads, where all processes are reversible, including the relation of the local to the global. They see that Serres has located in Lucretius the birth of the physics that must accommodate the irreversible (dissipative structures) as well as the reversible, in the science of mastery over nature.

All laminar flows can become unstable past a certain threshold of velocity, and that was known just as the productive nature of organized forms, of bifurcating evolution, of what we call dissipative structures, was known. One must ask how an abstraction of this knowledge could have been made to describe the world in order, subject to a universal law. We already know one answer given by Serres. Classical science is a science of engineers who knew, of course, that their flows were never perfectly laminar, but who made the theory of laminar flow perfectly controllable and directable, the only flow for which knowing is controlling. (*H,* 154)

In *Critique,* Prigogine and Stengers praise the force of Serres the commentator, who upends the designation "classical" in the history of science's "style." Girard also approves of Serres's insistence that there is myth in science, and adds to the flames by emphasizing the more provocative tag to Serres's formula, "et reciproquement."

If Girard and Prigogine and Stengers speak from different places on Serres's itinerary, they praise the same style, in the same "style." It is clear that Girard enjoys the way that Serres upends the relation of myth to science, and it is clear that Prigogine and Stengers take pleasure as well.

> Thus Leibniz was unequivocally a "pre-Newtonian." This is a condemnation, moreover, that is sufficiently justified by his rejection of the principles of inertia and of interaction at a distance—in short, of Newtonian physics. In the face of this condemnation, we can make three remarks.
>
> In the first place, one might well ask, solely based on the facts, whether it is not the history of physics that has "missed" Leibniz. (*H,* 139)

Girard's most moving defense of modern culture is identifying it as the period where "victims have rights." Yet the last stage of the decomposition of sacrificial practices (accusing others of that which they are not uniquely guilty) can be delayed by one last round of accusing each other of scapegoating, righteously defending the innocent. Here the age of suspicion in philosophy and the sign of the Paraclete in Girard are one. But O woe unto those who missed Leibniz. This style of upending the status quo common to Girard and Prigogine and Stengers is not different from the designation of "classical" to physics, to demonstrate at once the obsolescence of the subject and the modernity of the speaker.

At the conference at Stanford two years later, both Girard and Prigogine stay "on message." "Disorder and Order in Mythology" and "Order Out of Chaos" can easily be sorted to their proper authors. Girard and Prigogine speak ex cathedra on the topics they own, but Serres delivers in "Dream" what was to be the last word of the conference as poetry, not commentary. It is now time to suggest why.

> When René Girard asked me to be the last speaker, I did not view this as an unexpected honor, but as the painful duty of becoming the functionary of synthesis. How can one express the synthesis of diverse discourses, each of which already contained or expressed, in its own genre, a synthesis? How could I express it? For the moment I have not answered this question. I have therefore chosen to narrate the synthesis

in a language that will abstain from using any technical vocabulary. In
other words, instead of accumulating the languages of the mathematician, the physicist, the biologist, the sociologist, the historian of religions, etc., I will try to be none of these. Instead of more: less; instead
of addition: a subtraction; instead of the full: the empty. I will speak,
then, as naively as possible, and I have resolved to speak as if in a dream.
(225)

Although this is perhaps the most polite way to charm such a potent gathering,[12] Serres's disingenuous explanation won't account for other examples in this period of what moves forward in his ensemble of writing practices to become his dominant *style*. When Serres puts aside demonstrations
that turn the tables, he develops another consequence of his early contribution to communication theory first introduced in the late sixties, the
exclusion of noise or the third person that guarantees transmission, communication.[13] The motive of the new model of poetry rather than commentary becomes, "How might one communicate without excluding or
upending someone, how might one speak to all?"

"Dream" is a parable, which speaks approvingly of the Tower of Babel as
a sign of the localness of order amid a larger disorder, order proceeding
from disorder, sometimes.

One organism speaks instead of taking refuge in the redundant order of
instinct; facing the gusts of circumstances, it spreads out everywhere
and has an unstable history. The amount of sound and fury would also
speak the flexibility, power, and sophistication of a given technology:
there is very little noise in a lever, some more in a clock, and the topography of a motor is already designed in relation to the chaos of the boiler
or cylinder. The distance that separates the mechanical and the living
worlds is a distance that consists of contingencies, of handling unrelated
multiplicities, of flexible functioning when there is turbulence, of
returning to a state of equilibrium, in unpredictable ways, after an accident. This amount of sound and fury would also speak the refined
progress of science, the open politeness of a civilization or the sublimity
of a work of art. It would show, finally and above all, the simple happi-
ness of living together within such a city, the subtle pleasure of inventing, in plurality, one's behavior, one's language, one's own singular
work and private existence, one's very body.

"Dream," along with *Le Parasite,* mark Serres's turning away from demonstration to creation. Serres subsequently spends more time writing philosophy, not about it. Instead of a conflict over the best hypothesis for the
philosophical work discussed, Serres establishes a working relation within
philosophy by imitating it, positively.

One of the best examples of the positive reciprocity in his lifelong sharing of ideas is with Girard. *Rome: Le livre des fondations* (1983) is certainly his
most Girardian work, as he retells the myths of (sacrificial) origin sur-
rounding Rome. He "likens" his work to Girard's, more than he demonstrates the scapegoat hypothesis. He does not tediously quote Girard, but
shares his ideas. In return Girard's book of this period, *Le Bouc émissaire*
(1982), thanks Serres openly for showing him the same passages in Pliny
that Girard then uses to establish his reading.

The differences between the two books are instructive. Girard has
never been more precise in patiently answering any conceivable objection
to his hypothesis, as he carefully builds his argument step by step. Yet
Girard's characterization of his own generation of intellectuals is instructive.

> Si vous voulez dire par là que j'ai toute la combativité des intellectuels
> de ma génération, je vous l'accord volontiers. Et mes défauts person-
> nels; je l'ai déjà suggéré, donnent à certains de mes propos des réso-
> nances plus dures qu'il ne serait souhaitable et, de façon générale,
> nuisent à mon efficacité.[14]

The respective *styles* of Girard and Serres are very different, yet they agree
on the competitive and combative character of the intellectual climate of
the second half of the twentieth century. We need a full-scale demonstration of their intellectual amity over thirty years,[15] set against these dominant intellectual *styles* of enmity.

In earnest of such a project, we might conclude in suggesting that Serres's formulation of *le tiers exclu* in the late sixties needs to be set in relation to Girard's early model of triangular desire, which suggests an
emerging relation between rivals that excludes their amorous object in
Mensonge romantique et vérité romanesque (1963). At the conclusion of such
a comparison, we would understand the remarkable serenity of *Je vois
Satan tomber comme l'éclair* (1999), where Girard detaches his model from
"deterministic traces"[16] as the comradely reflection of the equanimous
style of Michel Serres.

NOTES

1. The papers themselves were collected in *Stanford Literary Studies,* vol. 1
(1984); two of the discussions were transcribed, as well as ensuing discussions from
some of the papers, which give some sense of the sharpness of exchange.

2. Serres's most elegant formulation might be, "drawing the *maximum* number
of results from a *minimum* number of suppositions" (C, 144). Girard: "To earn the
glorious title of scientific . . . [a hypothesis] must combine the maximum of actual

uncertainty with the maximum of potential certainty." *The Scapegoat,* trans. Yvonne Freccero (Baltimore: Johns Hopkins University Press, 1986), 98.

3. René Girard, "Michel Serres: Interferences et Turbulences," *Critique* 35 (January 1979); other contributors included Shoshana Felman, Regis Debray, Christiane Fremont, Pierre Pachet, Christiane Rabant, M. A. Sinaceur, Michel Pierssens, and Claude Mouchard.

4. Prigogine and Stenger note the *turba/turbo* distinction in "Postface: Dynamics from Leibniz to Lucretius" (*H,* 153); Girard alludes to it as well in his paper to the Stanford Conference: "Disorder and Order in Mythology," in *Disorder and Order* (Stanford: Anma Libri, 1984), 86.

5. This remarkable comment on Girard appears as the end of a paragraph. In the translation for *Hermes,* it appears as a footnote (*H,* 110n), which somewhat diminishes its remarkable and sudden appearance.

6. Until the publication of *Des choses cachées depuis la fondation du monde* (Paris: Bernard Grasset, 1978).

7. The Japanese *renga* is a sequence of linked poems in which units of two or three lines are written by two or more poets. Any given link must make a poem with that which precedes it. See Charles Tomlinson, *Renga* (New York: George Braziller, 1971).

8. Girard, "Michel Serres," 24–25.

9. Ibid., 26–27.

10. René Girard, *Violence and the Sacred,* trans. Patrick Gregory (Baltimore: Johns Hopkins University Press, 1977), 223–49.

11. Ilya Prigogine and Isabelle Stengers, "La Dynamique, de Leibniz à Lucrèce," *Critique* 35 (January 1979): 35–55. The English translation ("Postface," *H,* 137–55) is slightly different, adjusting to English readers.

12. In a mock-serious note of jealousy, Heinz Von Foerster gave *his* version of what a synthesis would be like, if he had been given the last word (179).

13. See "Platonic Dialogue," *H,* 65–70.

14. René Girard, *Quand ces choses commencerent* (Paris: Arléa, 1994), 177.

15. When one notes Serres's successive academic positions in America (Johns Hopkins, SUNY Buffalo, Stanford), it is hard not to see Girard behind him. *Rome: Le livre des fondations* thanks Girard publicly.

> Par le livre présent et, si la vie ne m'est pas trop dure, par quelques autres qui suivront, j'adresse mon remerciement à la communauté des historiens qui m'accueillit, voici treize ans, quand la groupe de pression alors au pouvoir m'expulsa de mon vieux paradis: la philosophie. Ce qui me fit la vie dure. . . . Par le même, je remercie René Girard qui, dans les mêmes circonstances, m'accueillit, quasi réfugié, dans l'hospitalière Amerique, et qui, alors, m'enseigna les idées vraies ici développées. (7)

In return, we have that fine introduction Girard wrote for Serres's *Detachment,* trans. Genevieve James and Raymond Federman (Athens: Ohio University Press, 1989), which gives the force of his support for Serres's work throughout his career:

When an idea is new it inevitably falls between existing categories and it may go unnoticed for a long time; it may even look irrelevant and silly to "serious" researchers. Michel Serres is not an author for those people whose intellectual life consists in "keeping up with the literature" in one of our constantly shrinking "fields" and in believing that steady progress is being achieved simply because, as the field gets smaller, the objects left in it look larger. (viii)

16. In the introduction to *To Double Business Bound* (Baltimore: Johns Hopkins University Press, 1978) Girard reviews his collection of essays, noting what Burke called "deterministic traces." More than influences, such traces reflect the audiences Girard tried to capture: structuralist, poststructuralist, etc. When Girard presents the mimetic hypothesis in *Je vois Satan tomber comme l'éclair,* he derives it clearly and peaceably from the religious tradition, leaving his skirmishes with contemporary theory behind.

"INCERTO TEMPORE INCERTISQUE LOCIS"

The Logic of the Clinamen and the Birth of Physics

HANJO BERRESSEM

> *La bête imprévue* Clinamen.
> —Alfred Jarry

In the work of Michel Serres and Gilles Deleuze, the Lucretian clinamen is a shorthand for the logic of nonlinear dynamics.[1] Jacques Lacan uses it to think the logic of trauma. In the work of Jacques Derrida, it designates the irreducible complexity of writing. From feedback loops between these reference I will, in what follows, develop the poetics of what I propose to call the "intelligent materialism" (a materialism that considers matter as "autopoietic") that informs the writings of Serres and Deleuze.

HISTORIOGRAPHY

> *Invent liquid history and the ages of water.*
> —Serres, The Birth of Physics

Let me start with a short archaeological reconstruction. (This is, I think, appropriate for an investigation into Serres's work, which is itself fundamentally archaeological. Throughout, in fact, I will provide ample bibliographical and intertextual references in order to highlight that the discursive sites covered by my investigation are invariably "material" and "local.")

FLASHBACK THEORY

The year is 1977. In 1967, Jacques Derrida's *Of Grammatology* had argued the materialism of the sign. In 1970, Michel Foucault's "The Discourse on Language"—written partly with Serres in the conceptual background—had argued the materialism of history. As Foucault notes, "we must accept the introduction of chance as a category in the production of events . . . the introduction, into the very roots of thought, of notions of *chance, disconti-nuity and materiality*. This represents a triple peril which one particular form of history attempts to avert by recounting the continuous unfolding of some ideal necessity."[2] (Serres, who taught with Foucault in the 1960s, is referenced twice in *The Archaeology of Knowledge;* Serres includes two long articles on Foucault's work in *Hermes I* [1968] and uses the expression "les mots et les choses"—no longer an innocent term "after Foucault"—in *The Birth of Physics*). In 1972, Gilles Deleuze and Félix Guattari's *Anti-Oedipus* had argued the materialism of the unconscious (one reference to Serres in *Anti-Oedipus;* a number of references to *The Birth of Physics*—in which Serres explicitly states that "the id is material" [B, 105]—in *A Thou-sand Plateaus* [1980]). In 1973, Jacques Lacan's *The Four Fundamental Con-cepts of Psycho-Analysis* had argued the materialism of the language of the unconscious. In 1976, Jean Baudrillard's *L'Échange symbolique et la mort* had argued the immaterialism of a culture of simulation in which the "real has become the rational," a statement Serres does not stop arguing and polemicizing against. The stage was set, then, for 1977, the year in which Serres's *The Birth of Physics* and *Hermes IV: La distribution* argue the intelli-gent materialism of the world. (Before these publications, Serres's world had been a world of thermodynamics and cybernetic noise, although chaotic clouds had already drifted in, to finally rain themselves out at the programmatic beginning of *Hermes V* [1980], a meditation on Robert Musil's "lecture on the weather" that opens up *The Man without Qualities.*) The year 1977 is when the weather holds its entry into philosophy.

FLASHBACK SCIENCE

The year is 1979. In 1963, Edward Lorenz's paper "Deterministic Aperi-odic Flow" had argued a world of strange attractors. In 1971, D. Ruelle and F. Takens's paper "On the Nature of Turbulence" and in 1975 J. Gol-lub and H. L. Swinney's paper "Onset of Turbulence in a Rotating Fluid" had introduced chaos into turbulence and turbulence into chaos. In 1977, Ilya Prigogine, together with Grégoire Nicolis, had written *Self-Organiza-tion in Non-equilibrium Systems: From Dissipative Structures to Order through Fluctuations*. In 1979, Lorenz had presented his "idiomatic" paper: "Pre-dictability: Does the Flap of a Butterfly's Wings Set Off a Tornado in Texas?" The year 1979 in when the weather holds its entry into science.

What makes Serres's poetological chromatics so unique is that they con-tinuously slide between "the weather of science" and "the weather of phi-losophy." In fact, one might say that there are literally two Serres. One, written from front to back, represents the scientist, the other, written from back to front, represents the poet. In the unilateral space unfolding in this chiasm, Serres writes the science of poetry and the poetry of science, constantly on a line of flight before the specter of dualism. His "northwest passages" between the two cultures result in sentences like "the hymn to Venus sings in praise of voluptuous pleasure" (*B,* 107), sentences that are as poetic as they are, in their specific contexts, scientifically precise.

SWERVE INTO CHAOS Influences Plus Confluences

> *Either I am seriously mistaken, or this is materialism.*
>
> —*Serres,* The Birth of Physics

Although *The Birth of Physics* is an important pillar in the construction of the intelligent materialism that today informs much of the theoretical scene on both sides of the "cultural divide," Serres's presence has long been a hidden one. References in the works of other writers are generally subtle and tenuous, and in the multiplex discursive "attractorspace" bundled under the name of poststructuralism, he exists mainly in footnotes and as someone who is "paracited." (He himself, of course, reciprocates this by denying— rather flatly and obsessively, one might note—any influence by other thinkers, especially in the often autobiographical *Conversations on Science, Culture, and Time.*) Derrida's "My Chances/Mes Chances: A Rendezvous with Some Epicurean Stereophonies" (1982),[3] for instance, makes ample use of the clinamen (in the work of Lucretius, the clinamen designates the "smallest possible angle" by which an atom deviates from the straight line of the fall of the atoms through a laminar void; an "infinitely small deviation" [*B,* 91] that marks the beginning of the world as atomic turbulence), but Derrida is curiously silent about Serres, who had provided, in *The Birth of Physics,* a fundamental rereading of the clinamen. (Similarly, by the way, Derrida's text, so full of chance meetings, is silent about Lacan's use of the clinamen in *The Four Fundamental Concepts of Psycho-Analysis* [1973].) Harold Bloom had used the clinamen in *The Anxiety of Influence* (1973), which means before the publication of Serres's book; providing, ironically from within a Derridean context, the theory of the specific anxiety of which Derrida's silence about Serres might actually be speaking. As Derrida notes, in staking the "Accidental" against the "Occidental": "throughout the history of Occidental culture the Democritian tradition, in which the names of Epicurus and his disciples are recorded, has been submitted since its origin . . . to a powerful repression";[4] the resonant word, of course, being "repression."

The rediscovery of atomist materialism, then, is not Serres's original contribution. Atomism had been in the air some time before 1977 and Lucretius had been discovered as an intellectual forefather before Serres's massive intervention. One especially interesting line of tradition goes from Henri Bergson's *Extraits de Lucrece avec un commentaire, des notes et une etude sur la poésie, la physique, le texte et la langue de Lucréce*[5] to Alfred Jarry, who learned of it in Bergson's philosophical lectures and who uses it in *Gestes et opinions du Docteur Faustroll* and elsewhere to ground the science of pataphysics.[6] Add to this Karl Marx's dissertation on the "Difference between the Democritean and the Epicurean Philosophy of Nature,"[7] and you have a number of important references for Deleuze, who talks of the clinamen and of its relation to multiplicity in "Lucretius and the Simulacrum" (in *The Logic of Sense*, originally published in 1961). It is probably through Deleuze's essay that the clinamen had swerved into Lacan's *Four Fundamental Concepts* and into Bloom's *Anxiety of Influence*. In fact, Deleuze's essay might well have paved the way for Serres's own Lucretian investigation. (Throughout their careers, Deleuze-Guattari and Serres were interested in similar things. In particular, both share a fascination with modern science, from Réne Thom's catastrophe theory to nonlinear dynamics. Deleuze quotes Serres extremely favorably on Leibniz [the references are to Serres's *Le Système de Leibniz et ses modèles mathématiques*][8] in *The Fold* [1988] and on various grades of multiplicity in the final chapter, "From Chaos to Brain," in *What Is Philosophy* [1991]: "There would be two infraconsciousnesses: the deeper would be structured like any set whatever, a pure multiplicity or possibility in general, an aleatory mixture of signs; the less deep would be covered by combinatory schemas of this multiplicity."[9] This is Deleuze's version—or maybe even his transposition?—of Serres's concept of pure and ordered multiplicities from *Genesis* [1982]—"the cosmos is not a structure, it is a pure multiplicity of ordered multiplicities and pure multiplicities" [*G*, 111]—into psychic space.)

What makes "Lucretius and the Simulacrum" so crucial is that it proposes a nonlinear and dynamic philosophy (a "chaotics" *avant la letter*) in which the logic of the clinamen does not only allow "to think the diverse as diverse,"[10] but in which it comes to function, in the context of the idea of nature as a complex machinic system, as "the principle of the diverse and its production"[11] as such. (Serres echoes this sentiment when he states that "the logic of . . . dualism . . . must be opened to plurality" and that what is fatal is "bringing down the multiple to two, and the specific to the general" [*B*, 98]; the general, of course, being a pun Deleuze and Guattari would later use to designate in general any "military" power of overcoding.)

Already in this "early" text, Deleuze proposes that nature is, like any complex open system, forever incomputable, because "it does not assemble its own elements into a whole,"[12] a fundamental diversity Deleuze and Guattari would later express by the formula $n - 1$, which they use in *A Thousand Plateaus* to describe the topology of the rhizome, which "constitutes linear multiplicities with n dimensions having neither subject nor object, which can be laid out on a plane of consistency, and from which the One is always subtracted [n − 1]."[13] In such "chaotic" systems, the whole is always less than the sum of its parts.

Deleuze stresses in particular Lucretius's statement that the clinamen occurs at an indeterminate moment ("incerto tempore") and in an indeterminate place ("incertisque locis") from which follows that it "takes place" in "a smaller time than the minimum of continuous, thinkable time," so that it comes to designate an impossible—always already too swiftly passed—origin and, as a result, a fundamental rather than a merely supplementary state of complexity.[14] As Deleuze states, it "has always been present: it is not a secondary movement, which would come accidentally to modify a vertical fall. It has always been present. . . . The clinamen is the original determination of the direction of the movement of the atom."[15] As such, "the clinamen manifests neither contingency nor indetermination. It manifests . . . the irreducible plurality of causes or of causal series, and the impossibility of bringing causes together into a whole."[16] As a figure of irreducible complexity, the clinamen also designates, for Deleuze, a fundamental positivity: "The multiple as the multiple is the object of affirmation, just as the diverse as diverse is the object of joy."[17] As Serres would put it later, it designates "nascent nature in joyous pleasure" (*B*, 111).

Although it is not originary (but then what ever is?), Serres's Lucretian intervention is immensely far-reaching because it sees in Lucretian physics a premonition of "postmodern science," in particular the science of nonlinear dynamics, which he sees "already" embodied in *De rerum natura* and which he reads "out of" (as well as, of course, retrospectively, "into") Lucretius. For Serres, the concept of the clinamen already "contains" the logic of nonlinear dynamics (a science, by the way, which marks the most notable blind spot around which Serres's work revolves; a work that to my knowledge nowhere mentions the name of Lorenz and only very sporadically that of Prigogine (*H*, 60), Thom,[18] or other notable figures. (In *The Birth of Physics,* he talks about nonlinear dynamics as "the new science" or "*the current state of the sciences*" [*B*, 64, 85]. Another way of keeping his references extremely vague is by talking about "present-day scholars" [*B*, 84] rather than mentioning specific names.)

From the "other side," the acknowledgment is more transparent. In *Order Out of Chaos,* Prigogine and Stengers stress, from out of nonlinear dynamics itself, the importance of Serres's rereading of Lucretius, especially in relation to the problem of turbulence, which they, like Ruelle and others, consider as the node between Lucretius, fluid mechanics, and nonlinear dynamics.[19] They also write on Serres in *Critique: Fleuves et turbulences* (1997) and provide the "Postface" to *Hermes: Literature, Science, and*

Philosophy. In *A Thousand Plateaus,* Deleuze and Guattari stress the importance of Serres's relation between the clinamen and the theory of fluid mechanics: "The strength of Michel Serres' book is that it demonstrates this link between the clinamen as a generative differential element, and the formation of vortices and turbulences in so far as they occupy an engendered smooth ['vectorial, projective, or topological'] space."[20]

In fact, in Serres's writing, nonlinear dynamics seems to be born, like Lucretius's Venus, out of the foam of fluid mechanics. As Prigogine notes, "Michel Serres has recently recalled that the early atomists were so concerned about turbulent flow that it seems legitimate to consider turbulence as a basic source of inspiration of Lucretian physics."[21] Because "the transition from laminar flow to turbulence is a process of [spontaneous] self-organization," the notion of an intelligent materialism is "not so far from the clinamen of Lucretius."[22] Somewhat ironically, Prigogine praises in Serres's intervention precisely the spirit of "connectionism" for which Sokal chastises in particular Deleuze;[23] the fact that "in Lucretian physics we thus again find the link we have discovered in modern knowledge between the choices underlying a physical description and a philosophic, ethical, or religious conception relating to man's relation to nature."[24]

THE LOGIC OF THE CLINAMEN

> There is a nature to things, a process of emergence, which is enough.
> —*Serres,* The Birth of Physics

In order to read Lucretius "with" nonlinear dynamics, one of the most important requisites is an intelligent notion of chaos. Accordingly, Serres starts his Lucretian meditation by unfolding in detail the two seemingly divergent modes of chaos that inform the Lucretian text. The first of these is the "ordered chaos" of the laminar flux that is disturbed into disorder by the clinamen: "Laminar flow, the figure of chaos, is at first sight a model of order. . . . Turbulence seems to introduce a disorder into this arrangement. . . . Disorder emerges from order" (*B*, 27). This disorder is the chaos of the Brownian background noise out of which, subsequently, temporary and local orders will emerge and that will continue to rumble through any form of order. This passage is the one from a turbulent, pure chaos (*turba* [28], whose image is turbulence) to a deterministic chaos (*turbo,* whose image is the vortex; see also 175–76). As Serres notes, "the origin of things and the beginning of order consists simply in the narrow space between *turba* and *turbo* . . . between *turbulence* and vortex. . . . The first is simply disorder and the second a particular form in movement"

(28). This movement seems to be "precisely the reverse" (27) of the first: "several orders emerge from disorder. . . . This seems contradictory. . . . Order or disorder, it is difficult to decide" (27). What is the logic of this process by which order becomes chaos and chaos becomes order? And what is the function of the clinamen in this logic?

Both of these questions lead back to the curious temporality of the clinamen Deleuze had stressed. The logical difficulty of the process stems from the fact that the two modes of chaos contract (both in the sense of drawing together and creating a legal, or better natural, contract) two moments that are generally considered to be successive. According to a classical chronology, the first moment of order (which is, according to Serres, a chaos disguised as order: the laminar flux, "the streaming chaos, the laminar flow of elements, a parallel flow in the void" [B, 30]) designates a state-time before the beginning (variously that of the world, of the subject, or of language),[25] while the second (the Brownian disorder, "the cloud-chaos, a disorganized fluctuating, Brownian mass" [B, 31]) designates a state-time after the beginning. In contracting this chronology, the logic of the clinamen comes to designate (1) the complexity of the "sudden change" from the one to the other and (2) the two different logics according to which the two modes of chaos function: "with declination, the vortex appeared against the backdrop of the first [laminar chaos]; now it appears against the backdrop of the second [the Brownian melée]" (B, 31).

About 1: In terms of temporality, the impossibility of thinking "the time of the clinamen" implies, as Deleuze had noted, the impossibility of thinking an origin. According to the logic of the clinamen, the moment of origin recedes, fractally, into ever smaller, ultimately infinitely small "zones of indeterminacy." Serres stresses this when he notes that the clinamen is the figure of both "the potential infinitely small and the actual infinitely small" (B, 4). What this means is that every designation of a moment of origin will be merely an approximation (it can never be infinitely accurate), which in turn means that whatever originates from such an incomputable origin will have "initial conditions" that can never be fully known. (See in this context also Deleuze's concept of the "dark precursor," an object that brings together disparate series without being in any way "originary.")[26] Another way of saying this is that chance events are always faster than their computation. As Serres notes, conflating the temporal and the spatial registers: "at some point [in space or time], that is to say by chance, a deviation, a very small angle is produced" (B, 11).

In marking that "turbulence appears stochastically in laminar flow" (B, 6), the clinamen interferes in the laminar flow "too fast" to allow for a separation into two successive moments, which is what Deleuze meant when he stated that the clinamen "has always been present: it is not a secondary movement, which would come accidentally to modify a vertical fall." If this is one side of the chronology (order becomes disorder), the other side is that the clinamen is immediately part of the beginning of the formation of "order" (the vortex: *turba*), as opposed to disorder (turbulence: *turbo*). As Serres notes, the "spiral order" of the vortex, which is the order of a deterministic chaos, begins already "in the infinitely small declination" (*B*, 91). At the same time that order becomes disorder, disorder becomes order, which is to say that the difference between these moments is infinitely small.

About 2: A similar "contraction" reverberates through the logical structure of the *clinamen*. Like the certain particles, which show both particle and wave properties, the clinamen is two things at the same time. As an infinitesimally small angle ("the minimum angle of formation of a vortex, appearing by chance in a laminar flow" [*B*, 6]), it is "digital" ("The *clinamen* is thus a differential, and properly, a fluxion" [4]). "At the same time," as the "origin" of turbulence, it is "analog." This is why the moment of the beginning of turbulence is that of an originary "differance": "the vortex arises by a *fluxion* in the first hypothesis . . . and by *fluctuation* in the second" (31). The first hypothesis-model, which deals with the solid-static ["solid mechanics" (7)], "opens a classical knowledge, in which disorder is minimized" (31) and leads to "infinitesimal calculus, the science of fluxions" (31). The second model, which deals with the fluid ["fluid mechanics" (11)], leads to the idea of a turbulent world: "order by fluctuation has become our problem" (31).[27] Again, these two models are contracted. For instance: although modern science favors the fluid, conscious thought has an affinity toward digitalization. Actually, if one considers "the other model [the ordered chaos of the cataract] . . . [as] only a localization of the first [the chaos of stochastic fluctuations]" (137), one can state that "the chaos-cloud is reality, the present real. The chaos-pitcher is its epistemological model" (138), so that in this context the clinamen does not only contract the logic of the digital and the analog, but also that of the theoretical (fluxion) and the practical (fluctuation): "The *clinamen* . . . is also the passage from theory to practice" (83). Ultimately, it contracts knowledge and the world.

Because it is spanned out between a stochastic and a deterministic chaos, any autopoietic system that emerges from turbulence is always "unstable and stable, fluctuating and in equilibrium, is order and disorder at once" (*B*, 30). Turbulence is "productive and destructive, as the *clinamen* is formative and declining" (92). In this context, "formation" refers to the clinamen as a generative force, while "declination" refers to the fact that, looked at from a "hydraulic" rather than a geometric angle, the clinamen introduces an *inclination* in a horizontally balanced plane, which implies that it causes an entropic *declination* toward death and stasis ("this final equilibrium from which no genesis can emerge" [37]) even while it creates turbulence, and thus life ("to *exist rather than* is to be in deviation from equilibrium" [21]). From this perspective, the clinamen introduces life through a declination of the atemporal plane of nonbeing ("It is the slope that begins with a loss of equilibrium, with a difference in relation to this pre-equilibrium that is homogeneous" [33]), so that it "grants being" (61) even while "it leads back to phenomenal non-being" (61).

The aquatic image of this twofold dynamics is that of a river flowing downstream with vortices that are stable and that in places even move upward: "rivers flow vortically, the vortices fluctuate, and all of physics is here. . . . A single movement, *quo motu* determines at once the formation and the resolution. And a single force, too, *qua vi,* compels their aggrega- tion and their dissolution" (*B,* 92–93). The *clinamen* contracts birth and death in these double dynamics: "theorem of the world: neither nothing- ness nor eternity. Neither straight line nor circle. Neither laminar flow nor stable cycle. Nature, that is to say birth, that is to say death, is the line inclined by the angle that produces a global vortex, which the wear of time brings back to the straight" (*B,* 58).

What is still missing in order to successfully map the logic of the clina- men and that of nonlinear dynamics is a cybernetics of the clinamen. Such a cybernetics is also implied in the double dynamics of the two modes of chaos. In terms of information theory, if one once more "expands" the gen- eral dynamics (order becomes chaos becomes order) for the sake of clar- ity, the movement goes from a state of laminar simplicity, "redundancy" (*B,* 146), and no-sense: ("Chaos . . . is non-sense . . . the absence of a sign, the absence of a signal" [144]; "the irreversible is without memory" [148]; "the fall is without memory, it is without code. Nature does not code the universal. Whatever their initial condition may be, things fall [150]; "this is the zero state of information, redundancy. The chain of causation, the fall of atoms, and the indefinite repetition of letters" [109]) to a state of highest complexity ("maximal improbability" and "minimal redundancy" [146]), pure multiplicity and all-sense ("multiple aleatory collisions within the infinite void of space send disordered atoms moving in *all* directions" [144]) to a state of "deterministic chaos," which designates the "space and time" of the code. It is here that "pure multiplicity" is organized into metastable, "ordered multiplicities" ("meta-stable vortices" [36]), an orga- nization that implies the creation of meaning between the borders-thresh- olds of the equally nonhuman states of no-sense (a state of lowest informa- tion content and lowest entropy) and all-sense (a state of highest information content and highest entropy), both of which, because there is no place for a code in either, are barred from the production of meaning. ("The singular and the whole either produce no information or infinite information, which has no sense either" [147], "a maximum improbability, a minimal redundancy. Everything comes from the two instances of chaos that mark the two thresholds of disorder" [146].)

Only the space between provides meaning (the production of meaning is autopoietic), and with it, memory: "the clinamen sets the first coding, it introduces a new time, writing, memory, the reversible of the negentropic" (B, 150). Taking up the hydraulic image of the river flowing downstream, Serres notes that on its way down the arrow of irreversible time, both the body and the mind "climb up" an overall entropic inclination: "things and words are negentropic tablets and by declination they escape, for the time of their existence, that is to say for as long as the code is memorised, the irreversible flux of dissolution" (150).

At this point, the clinamen contains the complete logic of nonlinear dynamics. It is based on a differentiated notion of chaos (pure or deterministic); the systems that it describes are far from equilibrium (laminar or turbulent); it accounts for their "sensitivity to initial conditions"; it incorporates a "hydraulics" (entropy or negentropy), a theory of self-organizing production (formation or dissolution), and a theory of coding (digital or analog).

Most generally, the logic of the clinamen postulates a fundamental complexity of the world, a concern that also lies at the heart of *Genesis* (1982), which is Serres's ultimate tractatus on complexity and multiplicity. More than a scientific historiography, it is a poetic pamphlet against rationalism that shares with Félix Guattari's late pamphlet *Chaosmosis* (which proposes a "generalized ecology—or ecosophy"[28] and which contains numerous references to chaotics, such as autopoesis, fractality, strange attractors, multiplicities, emergence, cartographies, and complexification) a general love of indeterminacy. (Drawing on his and Deleuze's earlier work on machinic systems, Guattari argues that the "notion of autopoiesis—as the autoreproductive capacity of a structure or ecosystem—could be usefully enlarged to include social machines, economic machines and even the incorporeal machines of language, theory and aesthetic creation"[29] because "every species of machine, is always at the junction of the finite and infinite, at this point of negotiation between complexity and chaos.")[30]

For both Guattari and Serres, the objective is to keep the complexity of the system alive and to never reduce complexity to dualism. As Serres notes, less polemical than usual, "the logic of yes and no, dualism, and the dual, that is to say life and death, must be opened to plurality" (B, 98). In the reference to constant metamorphosis and morphogenesis, atomist materialism is related to movement and life, whereas a system based on logical dualism, which leads to strict laws of inclusion and exclusion, is related, in Serres's overall polemics, to stasis and death: "The laws are the same throughout, they are thanatocratic" (109). Ultimately, "the law is the plague. Reason is the fall. The reiterated cause is death. Repetition is redundancy. And identity is death. . . . Turbulence disturbs the chain. It troubles the flow of the identical, just as Venus disturbs Mars" (109–10).

The counterproject is to think (of) the world as a complex, immanent system in which "nothing is exterior to things themselves" (*B, 54*). For such a project, one needs a "physics of immanence" (54) (a physics based on a "combinatory topology" [98] rather than "universal laws"), which is what both Lucretius and nonlinear dynamics offer. In Lucretius's text, Venus is the figure of such a physics. She "is not transcendent, like the other gods, she is immanent to this world, she is the being of relation" (123). Only such an immanent physics allows to think the autopoiesis of infinitely many infinitely complex systems: "The mathematics of the Epicureans . . . is a science of images: neuter producing infinite multiplicities of form. Auto-productive forms" (106). Repeatedly, Serres stresses that such an immanent physics cannot be contained in the ideal space of the laboratory because "the laboratory, and every closed system, are a protection against turbulence" (68). In a universe in which everything is fluid (not only the fluid contained in the vessel "but *the vessel itself is a flow,* although thicker and more complex" [69]) one needs "a physics of open systems" (79) that is itself open to the world and to its materials. This claim calls for a return to the logic of materiality; in particular to that of an intelligent materialism: "the hatred of objects at the root of knowledge, the horror of the world at the foundation of theory" (131).

CLINAMEN, CHAOS, CHANCE, AND TRAUMA

> *The soul is a material body, the body is a thing
> . . . psychology is just physics.*
>   —Serres, The Birth of Physics

Most of the references to the clinamen in recent theory deal with the entry of chance into an ordered universe and the subsequent breakup of order and chaos into a universe lodged between the probable and the exceptional; a universe in which order suddenly finds itself a highly improbable state of affairs. These problematics goes back to Aristotle's *Physics* in which Aristotle (symptomatically in a refutation of Epicurean, and thus inherently materialist claims) differentiates between the realm of chance and the realm of necessity.[31] Although Aristotle still differentiates between the realm of chance and chaos on the one hand and the realm of necessity and order on the other, already at this point, things are more complicated: To account for various aspects of chance, Aristotle subdivides chance events into a group that is related to human beings (these, which might be rendered as "luck," "fate," or "accident" he calls *tychē*) and a larger group that concern the world at large (these, which are generally rendered as "chance" or "contingency," he calls *automaton*). The *automaton*, then, designates the laws of probability, while *tychē* designates the individual subject's meeting with these laws.[32]

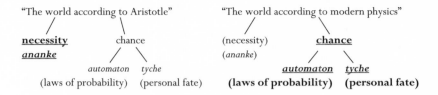

"The world according to Aristotle"

necessity   chance
ananke   automaton   tyche
        (laws of probability) (personal fate)

"The world according to modern physics"

(necessity)   **chance**
(ananke)   **automaton   tyche**
        (laws of probability) (personal fate)

While Aristotle is predominantly concerned with a "physics of necessities" that can disregard chance events ("where Aristotle could only regard chance as an interruption of a predetermined causal sequence, atomism allowed for contingency as the outcome of an indeterminate beginning),"[33] contemporary physics (aka nonlinear dynamics) is increasingly concerned with a turbulent world considered as a system organized by the logics of the *tych* and the *automaton:* a world considered as a deterministic chaos, with necessity a "lost ideal."

In general, the subject experiences the incomputability and the complexity of a turbulent world as chance. (In the light of modern "game theory" and "the theory of probability," chance is merely what the subject experiences as an unexpected and unforeseeable event: the name given to a structural, fundamental lack of computability in the system. As Laplace states in his essay on probability, "Given for one instant an intelligence which could comprehend all the forces by which nature is animated and the respective situation of the beings who compose it—an intelligence sufficiently vast to submit these data to analysis—it would embrace in the same formula the movements of the greatest bodies of the universe and those of the lightest atom; for it, nothing would be uncertain and the future, as the past, would be present to his eyes."[34] Only such a "Laplacian spirit" could provide a full computation of the multiplexity of events. Serres quotes Carnot's definition of chance as "the intersection of independent series" [*B,* 126], which again evokes Deleuze's idea of the "dark precursor.")

It is in this context that Lacan takes up Aristotle's terminology in his theory of the subject's forever missed and thus traumatic "encounter with the real," relating this missed meeting to the *tychē* and the *automaton* to the more general symbolic "network of signifiers," which, as he argues in the appendix to "The Purloined Letter" (a text Serres mentions in passing in *The Birth of Physics*), is inherently probabilistic. A superimposition of the Lacanian registers onto the Aristotelian ones results in the relationships shown in the accompanying table.

automaton → probability → language → symbolic → not arbitrary, "ordered multiplicity"

tyche → chance/fate → trauma → real → cause of repetition, "pure multiplicity"

necessity → order → madness → imaginary → phantasmatic hallucination of agency

In relation to psychic space and time, the trauma is an incomputable, *tychic* event that cannot be integrated into the psyche's "necessary" sequentialization of random series and into the *automaton* of language. As Lacan notes,

> The function of the tuché, of the real as an encounter—the encounter in so far as it may be missed—first presented itself in the history of psycho-analysis in a form that was in itself already enough to arouse our attention, that of the trauma.[35]

Like the clinamen, the traumatic event—ruled over by the "blind" chance designated by the *tychic*—happens "incerto tempore incertisque locis." (As Serres states, in another conflation of science and poetry, "the *eventa* slide on the *coniuncta,* history skids on matter" and "history flows around physics" [*B,* 125].) This is why for Lacan, the clinamen can come to designate the moment of a "primary trauma":

> If development is entirely animated by accident, by the obstacle of the tuché, it is in so far as the tuché brings us back to the same point at which pre-Socratic philosophy sought to motivate the world itself. It required a clinamen, an inclination, at some point. When Democritus tried to designate it . . . he says, It is not the μηδέν that is essential . . . but a δεν . . . He did not say, let alone.[36]

While the infinitely "small" time of the clinamen designates for Lacan the time of the "traumacore," it designates for Lucretius the birth of complexity. Can these two readings be reconciled?

For Lacan, the traumacore is an inaccessible (in Lacanian terminology: real) event that surfaces, "always already" after the fact and in a changed form (following the mechanisms of condensation, displacement and distortion), in the subject's systems of representation, in particular those of vision (in Lacanian terminology: the imaginary) and language (in Lacanian terminology: the symbolic). This retroactive temporality *(Nachträg-lichkeit),* which rules over the Lacanian logic of trauma and which is the temporality of psychoanalysis in general, is based on the idea that language has "always already" eclipsed the direct experience of the body. According to these chronologics, a return to moments of "pure multiplicity" is experienced by the subject (as an "ordered multiplicity") as a fragmentation and a descend into white noise. (As Serres notes, "*incerto tempore incertisque locis* . . . signif[ies] . . . simply aleatory scattering" and "collision and chance" [*B,* 112, 126].)

In Lucretian terms, the traumatic encounter is a "missed encounter" with the chaos of the laminar flux as represented by the chaos of turbulence. While the laminar state of nonbeing is related to the concept of inertia *(Reizminimierung)* ("the eternity of the atomic stream is the equivalent of the principle of inertia, recognized by the Epicurians" [*B*, 46]), the moment of birth designates the "emergence" of time and life ("Time is the interruption of rest" [48]), but also the birth of death as a state contracted to life. As Serres notes, "death, defined rigorously by a rupture is . . . *like an atom without a clinamen.* . . . Death is a limit, it is the inverse singularity of the place of birth" (184–85). Every meeting with chaotic shocks is thus a meeting with death (turbulence as the figure of laminarity), but at the same time a meeting with the beginning of life (turbulence as the figure of the opening up of multiplicity). Because of this contraction of the logics of the end and the beginning of life, the traumatic *Reizüberflutung* is both terrible (from the retrospective position of the subject) and at the same time desirable (from the position of what Lacan calls the subject of *jouissance,* which is, strictly speaking, not a subject at all, but a material, or, as Deleuze would say, machinic corporeal assemblage). If the trauma is understood as an onrush of stimulation or irritation, the ambiguity of the German word Freud uses in this context, *Reiz,* which also means "lure," "attraction," "charm," and "temptation," implies that one side of the trauma is related to this, however painful and violent, *jouissance.*

Up until now, there is no discrepancy between the Lucretian and the Lacanian logic in terms of the general position and structure of the trau-macore. In both logics, a complete return to the trauma time and trauma site is impossible (for Lacan, because the systems of representation have always already interfered with the experience according to the temporality of retrospection, for Lucretius, because the "initial conditions" of the traumatic event can never be fully computed and thus recreated or re-experienced). In both logics, the "traumatic" moment of the clinamen designates a blind spot in the subject's history (which is why history is, as Foucault had stated in almost identical words, forever incomplete: "History is chance, aleatory and stochastic. . . . The capricious effect of an operation depending on chance is made regular by the sufficient repetition of this operation. History is formed of syrrhèses, of systems, of orders, originating from this endless cloud. The recognition and description of these emergences" [*B*, 164]).

There is, however, a discrepancy in terms of the "traumatic logic" that Lacan develops from these givens. This discrepancy has to do with the intervention of the code and of language into the traumatic logic. In particular, the discrepancy has to do with what happens when one considers, as do Lucretius and Serres, things and language to come into existence simultaneously. What does it mean for the traumatic logic when "language is born with things, and by the same process" (*B,* 123)?

According to Lucretius, who equates atoms and letters (it is this analogy, which, surprisingly, Deleuze does not mention, that allows for the meeting of atomism and cybernetics), the clinamen marks "the birth of things. And the appearance of language" (*B*, 23). As Serres states, "in the cataract of the meaningless, in which the atom-letters rush towards their fall, here is the birth of meaning" (78). This implies that, for an intelligent materialism, "nature is coded" (140), from the beginning and down into the infinitely small. In Lucretian terms, "atoms, as we know, are letters, or are like letters. Their interconnection constitutes the tissue of the body, in the same way as letters form words, empty spaces, sentences and texts" (141).

Unlike Lacan, for whom the realm of the material "real" is strictly excluded from the realm of representation, an intelligent materialism proposes that "writing appears in things, it appears from things" (*B*, 149). In fact, it lies at the core of any process of emergence (autopoiesis), because material writing is "negentropic. It is memorised information in the core of connections" (149). Curiously reminiscent of Derrida, but at the same time very unlike him, an intelligent materialism proposes that "everything that exists only exists in the form of writing and code" (149). This is why an intelligent materialism considers the world as "a network of primordial elements *in communication*" (123), which means, once more, that it is an open, immanent system (if nature is a "communicating ensemble," then "it is absolutely necessary that these vortices be in relation to another" [94]). According to an intelligent materialism, then, both the material body and the mind are cybernetic codemachines in which, as Deleuze notes, "writing . . . functions on the same level as the real, and the real materially writes."[37]

"Circumstance" (by which Serres means something similar to what Deleuze calls "a life," a "cohering" system amid a turbulent world, or, in the words of nonlinear dynamics, an "island of order in a sea of disorder")[38] "and its coding are the place where writing emerges as the mnemonic preserver of this initial condition by chance within the interconnections of things themselves" [*B*, 149]). From such a position, the logic of trauma can be prolonged from the field of discourse into that of materiality, which means that the field of the real is no longer excluded from its logic.

As the atoms are letters, the clinamen can come to designate the birth of the world (the laminar flux disrupted in the "atomic" trauma of the clinamen [*Reizüberflutung*], which concerns the atomlevel and the multiplicity of the mattermachine) as well as that of the subject; both its "real" birth [the "motherchild unity" disrupted in the trauma of birth, which concerns the organ level and the multiplicity of the "bodymachine"] as well as its symbolic one (the imaginary unity disrupted in the trauma of the entry into the signifier, which concerns the letter level and the multiplicity of the "meaningmachine").

A Lucretian or "immanent traumatics" might thus account for the fact that the intensities of sudden, violent chance events are stored in various ways in the psychomaterial archives of the subject. They are "impressed" into the landscapes of thought and writing (where these impressions—or, more precisely their flashes—are transferred, at least partly, into the landscape of conscious and unconscious memories), but they are also impressed into the neuronal landscape (often to such a degree that they can no longer be accessed except in the sudden flashes of what is not quite correctly called *memoires involuntaires*) and into what might be considered muscular and visceral archives—archives of the flesh—with their own mnemonic operations; a field that is eclipsed from a Lacanian traumatics, in which these intensities are "always already" significations. Maybe, however, they cannot be treated as such.

As Serres notes, "our writings, our memory, our histories and our times are negentropic, go back to the initial conditions, preserve them and maintain them, *as* nature has shown them to us. History is a physics, and not the other way around. Language is first of all in bodies" (*B,* 150). This is a lesson psychoanalysis might learn from physics. An intelligent materialism proposes a continuity between the material and the psychic which is missing in psychoanalysis and deconstruction. According to an "immanent physics," the text that extends from the world to the page is a continuous one, which is why "the senses are faithful" (49). In fact, "physics is faithful to the world, since the formation of its text is isomorphic with the constitution of the natural tissue" (159).

SWERVE INTO LITERATURE

> *Every non-physical interpretation of the* clinamen *remains essentially idealist.*
> —Serres, The Birth of Physics

The poetic potential and power of trauma and the clinamen lie in the fact that they are responsible for the failure of a "total recall." The subject that emerges from the multiplicity of nature-life as a mixture of *automaton* and *tych* (the "chora" in *Hermes IV*) is, like nature, "incalculable . . . measureless. It always exceeds the machines' capacity for calculation" (*G,* 127). It is, according to an intelligent materialism, always more than what we generally consider as language (or, stated differently, language is always more than "itself"). It partakes of the real not as a pure cut (as in the Lacanian, and, over long stretches, also the Derridean topology) but as a complex and chaotic force-field.

Deleuze and Guattari have taken account of this in the unilateral topology of what they call the "plane of immanence," which is modeled on the unilateral topology of the "projective plane" and which allows them to think the material and the informational as part of the same space.[39] Such a topology of immanence finds its "space of thought" *(Denkraum)* in a field of discursive-intensive attractorspaces. Its perspective point is a truly fluid, turbulent, material poetics in which microscopic, unconscious perceptions constantly cascade into the realm of language, while, just as constantly, conscious perceptions become imperceptible. In a Lucretian context, such a theory attempts to consider physical and psychic "inclinations" as happening on the same "projective plane."[40]

Although both Lacan's and Derrida's theories have a "space" for intensive, material complexities, they tend to consider only the complexities of the field of language and representation. In fact, Derrida's critique of Lacan is related to the fact that Derrida considers dissemination as more multiplicitous than Lacanian psychoanalysis. As he notes, "if I stress the multiplicity of languages . . . [a]s I make my way from digression to deviation I wish to demonstrate a certain interfacing of necessity and chance, of significant and insignificant chance: the marriage, as the Greek would have it, of *Anakè*, of *Tukhé* and *Automatia*."[41] In fact, Derrida sees in Lucretius's text a "theory of literal dissemination."[42] which he stakes, as an "atomystique of the letter,"[43] against the "necessity" of psychoanalysis finding itself; against Lacan's presumably "predetermined return [of the letter] to the point of departure despite all random incidents."[44]

According to Derrida, psychoanalysis argues from the position that "there is no chance in the unconscious. The apparent randomness must be placed in the service of an unavoidable necessity that in fact is never contradicted."[45] Even though I have shown that the notion of chance is more important in Lacanian theory than Derrida makes it seem, Derrida's intervention rightly points to the molar order of the theoretical matrix that "contains" this chance.

Rather than to address (or dis-address) the debate between Derrida and Lacan in more detail, however, I want to propose that the debate might already have been superseded by other, more pertinent ones. In the light of an intelligent materialism, the question is not so much whether a discursive unconscious is an island of order in a sea of disorder, or whether everything is a giant, free attractorspace in which the only rule is that of "destinerring."[46] Rather, the question is how to think a "material (machinic-informational) unconscious."

In this context, Serres's book is an important nexus in the development of a theory and a narratology that is inspired by an intelligent materialism. One might think here of such diverse texts as those of Charles Brockden-Brown's *Edgar Huntly* (in which the Lucretian concept of swerving defines the plot at many catastrophic places) or Witold Gombrowicz's *Cosmos* (symptomatically present in Deleuze's *Logic of Sense* for precisely this reason), or one might think of the turbulent poetics of Thomas Pynchon's *Mason and Dixon,* in which the vortex is one of the leitmotifs; from hair vortices to the vortex at the Pole through which one enters a "Hollow Earth." (These vortical poetics mark in Pynchon's work a change from entropics to nonlinear dynamics. Pynchon on multiplexity sounds exactly like Serres on multiplicity, and both oeuvres share a trajectory that leads from the second law of thermodynamics through cybernetics to chaos theory.) One might also think of Harold Brodkey's description of "bundles of times traversing subjectivity" in *The Runaway Soul:* "I think of people as bunchings and bouquets of velocities. . . . What if each thing in the universe were a hypothesis about velocity—a manifestation of a hypothesis in an actuality of present-tense moments. A person is a knot of velocities of different kinds and has an overall velocity, while the velocities of the smaller parts continue in currents and branchings, magnetism, collisions."[47] Or again, one might think of the complex "data dance" of recent digital texts; plastic texts that create complex systems through the incorporation of random programs into the code or by creating direct feedback loops between text and user.

In far-from-equilibrium systems, such as life or a novel, small, seemingly random microevents can cascade into macroevents (according to the logic of positive feedback loops within the system; so-called butterfly effects) and throw the system, seemingly without rhyme and reason, into other, unsuspected states. Such events produce bifurcations and seemingly inexplicable, catastrophic changes. Life is such a far-from-equilibrium system. It takes place within a complex and infinitely intricate network of attractors that interact according to the dynamics of a deterministic chaos. Emerging, it creates, out of randomness and turbulence, symbolic regulations that form, in locally and temporally bounded regions, islands of order. Thinking such complex systems as the weather, the cloud, the bifurcations of lightning and aquatic and atmospheric vorticisms, Serres's writing asks philosophy to address once more such complex systems of becoming and of self-organization. If nonlinear dynamics, literature and "poststructuralism" attempt to think new alignments of order and chaos and new translations between the "two (or more) cultures," Serres's and Deleuze's intelligent materialism should become major references.

NOTES

1. In this essay I will use the neutral term *nonlinear dynamics* rather than shift between *chaos theory* and *complexity theory,* which, though often considered interchangeable, have a different semantic feel.

2. Michel Foucault, "The Discourse on Language" in *The Archaeology of Knowledge,* trans. A. M. Sheridan Smith (New York: Pantheon, 1972), 231; emphasis added.

3. Jacques Derrida, "My Chances/Mes Chances: A Rendezvous with Some Epicurean Stereophonies," in *Taking Chances: Derrida, Pyschonanalysis, Literature,* ed. Joseph H. Smith and William Kerrigan (Baltimore: Johns Hopkins University Press), 1–32.

4. Ibid, 18.

5. Henri Bergson, *Extraits de Lucrece avec un commentaire, des notes et une etude sur la poésie, la physique, le texte et la langue de Lucréce* (Paris: Delgrave, 1884).

6. *Oeuvres complètes d'Alfred Jarry,* vol. 1 (Lausanne: Éditions du Grand-Chene), especially chap. 34, called "Clinamen," 292–97. For other contexts, see especially Noël Arnaud, *Alfred Jarry: D'*"Ubu Roi" au "Docteur Faustroll" (Paris: La Table Ronde, 1974).

7. Karl Marx and Friederick Engels, *Collected Works,* vol. 1 (New York: International Publishers, 1975), 25–108.

8. Michel Serres, *Le Système de Leibniz et ses modèles mathématiques,* 2 vols. (Paris: Presses Universitaires de France, 1968). In the book, whose shadow looms large in Deleuze's *The Fold,* Serres traces a complex theory of multiplicity (implication, complication, explication) and "infinitesimal calculation" in the work of Leibniz. See for instance "revenons sur le terme *complexion,* et notons à quel point sa famille sémantique va dominer la pensée ultérieure. Le monde et le système de Leibniz sont essentiellement complexes et compliqués, somme si le baroque avait trouvé là sa logique, sa mathématique et sa métaphysique" (2:418–19). There are three mentions of the clinamen in the book (1:303, 324, 381), as well as one of Lucrece (1:381), plus a number of mentionings of the spiral vortex (for instance 1:226 and 2:754).

9. Gilles Deleuze and Félix Guattari, "From Chaos to Brain," in *What Is Philosophy?* trans. Hugh Tomlinson and Graham Burchell (New York: Columbia University Press, 1994), 205.

10. Gilles Deleuze, *The Logic of Sense* (New York: Columbia University Press, 1990), 266.

11. Ibid.

12. Ibid.

13. Gilles Deleuze and Félix Guattari, A *Thousand Plateaus: Capitalism and Schizophrenia,* trans. Brian Massumi (Minneapolis: University of Minnesota Press, 1987), 21.

14. Deleuze, *The Logic of Sense,* 270.

15. Ibid., 269.

16. Ibid., 270.

17. Ibid., 279.

18. "Archimedes and Lucretius, as the predecessors of René Thom" (*B,* 20). See also "Prigogine, the deviation, open system, vortices once again, dissipative structures, hence Thom and the mathematisation of the model. Thom, the new Leibniz and the new Archimedes, in relation to these new Epicurians" (*B,* 37) and "Atomist physics is . . . an architectonics of the opening . . . Lucretius is among us, he speaks the same language as we do, his feet on the same earth" (*B,* 78). See also his expression "the new pact with nature" (*B,* 113).

19. Ilya Prigogine and Isabelle Stengers, *Order Out of Chaos: Man's New Dialogue with Nature* (Boulder, Colo.: New Science Library, 1984).

20. Deleuze and Guattari, *A Thousand Plateaus,* 361, 489.

21. Prigogine and Stengers, *Order out of Chaos,* 141.

22. Ibid.

23. In the science wars, Serres figures only as a minor figure. Sokal, apart from a whiff against Serres's northwest passages, is silent about him. Alan Sokal and Jean Bricmont, *Intellectual Impostures* (London: Profile Books, 1998): "Serres goes on to apply the 'Gödel-Debray principle' to the history of science, where it is as irrelevant as it is in politics" (170).

24. Prigogine and Stengers, *Order Out of Chaos,* 304.

25. For the "physical conceit" of atoms as letters see especially *B,* 136–37.

26. "Thunderbolts explode between different intensities, but they are preceded by an invisible, imperceptible *dark precursor,* which determines their path in advance but in reverse, as though intagliated. . . . There is no doubt that *there is* an identity belonging to the precursor, and a resemblance between the series which it causes to communicate. This 'there is,' however, remains perfectly indeterminate." Gilles Deleuze, *Difference and Repetition,* trans. Paul Patton (New York: Columbia University Press, 1994), 119.

27. In the following I will use the more common term *fluid mechanics,* although a better term may be *fluid dynamics.*

28. Félix Guattari, *Chaosmosis: An Ethico-Aesthetic Paradigm,* trans. Paul Bains and Julian Pefanis (Bloomington: Indiana University Press, 1995), 91.

29. Guattari, *Chaosmosis,* 93.

30. Ibid., 111.

31. *The Works of Aristotle,* ed. W. D. Ross, vol. 2 (Oxford, Clarendon Press, 1930). "Thus to say that chance is a thing contrary to rule is correct"; "chance is unstable" (197). For a discussion of *tuch* and *automaton,* see Cynthia A. Freeland, "Accidental Causes and Real Explanations," and Lindsay Judson, "Chance and Always for the Most Part," both in *Aristotle's Physics: A Collection of Essays,* ed. Lindsay Judson (Oxford: Clarendon Press, 1991), 49–72, 73–99.

32. Commenting on one of his seminars, in which he had talked about the *tychic,* Lacan notes that some people thought that he had been sneezing all the time.

33. David Webb, introduction, *B,* vii–xx, xii.

34. Pierre Simon, marquis de Laplace, *A Philosophical Essay on Probabilities* (New York: Dover, 1951), 4.

35. Lacan, *Four Fundamental Concepts of Psycho-Analysis,* trans. Alan Sheridan (New York: Norton, 1978), 55.

36. Ibid., 63–64.

37. Deleuze and Guattari, *A Thousand Plateaus,* 141.

38. Gilles Deleuze, "Immanence: A Life," in *Pure Immanence: Essays on a Life* (New York: Zone Books, 2001), 25–33.

39. See my "Matter That Bodies," *Gender Forum* 6 (2002), http://www.gender-forum.uni-koeln.de.

40. "Atoms . . . are letters. Their interconnection constitutes the tissue of the body, in the same way as letters form words, empty spaces, sentences and texts" (*B,* 140).

41. Derrida, "My Chances/Mes Chances," 6.

42. Ibid., 8.

43. Ibid., 10.

44. Ibid.

45. Ibid., 24.

46. Ibid., 16. See also Serres's use of the concept of the "chora" in *LD*.

47. Harold Brodkey, *The Runaway Soul* (New York: Farrar, Straus and Giroux, 1991), 53.

LIQUID HISTORY

Serres and Lucretius

STEPHEN CLUCAS

> *Everything moves, in appearance, and nothing is motionless. Always uneasy, I am in search of history.*
>
> *[Tout bouge, en apparence, et rien ne remue. Inquiet, toujours, je suis en quête de l'histoire.]*

In *La Naissance de la physique dans la texte du Lucrece: Fleuves et turbulences,* his fluid and mercurial improvisations on themes derived from *De rerum natura,* Michel Serres presents his readers with a characteristically centrifugal narrative. Beginning as an unorthodox history of Western science, which seeks to overturn the dominant historiographical model of the "scientific revolution" by identifying an unvarying set of constants underlying scientific thought since the Renaissance, his meditations bifurcate into more general reflections on the nature of subjectivity, ethics, and social and historical process. For Serres the dynamic physics of turbulence and chaos, or rather the complexity of a world system seen as a "vortex of vortices" (*N,* 65), becomes the shifting foundation for a global theory of both man and nature.

Serres begins by arguing, counterintuitively, that the ancient atomistic doctrines of Epicurus and Democritus were, contrary to the beliefs of historians of ancient Greek science, underpinned by a mathematical system. He argues against the idea that ancient atomism was unscientific, not "science of the world" but "an impure mélange of metaphysics, political philosophy, and reveries on individual liberty projected on things themselves" (*N,* 10). He does this by arguing that the clinamen—or minimal deviation from rectilinear free-fall that allows atomic collision, and thus material creation—was not (as has widely been held) a logical, geometrical, physical, and mechanical absurdity (9), but an anticipation of the differential calculus (11) and fluid dynamics, the clinamen being seen as "one of the first formulations of what we call a differential" and the "least conceivable condition for the first formation of turbulence" (13). Rereading the famous passage that opens second book of *De rerum natura,* "Suave mari magno," in which a spectator standing high on a cliff delights in watching the "heavy stress" of the unfortunate seafarers below in the stormy sea, Serres sees the passage not as "a rhapsody of egoistic serenity" but (concentrating on what he sees as a culturally obliterated phrase from the passage "turbantibus aequora ventis"—"the whirling winds are lashing the surface") as an image "recalling the *dine* [or vortex] of Democritus" (14).[1] Lucretius's poem, and the ancient atomistic hypotheses that it articulates in poetic theorems, is rescued from claims of absurdity by "abandoning the general framework of solid mechanics" and turning instead to the "science of fluids" or hydraulics, which draws Lucretius close to "our world" and the chaotic physics of turbulence (14).

This opens the way to the next stage of his argument, that Archimedean mathematics was the analogical basis of the atomistic philosophy of Epicurus and Democritus. Archimedes, he says, provided a "global system" that "describes with mathematical sophistication the physical model of the Epicurean world" (*N,* 20–21). Alluding to the ancient prohibition of *metabasis* that forbade the importation of rules between different sciences,[2] Serres notes that the Greeks strongly rejected the mixture of mathematics and physics that has been commonplace since Newton's *Principia.* The Greeks, Serres argues,

> produced a rigorous formal [mathematical] system and a discourse of nature as two separate linguistic blocs, like two disjoined ensembles. And as they operate with completely different proper names, no one has realized that they are structurally isomorphic. (21–22)

This (with a little rhetorical force) allows Serres to argue that "in a technical sense the atomic universe is Archimedean" (*N,* 24). His insistence on the structural isomorphism of mathematics and nature is underlined by an inventive analogy between Archimedean geometry and Lucretius's poetics of storm and whirlwind. The *salinon* (σαλινον), a "curious form" created by four semicircles, three of which have their respective diameters in alignment, and the fourth having a different alignment, is chosen by Serres as an emblem of the turbulent physics of the ancients.[3] Examining the etymological speculations of earlier mathematicians beginning with Isaac Barrow, who thought it was derived either from the word *salinum* (salt cellar) or *selinion* (lunule), Serres's own etymology reflects his project of collapsing Archimedean mathematics and Epicurean atomism, and his choice of Lucretius's poem as a poetic expression of the mathematics and physics of turbulence. He suggests that σαλινον is derived from the word σαλος, which signifies, Serres argues, "the agitation or the breaking of waves, turbulences of the sea and disturbances of the soul. The trembling of the earth, unease." The verb σαλευω *(saleuo)* signifies "to shake or disturb, to agitate, to ruin, to get a horse moving; to be balanced, as in a boat; a rolling movement; being uncertain, hesitant, and troubled." "The semantic atmosphere here," Serres says, "is Lucretian, but also Archimedean." He compares the *salinon*'s "fluctuating curve, the disequilibrium of the swell" to one of Lucretius's whirling winds, "turbantibus aequora uentis." The curve in fact becomes not just an analogy, but a "matrix or pure model" of Lucretius's poetic statement, as well as a "distant ancestor" of modern turbulent systems (*N,* 29–30). This metonymic moment describes a gesture that will be repeated at different scales throughout the book: Archimedes is folded into Epicurus, Epicurus into Lucretius, mathematics is folded into poetry, and antiquity is folded into modernity. Lucretius's poetry in a real sense "contains" or expresses the theorems of Archimedes. For Serres poem and theorem are closely related, and he sees his own poetic mode of argumentation as "transposing, exporting, translating the work of mathematicians" into another discursive register (*C,* 74). In his first scalar shift of the book, Serres abruptly introduces the notion that subjectivity follows the same Lucretian laws of turbulence as the physical universe. For him the clinamen is subjective as well as objective process: "I am myself a variation, and my soul declines, my global body, open, adrift. It slides irreversibly down the slope. Who am I? A vortex. A dissipation which undoes itself. Yes, a singularity, a singular" (*N,* 50). The *salinon* then reemerges as a figure of a soul that has found its balance between turbulent extremes—the *ataraxia,* or emotional neutrality of stoic morality:

> The circle leaves the trough in the waves and passes between the two adjacent troughs including the same space carved out by the high and low waves. A stable ring which comprehends disturbance. A local figure of *ataraxia.* The circle does not calm the waters, it transforms their instability into a law. An elegant theorem. *Ataraxia* generalizes the *salinon:* it traces its path from the disturbances of the trough to the heights of the cliff top. The cycle of the happy Sisyphus. (*N,* 51)

Alluding to Lucretius's clifftop spectator, Serres suggests that the *salinon* represents a still point between extremes, or rather (since it does not "calm the waters") a stability within instability, a "space carved out by the high and low waves." This idea of the desirability of stability in turbulence (which characterizes the Lucretian and the modern chaotic physical universe) is repeated at various levels, or on various scales, throughout the book: nature, subjectivity, ethics, social and historical process are seen as complex but isomorphic structures.

Serres sees the history of science as an example of one of these isomorphic structures, a pattern of stability within instability. He sees the history of science since the revival of Archimedes in the Renaissance as a "chain of isomorphisms" (*N,* 197) that was only broken by the first genuine scientific revolution, that of nineteenth-century thermodynamics: "history flees in the face of the iteration of invariances," says Serres, "until finally a revolution: thermodynamics" [L'histoire fuit encore devant l'itération des invariances. Enfin, une révolution: la thermodynamique] (198). Lucretius's system was, according to Serres,

> a global model of such fecundity for the natural and physical sciences that it forms the horizon of four centuries of research. A horizon that is not, as one might think, concealed, but perfectly clear. Reviewed, reprised and redeemed by the great Renaissance figures, Leonardo, Stevin (the new Archimedes), and Benedetti. (47)

In a vastly simplified account of the scientific revolution, Serres sees the rise of Archimedean mechanism and atomism in the late sixteenth and early seventeenth centuries as a "restaging" of the science of antiquity:

> The modern scientific revolution consists in playing Archimedes (that is, the atomists) against Aristotle. Playing Stevin (whose whole oeuvre seems to have been written by the Syracusan philosopher). In the classical age that game became a strategy, and the particularity of experiences became a general theory. (47)

Unlike many historians of science, who have characterized this phase of scientific development as a radical rupture with mediaeval science, Serres argues that the themes of ancient natural philosophy persisted. "Scientific modernity," he suggests,

> did not enter history like a geological fault, but through the relaunching of a philosophy of nature diffused by antiquity. This fault is an artifact of the universities: those ecological niches designed for specialized animals. (*N,* 55)

His Lucretian "filiation" is thus extended, first to Kant's cosmology, and thence on to other modern scientific thinkers; he even goes so far as to suggest that Archimedes and Lucretius were "predecessors of René Thom" (author of *Structural Stability and Morphogenesis* [1972] and one of the founding fathers of systems theory in the biological sciences) (*LN,* 30), whom he calls "the new Archimedes." This filiation involves a "finite group of constants" operating through history of Western science, which are basically Lucretian and Archimedean in character:

> angle, variation, slope . . . functioning in relation to an equilibrium, an equator, a homogeneous or an indifferent [factor]: circles, vortices, balls, drops, pairs or rotations; two forces and extremes; and the ques-

tion finally of genesis. Vary these constants as you please and you will easily obtain the historical cluster. (*N,* 49)

One can locate local "fractures or discontinuities" in the historical development of post-Renaissance science, Serres argues, "but elsewhere I have found links or bridges. A tormented surface, but . . . underneath, [there is] a stable substrate" (*N,* 200). The discovery of these "quasi invariants" in the history of science leads him to reflect on the reductive nature of the schematizations of historical process, many of which are current today. "All my uneasiness," Serres says,

> stems from this: that I have discovered a relative stability where I was expecting a variation, a series of upheavals, stages, or ruptures, changes of paradigm, and so on. This is because we have ideas about history, one or more discourses of history, schemas that are in agreement with or opposed to it, but in each case, limited. The problem is we think of time as linear, no doubt because the line, which is dimensionless, seems to us, mistakenly, to be opposed to space, and thus as analogous to time. Thus history seems to us to be drawn like a curve, continuous and discontinuous, increasing or decreasing, straight or in zigzags, and so on. These silent models are naive, they are oversimplified, impoverished and of limited use in rendering an account of a formidable complexity, and especially that most complex multiplicity which we call history. The experience I have had has obliged me to change our ideas, to transform our theories. I believe that I have brought to light a quasi invariant of an extremely long duration, in which from the pre-Socratics until the present, there has been only the slightest variation. (199–200)

Serres suggests that we abandon linear history and the "old logic of causality" for a turbulent model of history that considers aleatory variations from states of equilibrium (a model that is close to his characterization of the Epicurean "global system"—which is a rapprochement between statics and dynamics). He thus sees history as a variant of the *salinon:* as a form that demonstrates the structural stability of cyclical turbulence. He opposes himself to historical models based on a simple "logic of resemblance and difference, contradiction and identity, continuous or discontinuous," which is a "simplistic logic of two values" (*LN,* 200). Serres argues that we need to *complicate* our view of historical change: "in order to comprehend history, and not only the history of science, [we need] a model that associates, combines and integrates different times together." Any history that does not attempt to do this, he says, "will be nothing but an abstraction" (*N,* 201).

The historiographical difficulties of Serres's history of quasi invariance and temporal multiplicity is manifest. His insistence on the stable sub-strate, or *longue durée,* of scientific thought has led him to make connec-tions between remote historical locations that some historians have (not unfairly) seen as anachronistic. Bruno Latour, the most devilish and yet most angelic of Serresean advocates, forced Serres to confront this difficulty head-on. His response is fascinating.

> If you take a handkerchief and spread it out in order to iron it, you can see in it certain fixed distances and proximities. If you sketch a circle in one area, you can mark out nearby points and measure far-off distances. Then take the same handkerchief and crumple it . . . Two distant points are suddenly close. (*C,* 60)

In this way, he argues, while "Lucretius and the modern theory of fluids are considered as two places separated by an immense distance . . . I see them as in the same neighbourhood" (*C,* 57).
"Classical time," he suggests,

> is related to geometry . . . [but] take your inspiration from topology, and perhaps you will discover the rigidity of these proximities and dis-tances you consider arbitrary. And their sim*pli*city, in the literal sense of the word *pli* [fold]: it's simply the difference between topology (the handkerchief is folded, crumpled, shredded) and geometry (the same fabric is ironed out flat). As we experience time—as much in our inner senses as externally in nature—as much as *le temps* of history as *le temps* of the weather—it resembles this crumpled version much more than the flat, overly simplified one. (*C,* 60)

Serres's conception of history is modeled closely on contemporary theo-ries of chaos and complexity, an apparently disordered set of phenomena that actually obeys surreptitious orderly forms:

> History is random, aleatory, and stochastic. It is cloud and noise. Huge populations, a parametric multitude exceeding all measure. History is ergodic. The capricious effect of an operation that depends upon chance finds itself regularized by a repetition sufficient for that operation. His-tory is the formation of syrrheses, of systems, orders, out of the cease-less cloud. The recognition and description of these emergences. That which emerges from noise can be a signal, and before long a language. Then the formation recognizes itself as such and describes itself. Mate-rial and signaletic turbulences maintain their clusters in and against the irreversible, hurled toward short-, medium-, long-, or extremely long-term conclusions in the fall that produces them. Local vortices—small, mediocre or immense, always engaged in transforming themselves or being transformed by the flux of events from upstream and down-

stream, by intrinsic forces, energies that make and unmake them. The old logic of causality becomes turbulent, effects return to their causes. This coherent model in history was history itself, as if it carried, carefully concealed within itself, the complex clocks that it needed. (*N*, 202–3)

This complex, chaotic, topological view of historical process, based on the notion of "folded or crumpled time" (*C*, 77), historical "folds" that bring remote historical instances into momentary proximity, and insisting on history as complex multiplicity of times (running at different speeds, locations, etc.), which he calls "clocks" *(horologes)*, while being rhetorically compelling is not always answerable to his practice, however, and many of his statements seemed embedded in the linear and chronological causality he claims to reject: thus he talks of "anticipations," "predecessors," "recalling," "reviving," and so on.

Serres's insistence on quasi invariance, which seems to be counterintuitive to much of contemporary historiography (although close in some respects to the French tradition of history of the *longue durée*), needs to be understood in the context of his global system and the cultural critique that underlies it. Using Lucretius's invocation of Venus as the tutelary deity of his fluid, atomic universe, Serres pieces together an argument that opposes a brutal, rigid, and violent rationalism presided over by Mars, with a new Venereal science of fluidity, turbulence, and love, which leaves nature "as she is, hazardous and complex" (*N*, 66). His appeal to the quasi invariants of history must thus be seen as a critique of Post–Industrial Revolution culture, which he sees as predicated upon a martial "logic of extremes" and a historiography of progress and decline (upward movement or entropy). The source of this "cultural logic" is the motor *(le moteur)*—which governs all levels of intellectual and practical activity:

The motor is constructed by the Industrial Revolution and its general systems of practice and theory. All questions—abstract or concrete— are brutally reduced either to ascent [*escalade*] or entropy. The motor, that is to say the producer of movement through a variation from an original equilibrium, the motor, that is to say, such and such a machine of fire or fluid. The cultures—but why do I speak in the plural?—the culture of fire and flood, of plethora and exhaustion, of vertical growth and brutal falls, of accumulation and drainage, where history, fatally and through the impregnable laws of matter, mounts and descends, like the sea tossed about by the circulations of the hurricane. Culture, where the elements are reduced to the energy of fire, succeeds forgotten cultures of invariances and earth, without inflation or deflation. (*N*, 81)

Serres suggests some theories "to draw us away from the tempest" of this culture of fire, with its violent oscillations between extremes. These theories he says, are "retrogressive"; they "propose that we return to minimal inclines, to flatter historical slopes" (*N*, 81). These theories are related to a utopian return from industry to nature, to the "slow metastabilities" of agriculture, and an embracing of "ancient ideas," especially the value attached to tranquility and equilibrium (this is particularly visible in the stoic strand in Serres's work, especially in the skein of ideas that he weaves around the ideas of "trouble" and "turbulence" as qualities in physics and ethics) (*N*, 82).[4] For Serres, Lucretius's *De rerum natura* (which he sees as a nested series of isomorphisms, importing the atomist concepts of its physical theories first into theories of perception, and thence into its reflections on history and social structure) is a paradigmatic text for his own antisystematic thought. In his 1982 work *Genèse*, for example, he reprised the themes of *La Naissance*, in the section on history and time, entitled "Naissance du temps," in which he links the pursuit of invariance to all the various disciplinary strands of his work:

> I am now seeking an invariant, I blindly seek a new stability, secret, perhaps unheard of. I am no longer speaking of variations, fall or circulation. I am speaking of transformations . . . without apparent laws, which are produced by the irregular bombardment of circumstances. I establish them in the inert world as much as in life, history, or culture. Everywhere multiplicity metamorphoses things. Does something stable, quasi-invariant exist in, by means of—in spite of multiplicities?[5]

Serres seems to ground his ideal of a turbulent nonsystem—at the level of history, ethics, and culture—on the chaotic and aleatory systems of the physical and biological world. "What I am seeking to form," he told Bruno Latour,

> to compose, to promote—I can't quite find the right word—is a *syrrhese*, a confluence not a system a mobile confluence of fluxes. Turbulences, overlapping cyclones and anticyclones, like on a weather map. Wisps of hay tied in knots. An assembly of relations. Clouds of angels passing. Once again, the flames' dance. The living body dances like that, and all life. (*C*, 122)

Lucretius makes him yearn nostalgically for a premodern interdisciplinary moment:

> Epicurus and Lucretius were fortunate, they did not know they were materialists—that word was invented much later by Leibniz. . . . Antiquity knew that age of freedom where philosophers were not exhibited in cages, penned up in little, well-appointed pigeonholes, for

defense and refuge. . . . The schools then were not burdened by the classification of ideas that closed down the possibilities of invention and history. (*N, 68*)

And yet there is, perhaps, a bad seduction involved in this nostalgia, and a hidden deviation waiting to produce a destructive turbulence within the heart of Serres's open system of multiplicities, his "Clouds of angels." "Can one conceive of a history where the invariants exceed . . . all variational process?" (*N, 198*), Serres asks rhetorically, and the truth is we can, but only perhaps at the cost of certain freedoms or possibilities.

In order to find "a global model that can account for quasi invariance" (*N, 202*), Serres looks to physics, where "every object in the world, insofar as it exists through a variation from equilibrium and in so far as it resists the tendency towards entropy, is a complex clock drawing together several times" (202). History itself is seen as an Archimedean or Lucretian phenomenon: "Equilibrium disturbs itself here and there, and these variations launch history" (220). History is itself a clinamen, a productive departure from equilibrium, a deviation from the free fall of immutability. In this model "the past, the present, the future, the dawn of appearance and death, tenacious illusions, are nothing but declinations of matter" (45), and "History is nothing but violence . . . inclinations, variations, ruptures of equilibrium; inclination in general begins a slope that runs toward death" (221). While Serres's view of history is complex and chaotic, it is still mechanical. The mechanisms may be more accurate reflections of the aleatory structures of human behavior, but they also have a cyclical inevitability. In place of "progress," "growth," and "maturation," Serres suggests "quasi-homeostatic circulations" or "temporarily fixed pseudoequilibral cycles" (73). His new history is chaotic, but not lawless; the "law of history" becomes "the Archimedean law of supersession" (69), and human desire, the motive force of history, becomes an indifferent term of an inevitable circulation:

> *Desire is the effect of degradation and its cause;* or *degradation is the cause of desire or its effect.* Because the concept utilized is *objective or subjective,* it forms a quasi-cyclical process, where *cause and effect,* producer and product, mover and moved change places. . . . A circulation, cause-effect in return, descends the declining slope, in broadening its lines of compensation and fall; it describes an endless spiral in deviation from itself, a turbulence that, in advancing, seeks and perpetually loses equilibrium. This is the precise nature of *the turbulent solution:* it is rigorously isomorphic with the natural genesis out of chaos. History is thus a physics. (222–23)

The logic of seeking models for history in physical process now become starkly apparent. For Serres a "separation between the discourses of physics, natural history, and history itself is no longer possible." History becomes part of a self-reproductive system:

> Inclination, instability, and instance as such is the mover without a first mover. All form, all order, produces or reproduces itself [*s'autoproduit ou s'autoreproduit*], mutations and variances, by means of temporarily stable or instable structures of self-regulation [*autoregulation*]. (*N*, 223)

Serres's idea of the self-reproductive and self-regulating system, like Niklas Luhmann's "autopoesis," seeks to apply systems theory to the processes of society and history, and the distinction between biological and social system ceases to be significant. Serres gives Lucretius the credit for this discovery:

> Lucretius discovered the processes in circular or semicircular causality. He discovered that there are two times, that of equilibrium and that of degradation, and that in history as in nature, things occur through the association of the two. Finally he discovered a third [time], that which relates the second to the first. History, like nature, consists of interchanges in three-part time. He discovered the efficacy of random fluctuation, and variation from equilibrium: one time surpasses another and is surpassed in its turn. Lucretius discovered the increase of complexity, when variation reappears in the course of the cycles of return to equilibrium. . . . He discovered that only insufficiency is productive. But also that production restores insufficiency. That labor, agriculture, navigation, and the arts compensate for the effects of degradation but increase its scope. Decline requires a dynamic adaptation, but that adaptation reinforces the decline. A spiral in three-part time, the reversible time of isonomy, the irreversible time of drift, and the productive time of compensation. (*N*, 223)

The problematic nature of a systems theory of history is highlighted by Serres's equivocations over the issue of historical progress:

> Finally, is it a question of progress? Yes, without doubt. The spiral increases itself in the opening of bifurcation, and the vortex amplifies its countermovement toward isonomy. Until it reaches a local highpoint, *cacumen,* summit, peak, Athens, here and now, mother of the arts, Epicurus and laws. But it is certainly not a question of progress. The quasi-cyclical process restores the City to its low point, plague and destruction. At the lowest point, it passes the relative place of the optimum. . . . Each progress, globally, is a loss. (*N*, 224)

History is thus both progressive and entropic: two countermovements and their interaction. In this model progress can only be a relative concept, one pole of a recursive quasi-cyclical movement from one temporary equilibrium to another. "The relation of order," Serres suggests "is never in equilibrium, it ceaselessly exceeds itself: *it is the trace of the spiral on one of its diameters—it doesn't matter which.* It is a particular case in the turbulent model of history, one in an indifferent disequilibrial series of exchanges. The necessary dynamic of force and violence" (*N,* 225). This reference to the "*necessary* dynamic" of force, together with Serres's vision of a global theorization that moves from matter to biological life and then to subjectivity, social process, and history, demands the exercise of caution.

While Serres's reflections on Lucretian physics and the turbulent, dynamic model of history that they provoke, or occasion, are invaluable insofar as they prompt us to seek less schematic ways of representing historical complexity, there are, I think, inherent dangers in Serres collapsing of physics, natural history, and history. The reduction of history to nature—even a complex and chaotic nature—is to replace various forms of teleological causality with a reified historical necessity, which threatens to reduce the scope for meaningful human agency, reducing it to mere instances of temporary disequilibrium. "In general," Serres says, "nature seeks an equilibrium in the midst of fluidity, and seeks fluidity through equilibrium. We call these fluctuations 'homeostasis' and 'homeorrhesis'" (*N,* 72); these two parameters are the oscillating poles of Serres's system, the extremes between which the turbulence of nature, history, and subjectivity emerge. But if, as Serres suggest, "ethics, correctly understood, is a physics" (225), where does that ethics find its resting place or its fulcrum? What meaning can ethics have in an indifferent system of fluctuations? Serres argues that "the physics of flux, the science of their law, and the Archimedean logic of maximal paths immediately produces a moral technology. That of equilibral ponderation, of equanimity" (69); that is to say, he draws an analogy (as the Stoics did) between physical balance and the balanced mind. But what is the "weight" of ethics? What is its "gravity"? For Serres the compensatory movements of history (or any other system) can never restore equilibrium, just as (for example) the war fought in Serbia could not restore the disequilibrium caused by genocide and the forced movements of population. But what does this tell us about the ethics of a putatively compensatory war? Surely it is not enough simply to say that it is "one in an indifferent disequilibrial series of exchanges" part of a "necessary dynamic of force and violence" (225)?

The inspirational power of Serres's thought is his gift for "putting two theses together in order to make them vibrate, through synthesis, ambiguity, paradox, or the undecidable" (*N,* 200). "It seems," he says,

> as if contradictions are separate from each other, as if they are repugnant to each other in the combat of reason and language, but contraries cohabit in the black box of things, so that if, one day, some subtle and

playful dialectician disconcerts you, you are silenced, you do not answer, you rejoin the children and play with the spinning top. (*N,* 41)

The spinning top, like the *salinon,* encapsulates Serres's ideal of stable fluctuation, an embodied proof of both the homeostatic and (as the top finally staggers, topples, and spins out of control) homeorrhetic principles, and it is Serres himself, no doubt, who is the "playful dialectician" making us reread Lucretius as an exponent of the "black box of things." The task of philosophy, Serres told Bruno Latour, is invention, or rather, "to invent the conditions for invention" (*C,* 86), and insofar as his thought compels us to rethink the complex nature of historical process, the troubled relationship between the disciplines and the affinities and tensions between poetic and scientific discourse, his work can be said to be in the process of inventing those conditions . . . and yet . . .

NOTES

1. On the philosophical history of this motif see Hans Blumenberg, *Schiffbruch mit Zuschauer. Paradigma einer Daseinsmetapher* (Frankfurt am Main: Suhrkamp, 1979), trans. Robert M. Wallace as *Shipwreck with Onlooker* (Cambridge: MIT Press, 1997).

2. See Steven J. Livesey, "*Metabasis:* The Interrelationship of the Sciences in Antiquity and the Middle Ages," Ph.D. diss., University of California, Los Angeles, 1982.

3. See W. Gellert et al., eds., *VNR Concise Encyclopedia of Mathematics* (New York: Van Nostrand Reinhold, 1975; reprint 1989), 175: "A salinon consists of two small semicircles of equal diameter *e* inside a large semicircle of diameter *d* and a further semicircle of diameter *d* 2*e* between them on the opposite side of *d*."

4. "How sweet still is the science of the sages, who from the safety of their hilltop, esteemed equilibrium" [Suave encore est la science des sages qui, du haut des cols protégés, estime les équilibres] (*N,* 82).

5. Michel Serres, *Genèse* (Paris: Bernard Grasset, 1982), 194.

SERRES AT THE CROSSROADS

ANDREW GIBSON

In part 1, chapter 4 of *Don Quixote,* there is a short paragraph that provides one of the defining moments of the new literary form, the modern European novel. Quixote has been riding on his way and singing Dulcinea's praises:

> He now came to a road branching in four directions, and immediately he was reminded of those cross-roads where knights-errant used to stop to consider which road they should take. In imitation of them he halted for a while, and after having deeply considered it, he gave Rocinante his head, submitting his own will to that of his hack, who followed out his first intention, which was to head straight for his stable.[1]

This is one of those crucial junctures early in the novel at which Quixote manifests his unassimilability, his irreducibility to modernity, his distance from the world and from the laws of the text in which he finds himself. At the crossroads, which is also the moment of crisis or decision, the moment that calls for determination in more senses than one, Quixote simply abandons the reins. As a consequence, narrative itself is imperiled, threatens to go into reverse, to return to its starting point, to nullify its own brief development and stifle its own prospects., in effect, to abort. This, of course, is something that Cervantes' novel cannot allow to happen. But the moment nonetheless helps to mark Quixote out—as from the beginning he must be marked out—as incongruous with his world. Not to understand what is signified by the crossroads, to take the crossroads as a point at which one merely surrenders, is to risk becoming a figure of fun. Quixote is defined from the very beginning as the man who recedes back into an alien past because he does not know how to negotiate an intersection of routes. This is the Quixote beautifully evoked by Foucault as the "diligent pilgrim" who nonetheless "never manages to escape from the familiar plain," who "travels endlessly over that plain, without ever crossing the clearly defined frontiers of difference."[2]

This quixotic crossroads stand at the beginning of a long tradition in the novel, a tradition in which what is crucial is precisely the topos of the crossroads as the figure of a crisis, of the moment at which there is crisis and a decision. But no one, any longer, will do as did Quixote: as regards the decision, their type might rather seem to be Bunyan's Christian. "Yes," says Good Will, at the beginning of *Pilgrim's Progress,* "there are many ways that butt down upon this [one]; and they are crooked, and wide; but thus thou may'st distinguish the right from the wrong, that only being straight and narrow."[3] Thus on arriving at the crossroads at the bottom of the Hill Difficulty, Christian will precisely "distinguish" the way "up the hill" that he must follow from the way Danger and the way Destruction, which lead Formalist into "a great wood" and, more evocatively, Hypocrisy into "a wide field full of dark mountains, where he stumbled and fell, and rose no more."[4] Christian's choices, however, are clear, necessary, and even foreordained. To come to a decision at Bunyan's crossroads, it would seem, is merely to choose a pathway between deceiving snares. From the Spanish picaresque to Defoe and Fielding to Dickens and Balzac, on the other hand, the crossroads is essentially secularized.[5] At the secular crossroads, not only does a structure, project, or trajectory have to take shape. The choice must be made in the absence of prior certitude, not least as to outcomes.[6] At the same time, the crossroads grows less important in itself than as figure, even as *implicit* figure, an implicit figure in terms of which, nonetheless, narrative does not cease to determine its own discursive limits:

> He stood and meditated—a miserable man. Whither should he go? . . . A man who has spent his primal strength in journeying in one direction has not much spirit left for reversing his course.[7]

This is Troy after Fanny's death in *Far from the Madding Crowd.* What remains crucial is the intersection of routes on the one hand and the decision on the other as in effect jointly composing a kind of narrative unit. At the crossroads whether literal or figurative, the complication of possibility becomes the resolved linearity of the actual. Whether the narrative is theological or secular, there is the moment of crisis, the moment of reduction to, or identification with, the single track. To fail at this moment is to risk simply returning with Rocinante to the stable. Even as crossroads become modern junctions—in Trollope's *The Prime Minister,* for instance—though it might seem "to the thoughtful stranger to be impossible that the best trained engine should know its own line," nonetheless "all do get properly placed and unplaced, so that the spectator at last acknowledges that over all this chaos there is presiding a great genius of order."[8] The crossroads that is quite distinct from Bunyan's theological crossroads, however, is not Fielding's or Balzac's secularized version, nor Trollope's modern, industrial complexification, but the crossroads as encountered in Robbe-Grillet: the crossroads that arrests progress rather than directing it, where one halts in uncertainty, where one chooses at the crossing only to find that one very quickly returns to it, where crossroads threaten to proliferate or repeat themselves indefinitely:

> He was at the crossroads already, and there was the white milestone (it was sixteen hundred yards to the big light-house at the end of the road). . . . The crossroads appeared immediately afterward: to the left the road to the farm, to the right a path that was quite broad at the outset.[9]

In *The Voyeur,* the figure of the crossroads recurs insistently and irrepressibly, like the malfunction produced by a computer virus. It is banished only to return again, soon if not at once. The crossroads can no longer be decisively left behind. It haunts narrative, threatening even to supplant it, to become the very figure of discourse itself. The abstract version of this would be Beckett's *Unnamable* wondering how to proceed, "by affirmations and negations invalidated as soon as uttered, or sooner or later," or perhaps by "aporia pure and simple."[10]

To produce a history of narrative as a history of the trope of the crossroads, then, would be to isolate four principal treatments: the quixotic, the theological-narrative, the secular-narrative and the postmodern aporetic. Serres's thematization of the crossroads is quite different. It conforms to none of these definitions and is as remote as is the quixotic from the other three. It also cuts, not only across the definitions themselves, but the system of thought according to which I have just produced them.[11] Indeed, it appears to emerge from a very different system of thought altogether, one, not least, that would break with the banal temporality according to which I have just constructed the progress of my historical fable; or, perhaps better, one that would raise questions about that temporality with reference to a *spatial* thought. The crossroads has been an insistent and crucial figure in Serres's writings. So much is clear from the significance Hermes has had for him. In interview with Raoul Morley, Serres insisted that when he wrote the Hermes series, he was not thinking of the Hermes associated with hermeneutics, the ambassador of the logos; not, that is, with a Hermes of the hermeneutic decision, a Hermes determining or determining on a single direction. Rather, he says he had in mind "the more classical God, Hermes, of communication, the god of transport, commerce, of sailors—the god whose statue was placed at the crossroads of various towns."[12] It is the point at which the statue of Hermes is placed that the philosopher will seek to occupy, not as a subject in relation to an object of

thought or knowledge, but as an *échangeur,* a point and instrument of transmission, of communication, a facilitator of circulation. The philosopher is
in this sense "mastropoetic": when Socrates was questioned on philosophy
in Xenophon's *Symposium,* writes Serres, he replied that it was *mastropoiea,*
"a trade of low repute in our society . . . the activity of the person who puts
into communication men and women";[13] less a hermeneutics, then, than
an erotics. The crossroads is the figure for this erotics. Equally, in *Hermès
II: L'Interférence,* Serres asserts that to circumscribe a given space or region
(or area or field), as I began by doing here, is of less interest or importance
than to establish or specify the points of confluence of lines. To consider
intersection is itself a heuristics, an exploration of what Serres follows
Bachelard in calling "complexité essentielle" (*LI,* 34). It is impossible to
proceed beyond or behind this complexity. For any linear or hierarchical
order is imported into knowledge only by means of distinctions improper
to it (*LI,* 39). In this respect, as we come after Bachelard, so, says Serres,
we are no longer Cartesians: for the segment and the sequence organized
according to simple chains, for the linear and univocal order of reason, we
have substituted a multiplicity of chains, tied to each other by a multiplicity of routes. The thinker's journey, writes Serres, is thus from crossroads
to crossroads. There is no overview of this journey, it has no totality and
cannot be diagrammed, lacks any global reference (*LI,* 65). In this context,
among the various comparable figures in Serres's work—the parasite, the
knot, the interchange, the third, the archipelago, Harlequin, the mosaic,
and so on—and given the fact that, as I shall suggest later, there is properly
no founding metaphor or metaphorical structure, no central metaphor in
Serres, the crossroads may provisionally be thought of as the primary unit
of knowledge, the primary element available to what Serres calls his plu-
ralist epistemology and of the texts he explicates.

The pluralism is crucial. For Serres, we have lost a sense of the paths
that invariably run from one local configuration of knowledge to another,
crossing as they do so. Spaces are "local knowledges." As such, they may be
understood quite literally with reference to natural history. This will help
distinguish the point of connection between spaces in my account of it
from, say, Bakhtin's concept of dialogue or heteroglossia. Equally, if, as I
suggest, Serres's conception of narrative involves a displacement or shift
from the temporal to the spatial, that shift is also toward a reassertion, in
the wake of contemporary antirepresentationalism, of certain material
bases for narrative. The reference away to natural history helps to explain
the connection. The spaces of knowledge are or can be thought of as materially grounded. Natural history, for instance, deals precisely with local
knowledges, concrete locations traversed by the observer and inhabited by
the observed. These knowledges are abstractions of and from "lieux sensibles." Contemporary ecological science in particular has become the sci-

ence that thinks the relation between such locations, "par ensembles inter-spécifiques et selon les entrelacs de la diversité" (A, 41). Local knowledges can no longer be contained within a global configuration or homogeneous space of knowledge. Rather, knowledge increasingly appears to function only in pockets or as it is distributed haphazardly in a plurality of spaces. The space of knowledge is "in tatters." The real is *sporadic*. So, too, ratio-nalities are sporadic. They are islands in a noisy, disordered sea, with routes between them.[14]

The importance of a concept of intersection or inter-reference should thus be self-evident. The concept recurs insistently in Serres's work, and the crossroads is precisely a crucial figure for it—though it is worth not-ing, by way of anticipating my later argument, that it is not in fact a figure that quite works, at least, alongside the figure of the archipelago of ratio-nalities. Two important specifications are necessary. First, the crossroads is not exactly a simple figure: in graphic terms, it does not have the clarity and simplicity of Bunyan's cross, with Danger on one side, Destruction on the other, and the right way between them. It is rather represented in the Greek χ, the *chi*- of *chiasmus*, in which the intersecting lines are neither straight nor equivalent to one another, in which one line in particular is "errant"—to use a term from Serres—or wandering. As Serres says of the parasite, so too of the χ or crossroads: it is not a figure that indicates or implies the establishment of an equilibrium.[15] Second, the crossroads is not a point of disjunction or decision. It is perhaps above all in this respect that Serres thinks the crossroads quite distinctively: it is a point of junc-tion, a point where things meet or come together, and hence one where neither judgment nor doubt is in question, but rather the event of connec-tion. It is thus that Serres thinks the crossroads in relation to narrative in the essay "Discours et Parcours" in *Hermès IV: La Distribution*. The essay forms part of a post-Kantian aesthetic program that Serres himself tells us he began to develop in *Hermès II*, and that struggles to take account of the "proliférations multiples d'espaces" for aesthetics (LD, 201). Within this aesthetics, narrative emerges as a form of "inter-diction," of saying between: that is, of articulating what passes between multiple and hetero-geneous spaces.[16] It joins things together, ties knots, constructs bridges, establishes relays between spaces determined as radically different.[17] Its primary element would thus not be the building block placed in a linear or vertical relation to others, as has so insistently been the case in narrative theory and notably in narratology. It would be the point of juncture between spaces.

In "Discours et Parcours," Serres's principal instance runs immediately counter to the history and typology I sketched in at the beginning of this essay. In the Oedipus narrative, at the crossroads at Megas, Oedipus meets Laius and Laius's herald Polyphontes and kills them. For Serres, this cross-

roads is the very figure of the Oedipus narrative itself. Oedipus is journeying from the Corinth of King Polybos, who has adopted Oedipus as his
own to consult the Delphic oracle. At Megas, the road from Corinth
encounters the road to Thebes: "Thebes, City of Light," as Sophocles' cho-
rus have it, where "from the Pythian House of Gold \ The Gracious voice
of heaven is heard,"[18] but also a Thebes that will fall victim to the ravages
of the Sphinx. In addition, one of the roads that cross at Megas leads to the
Delphi for which Oedipus was aiming—Delphi at Parnassus, home of the
oracle and the temple of Apollo—and another leads to Daulis, where
Tereus ate the flesh of his son. On the one hand, writes Serres, Delphi,
knowledge, meaning, language, the sacred and the conscious; on the other
hand, ignorance, blindness, and the unconscious. What is crucial, here, is
the connection of the disconnected: the past that is Corinth and the future
that is Thebes, Delphi and Daulis, the Apollonian and the unconscious,
father and son, the incestuous relation. But it is also a connection or a relay
across a broken threshold of speech and language. The narrative, says Serres, turns inside out, like a glove, and reveals its essential function, the
essential function of narrative. This function is, in Serres's nicely judged
phrase, the weaving together of a complex, "la mise en place de séparations entre espaces et leur liaison difficile" (*LD,* 204). To put it differently:
the mythical and psychological dimensions of the Oedipus narrative are
inseparable from its topography, a set of relationships between the indige-
nous and the foreign, the selfsame and that against which the selfsame
defines itself. Or, to put it differently again, the mythical and psychological dimensions, the knowledges in circulation here as anywhere in narrative, are local knowledges inseparable from *lieux sensibles* (*A,* 41). Narrative
does not choose among such knowledges. Nor does it privilege one over
another or generalize or universalize one at the expense of another as what
Serres calls a "science-reine." It rather institutes meetings at crossroads. Its
principle is that of the Sphinx. The law of the crossroads is the law of the
Sphinx, of the chimera, a bodily equivalent of the χ, a meeting of dis-
parates. Like the statue of Hermes, the Sphinx watches over a bisected
route, a roadway along which the Thebans can no longer pass. The principle of the Sphinx cuts definitively across the principle of linearity that I
referred to at the start. The Oedipus narrative, it would seem, tells the
story of the revenge of the crossroads, which is also the revenge of the
Sphinx; and narrative itself is equally the chimera beyond which there is no
going, which Oedipus himself imagines he has gone beyond, only to be
cruelly and catastrophically undeceived.

   The Oedipus narrative, however, is what Serres calls mythic narrative.
It is also a story in which journeying plays a significant part. What of modern narrative, and modern narrative in which there would seem to be little or no vestige of the mythic or indeed the picaresque journey? Further-

more: in my reading of Serres's account of Oedipus, there is more than a faint residue of the Bunyanesque-allegorical—Delphi versus Daulis, Apollo versus Dionysus, and so on—which arguably corresponds to something that is there in Serres's own account. In other words, for all its fascination, what Serres says about the Oedipus story is not wholly consistent with the conception of narrative emerging in "Discours et Parcours." There is at least a vestige of hermeneutic practice in Serres's account of narrative, here, though it is also concerned to leave the last word to the Sphinx. Serres's study of the Rougon-Macquart series, on the other hand—of modern narratives, Zolaesque narrative—can be read as a different kind of operation relative to that same problem. Here again Serres asserts that mythic discourse is "une entreprise de tissage," a process whereby connections are established between places and spaces that are remote or isolated or inaccessible from, closed to, dangerous, and even deadly to each other. It is only once this process of "tissage" as both traced and performed by mythic narrative has been accomplished that science itself can begin (Z, 169). But, in Serres's phrase, as the logos is born out of the connection between these separate mythic spaces, so narrative is exiled from them, and passes over into what we call literature, which becomes the principal site for the process of connection itself. Thus we must conceive of reading Zola in terms of an immense voyage: the Rougons, the Macquarts, the Mourets, Lantiers, and Quenus spread out into the social body and set out for adventure, driven by the energy of their instincts through a variety of worlds that seem as heterogeneous to them as the lands of the Mediterranean do to Ulysses or the worlds joined at the crossroads at Megas do to Oedipus (Z, 189). The problem is how to find ways that bring these separate spaces together or effect passages between them. Like Homer's Mediterranean, Zola's Paris and Zola's France may be imagined—again—as archipelagoes, ensembles of disconnected spaces distributed sporadically. As contrasted to the "domaines de coupures" like politics, which establish and insist on separations, narrative insists on relations between these spaces. This is the power above all of the great figure of Nana. Nana circulates everywhere, from the brothels of the slums to the elite circles in which she plays the courtesan. For Serres, she appears to function precisely as a figure for narrative's desire for connection, an erotics, again, as distinct from a hermeneutics (Z, 242). But this is by no means the only respect in which Serres conceives of the Rougon-Macquart series in terms of the crossroads. Zola also institutes a labyrinthine network of crossings or intersections between the *savoirs*. The Rougon-Macquart novels put knowledges or sciences in communication with each other.[19] They bring Darwin into contact with Boltzmann and Maxwell, for example, and, indeed, with Nietzsche and Freud; and, beyond that, with mythic knowledge itself. There are incessant connections and disconnections between the spaces constructed by mechanics, topography, thermo-dynamics, genetics, economics, mathematics, biology, and mythology, a list that is by no means exhaustive. More remarkable still, and perhaps above all in the Zola book, Serres produces and sustains a discourse that keeps the terms of these multiple *savoirs* in circulation and effects junctures between them. The consequences of this are several: most obviously, per-haps, firstly, Serres's practice dissolves the unitary foundation or singular grid on the basis of which alone, according to Serres, any classical explica-tion de texte must necessarily proceed. Along with that—to go back to the case made at the beginning of this essay—it refuses the terms of a decision or choice effected as the consequence of rational reflection or in Olympian indifference. Third, it constructs the text in terms of multiple spaces the proportions of whose relations to one another are never definitively stabi-lized or fixed. Finally, the discourse establishes itself according to a princi-ple of the instability of all metaphors, and practices a kind of shifting or dis-placement, indeed, a mixture of metaphor throughout. The mixed or destabilized metaphor seems to me to be cardinal to Serres's work. More than any other philosopher or theorist, perhaps, he generates a desire to mix metaphors, a desire for "cross-metaphorization." I shall come back to this point toward the end of this essay.

The conception of narrative I have been describing is elaborated, ramified, or brought into new sets of relations with fresh material in Ser-res's book on Verne; in his account of Balzac's *Sarrasine* in *L'Hermaphrodite;* in his discussions of Merimée's *Carmen* in *Le Tiers-instruit* and of Maupas-sant's *L'Horla* in *Atlas.* Rather than describing or attempting to distinguish between these accounts, however, I want briefly to pursue three instances of the larger implications of Serres's conception of narrative with refer-ence to the texts in question. Firstly, aporia: it might seem as though the figure of the crossroads is a figure for an aporia. Puttenham's classical definition of aporia—a rhetorical figure indicating that someone "is uncer-tain how to proceed, in some difficult or doubtful matter"—appears almost explicitly to evoke hesitation at the signpost. But in fact, as I said at the beginning, aporia and the crossroads are quite distinct. It might appear that to think the narrative crossroads in Serres's conception of it is to think aporia in reverse, inside out or against the grain. But that would merely be to think the two figures within the same space or at the same site. Serres asks us to occupy a position different from that which produces both apo-ria and the certitude that aporia places at issue. That demand is part at least of what I take to be his covert effort to release *Sarrasine* from the grip of Roland Barthes in *L'Hermaphrodite.*[20] Serres points out that *Sarrasine* begins in hesitation, at the crossroads, as it were, with the narrator poised on the edge of joining the ball. But he is not there to designate an aporia. He rather belongs to what Serres calls the "régions précritiques," functioning as a kind of guardian or presiding spirit at the gates of narrative itself (*LH*, 62). To think the threshold, here—to think the crossroads—is to try at least to think narrative in relation to a space other than that of critique; critique, of course, implying a power of which the powerlessness of aporia is merely the obverse. For we are surely now at the end of the *parenthèse critique* and have begun to understand that the place occupied by commentary, critique, judgment, the norm or foundation is both less plausible and less interesting than that occupied by the things judged or criticized (*E*, 186). What Serres refuses is the vertical dimension, the elevation of critique *au dessus de la melée*, its assumption of what he calls the position of the tribunal as in Kant, the "last instance" before which the whole can be decided and whose foundering is aporia itself. To think the intersection is to resist both the illusory clarity of the vertical leap and the catastrophe of its failure. Furthermore—and this is crucial—to think the intersection is to attempt to think narrative or the work from the point of view of its production, of its "plongée précritique dans un espace multiplement orienté" (*LH*, 75). Balzac is not searching for criteria for judgment but for conditions that make productivity possible: "avant le métalangage du jugement, il faut bien construire une chose" (*LH*, 75). Here the work is always plural where critique is a monism. The critic—Barthes by implication—works according to a principle of exclusion that *Sarrasine* itself excludes. What critique could only ever articulate as the chilliness of aporia thus becomes "surabondance" or saturation, "éblouissante montage."[21] *Sarrasine* begins with a narrator described as "songeur." Equally, it ends as it began, with the enigmatic, with the sentence "Et la marquise resta pensive." There is no mechanical, hermeneutic progress from enigma to resolution of the kind Barthes was determined to discover in Balzac's text. Such a structure is merely a reflection of the operations of critique itself. But to say this is not to give the text over to irresolution. In Serres's terms, it rather returns it to the crossroads, the place of rich and complex exchanges.

For the bleak austerity of aporia, then—the thought that a parting or crossing of ways means less and not more, loss rather than gain—Serres substitutes the thought of the juncture as abundance or complexification. Equally, if, self-evidently, the crossroads is not a figure establishing or confirming an identity. Nor is it one that signals the dissolution of identity or death of the subject. Identity is rather projected as a point of intersection between multiple networks. At the beginning of *Sarrasine,* the condition of the observant, intelligent narrator on the threshold both of the ball and of the narrative is one of tremulous if anxious equilibrium. He lies at the intersection of frontiers, writes Serres, his body a point of intersection between extremes. He is the "sympathique"—a figure cardinal to narrative—who *is* the multiple of what he describes, even at the price of contradiction. He understands everything and can reject nothing. He will never be a philosopher of antithesis—nor a dialectician, we might add, with *Rome, the Book of Foundations* in mind.[22] The crossroads, then, is where identity yields to and must incorporate or recognize its intimate association with a radical exteriority. This conception—of identity as intersection—begins with Oedipus, who must struggle to adjust the violently disjoined selves that are connected at the crossroads. "Is this my voice \ That is borne on the air?" he cries after the revelation in *Oedipus Rex*. "Vient toujours le carrefours," writes Serres in *Les Cinq Sens* with reference to *Cinderella:* the crossroads always when the carriage in which you are traveling turns into a pumpkin (*CS,* 66). What identity must take into account is the principle of, or the potential for, reversibility that Serres insists on throughout his work. This is the gist of the discussion of *L'Horla* in *Atlas,* Serres's most protracted meditation on narrative and identity. In Maupassant's tale, he asserts, identity emerges as an ensemble of relations between different places. Madness and alienation consist in enclosing all space in a single place that is deemed to be interior. As such, they merely correspond to a system in which identity is construed as inwardness and depth, the other as exterior or outward. But Maupassant destroys that system: *L'Horla* rather establishes identity as a complex set of relations between a series of "intimate" or inward spaces and a series of external ones (*A,* 67). Furthermore, the spaces between which identity is a kind of juncture are virtual as well as real: places left, or once occupied, or places that may be occupied or frequented. If the crossroads is a figure for identity itself, it is not simply as a point of connection between spaces whose availability in the present can be assumed. It points toward or designates, but does not indicate the status of that which it designates. It is in this manner that, for Serres, in Maupassant, narrative itself becomes the very model *of* identity.

But there is also an ethics at stake here, as repeatedly throughout Serres's work. Literature, says Serres, in *Zola,* occupies language more *largely* than any of the logics. (This is not a value judgment, but simply the case.) For the same reason, literature is a "system of simulation" that is relatively faithful to what is at stake in the game for any of the knowledges—any of the *découpages*—at a particular point in space-time (*Z,* 171). Narrative will therefore stand relative to any given knowledge as a simulation of Bachelard's "complexité essentielle." As such, it resists *entêtement,* obstinacy, stubborn persistence, the fixed idea lodged in the head, the singular, homogenous space of the dogmatist. Like Hermes, narrative stands at the crossroads connecting what Serres calls "passions sectorielles" (*Z,* 12), "les niches écologiques, defendus bec et ongles," the *lieu sensible* conceived of as the only sensible place to be (*LD,* 206). For the same reasons, narrative differs from the principle of the academic discipline, which is that of town planning: "le travail universitaire cloisonné en sectes, reproduisant les rues et les quartiers . . . un impossible art de vivre" (Z, 16). Equally, narrative is the work that resists the principle of the work as mastery and destruction: in Serres's words, the work that claims that no other work is possible, that it stands alone as king, father and master of space. The crossroads always points elsewhere, to another relation. It is an open figure. It is also an intractable figure, one that cannot be reduced to the singular. It thus sets at issue, on the one hand, what Serres calls "the law of totality" and, on the other, "the axiom of closure," with their habitual sets of questions: is this complete, is it the last word, is it decisive, is it definitive and so on (Z, 38). Above all, perhaps, far from being reducible to or encompassed by the terms of critique, narrative would appear to be heterogeneous to them: heterogeneous, that is, to the theological structure of critique, its fetishization of the august position "où l'on a toujours raison, où l'on est le plus savant" (E, 195). Insofar as narrative itself has been understood in terms of the production or articulation of such a position—and a whole tradition of (above all, English) thought about the novel was only able to conceive of the latter in this way—it has merely been constructed as the mirror image of critique itself. With the thought of the crossroads, however, that construction loses its plausibility, and the image is dispersed.

In the end, however, if it is a useful figure, the crossroads is self-evidently also a strategic and therefore limited one, a point of departure but—as I said earlier—not a foundational metaphor. This has been clear from *Hermès II,* which will serve as a useful starting point for problematizing and subtilizing what I have said so far. In the first instance, then, the crossroads is not to be thought from the position of the traveler, as a point of disruption on a line. That is precisely to continue to understand it within a context that gives priority to linearity. By the same token, the crossroads is not to be thought of as a point that links heterogeneous and self-consistent spaces deemed in some sense to be original or come before it. That is to continue to give priority to the singular instance. Here, the metaphor begins to break down, to yield to another. Crossroads always refer away not to spaces as eventual destinations but to other crossroads in a great maze of connections without defined boundaries or limits. At length, the figure of the crossroads is swallowed up in two other metaphorical systems that are recurrent in Serres, the labyrinth and, above all, the *réseau,* or network. According to Serres, it is important to distinguish the latter from the technological model of the network: the crossroads is not a multiple flyover or spaghetti junction, in which roads do not cross, in which it is always possible to take a certain route without meeting any of the others (LI, 131). Furthermore: if to circumscribe a given space is of less interest than to address the points of confluence between lines, these points *are the regions themselves* (LI, 14). In other words, on a certain level, a given space appears as an intersection in itself: "des carrefours se connectent, où se jettent des sciences, qui sont elles-mêmes des carrefours et des noeuds de connexion" (*LI,* 67). By the same token, the metaphor of the crossroads is determinate insofar as in remaining obstinately horizontal, in contradistinction to the vertical dimension summoned up—as we saw earlier—for thought by critique, it reduces spaces and spatializations to a single plane and thus to commensurability. This in its turn is a reassertion of the position of domination that creates incompatibilities. For the latter are always asserted from that position, in an im-position of a language or a theory on the world; in other words, the imposition of a monism. Is it not possible, Serres asks, that the figure of the crossroads might turn out itself to be or at least to resemble such a monism?

However, spaces are "multiplement recouverts" (*LI,* 25): they overlap with each other, and there is a play of crossings within and between them, and within and between their overlappings. In this respect, crossings must be imagined, in Norbert Wiener's words, as "triplicated, quadruplicated" (*LI,* 29). What Serres is clearly concerned with here is a metaphor for a set of vertical relations that will be nonhierarchical. Crossings, then, must be thought in their instability and multiplicity and systems of crossings in terms of *enchevêtrements,* entanglings, as inter-referring or interfering with one another. If, for Serres, hierarchical order always implies the possibility of scrutiny, critique, observation, curiosity, and thereby a position of power, the "procès judiciaire" (*LH,* 62); if any linear or hierarchical order is imported into knowledge by means of distinctions improper or exterior to it; if the only proper exterior to knowledge is nonknowledge, the thought of the crossroads makes linear, hierarchical, global, or irreversible order unthinkable. It ruins all thought of a foundational metaphor. This is in keeping with our current emergence from "une période sombre où tout se décidait au-devant d'une dernière instance, préalablement choisie" (*LH,* 64). But if the crossroads works to exclude the possibility that any metaphor might have a foundational status, that must include itself. For to assert the foundational character of any given metaphor whatsoever is to reassert the possibility of a "science-reine." Furthermore, "mistakes, wavy lines, confusion, obscurity are part of knowledge." There is no system of knowledge that functions perfectly, "that is to say, without losses, flights, wear and tear, errors, accidents, opacity" (*P,* 12). This equally applies to the systems of metaphor inhabiting systems of knowledge. Thus the crossroads itself will necessarily be both an imperfect and a reversible metaphor. Hence a space may turn into a crossroads and a crossroads into a knot, and a crossroads in a network of routes may itself be a network of routes (*LI,* 131). Hermes may metamorphose into the parasite, the third (as in *le tiers-instruit*) or intermediary. For they are all mediators, says Serres, operators of change and transformation, but also all one figure, too.[23] The operation of change and transformation also takes place within its operators. The progress of Serres's work and the multiplications that that progress breeds themselves enact such metamorphoses.

In his concern with the instability of the metaphor, in an insistent mixing and overlapping of metaphors, a fading of one figure into another, Serres is notably distant from the terms of an empirical or commonsense logic. The distance might almost be described as quixotic. Finally, however: one way of conceiving of the relation between Serres's terms and a kind of thought represented, for instance, by narrative theory—systematic, taxonomical, or what, following Derrida, I elsewhere called *geometric*[24]—would be to suggest, not so much that Serres's conception of narrative "is quixotic," as that it incorporates Quixote or the quixotic *within* a thought of narrative; that is, it incorporates the quixotic as noise, disturbance, a principle of multiple overlappings, "complexité essentielle." To review one or two of my earlier points: the narrative unit may be thought of—as may narrative itself—as an *échangeur,* a nodal point for or means of transmission, of communication, of bringing together. The linear and vertical models for conceiving of narrative that have classically been more or less dominant may now be challenged with a conception of narrative as crossings, *tissage, entrelacs,* or, to return to an earlier quotation, "la mise en place de séparations entre espaces et leur liaison difficile" (*LD,* 204). It is thus that Zola brings Darwin into contact with Boltzmann, Maxwell, Nietzsche, and Freud. So, too, in Serres's account of Verne's work, voyages are conducted within three spaces: the literal, the space of the ordinary voyage; the scientific, the space of the intellectual or "encyclopedic" itinerary; and the initiatory, religious or mythic pilgrimage (*J,* 23). Thus in *Michel Strogoff,* for example, the plausibility of scientific space may yield to mythic or magical space, the "scène primitive," and vice versa (*J,* 41). But, beyond the tripartite division, a given space can splinter or proliferate to the point at which analogies with a variety of other "worlds" in a range of writers from Homer and d'Urfé to Faulkner and St John of the Cross become evident (*J,* 56). I have looked at this aspect of Serres's work on Verne before.[25] What needs to be added is a conception of "triplication," "quadruplication," and so on. The difficulty lies in finding a way of conceiving of or *writing* the "worlds" in question that does not establish them—perhaps even any two or more of them—on the same plane.[26] This is equally a difficulty with the crossroads as figure, in that, like any figure within a system of metaphor, its implications may appear fixed and its functions automatic. Insofar as the figure of the crossroads is wedded to a logic of commensurability, then, it must itself be problematized, deconstructed, subjected to the very process of enlargement or complexification that it might itself appear to represent.

NOTES

1. Miguel de Cervantes Saavedra, *Don Quixote,* the Ormsby translation, ed. Joseph R. Jones and Kenneth Douglas (New York: Norton, 1981), 42.

2. Michel Foucault, *The Order of Things: An Archaeology of the Human Sciences* (London: Tavistock, 1980), 46.

3. John Bunyan, *The Pilgrim's Progress,* ed. Roger Sharrock (Harmondsworth: Penguin, 1965), 59.

4. Ibid.,74.

5. On the choice of roads in Fielding in particular, see Simon Varey, *Space and the Eighteenth-Century Novel* (Cambridge: Cambridge University Press, 1990), 157–58.

6. Compare, in the novel of the road in particular, the corresponding fear "of going astray, of losing [one's] bearings in the wilderness." This fear is "a recurrent aspect of the picaro's essential situation throughout the history of the English novel." Lars Hartveit, *Workings of the Picaresque in the British Novel* (Oslo: Solum Forlag, 1987), 13.

7. Thomas Hardy, *Far from the Madding Crowd* (Harmondsworth: Penguin, 1981), 378.

8. Anthony Trollope, *The Prime Minister* (Oxford: Oxford University Press, 1974), 2:191–92.

9. Alain Robbe-Grillet, *The Voyeur,* trans. Richard Howard (London: John Calder, 1965), 71.

10. Samuel Beckett, *The Unnamable,* trans. by the author (London: John Calder, 1975), 7.

11. For a more detailed and developed attempt to use Serres's thought to elaborate a critique of the tradition and typologies of narrative theory, see my *Towards a Postmodern Theory of Narrative* (Edinburgh: Edinburgh University Press, 1996), 1–30, 111–16, 220–24.

12. Raoul Morley, *French Philosophers in Conversation* (London: Routledge, 1991), 50–51.

13. Ibid., 59.

14. See Josué V. Harari and David F. Bell, introduction to *H,* xii–xiv.

15. Morley, *French Philosophers in Conversation,* 59.

16. Percy G. Adams's work on the relationship between travel literature and the novel suggests that this particular conception of narrative is strikingly evident in the work of the travel writers (Marco Polo, Columbus, Raleigh, John Smith, Dampier, Careri, Hakluyt) who preceded the eighteenth-century novelists. Interestingly, Adams argues that, in the eighteenth-century novel, too, temporality is itself inseparable from a movement through space or spaces. See his *Travel Literature and the Evolution of the Novel* (Lexington: University Press of Kentucky, 1983), 184–85 and passim.

17. In this respect, narrative in Serres's conception of it is precisely distinct from Elizabeth Deeds Ermarth's conception of realist narrative as a power of abstraction and projection that produces a neutral time and space as the characteristic media of modernity. See her *Realism and Consensus in the English Novel: Time, Space, and Narrative,* 2d ed. (Edinburgh: Edinburgh University Press, 1998).

18. Sophocles, *Oedipus Rex,* in *The Theban Plays,* trans. E. F. Watling (Harmondsworth: Penguin, 1947), 30.

19. In this respect, the French "philosophization" of the picaresque as exemplified in *Rameau's Nephew* would clearly appear to bridge the gap between the picaresque and Zola. See A. R. Strugnell, "Diderot's *Neveu de Rameau:* Portrait of a Rogue in the French Enlightenment," in *Knaves and Swindlers: Essays on the Picaresque Novel in Europe,* ed. Christine J. Whitbourn (Oxford: Oxford University Press, 1974), 93–111.

20. See Roland Barthes, *S\Z* (Paris: Éditions de Seuil, 1970).

21. Ibid., 84, 95.

22. Serres, *Rome: The Book of Foundations,* trans. Felicia McCarren (Stanford: Stanford University Press, 1991). See 158: "If you are small, don't trust dialectics. The rude and common dialectic, with two values is only the master's logic. . . . It is the logic of immobility. Of stability and repetition that gives the appearance of movement. It is the logic of empire."

23. Serres, *Le Tiers-instruit* (Paris: François Bourin, 1991), 80.

24. Andrew Gibson, *Towards Postmodern Theory of Narrative* (Edinburgh: Edinburgh University Press, 1996), 3–8, 20–21, 32–33 and passim.

25. Gibson, *Postmodern Theory of Narrative,* 17–18.

26. It's tempting to suggest here that narrative theory, even thought itself, might have much to learn from one particular and paradigmatic narrative, Joyce's *Ulysses.*

"MULTIPLE PLEATS"

Some Applications of Michel Serres's Poetics

MARJORIE PERLOFF

"Style," Michel Serres tells Bruno Latour in the first of their "Conversations," is the sign of innovation, of passage into new territory" (*C*, 26). And yet, when it comes to poetry (or, for that matter, fiction), Serres has expressed little interest in innovative and experimental forms. The declaration, in the same interview, "I have never ceased to seek beauty" (26) is made in the context of a discussion about Serres's love of the Greek and Roman classics as well as for particular French philosophers and novelists. Asked about the authors he admires, Serres lists Plato, Aristotle, Lucretius, Pascal, Leibniz, La Fontaine, Balzac, Verne, and Zola (28). There is not a lyric poet on this list—an irony, given that, as Latour frequently reminds Serres, "the accusations of 'poetry' [have been] frequently leveled at your books" (44).

Serres himself has taken issue with this downgrading of the "poetic." "What a sign of the times," he remarks, "when to cruelly criticize a book, one says that it is only poetry! *Poetry* comes from the Greek, meaning 'invention,' 'creation'—so all is well, thank you" (*C*, 44). But like Roland Barthes, whose choice of subjects reveals him as having preferred almost every other form of discourse to lyric poetry, even as, paradoxically, his own writing became increasingly "poetic," Serres has never focused attention on lyric poetry, much less on the poetry of the late twentieth century. This is a curious anomaly given that, as I shall argue in this essay, Serres's analysis of *noise* in oral and written discourse is extremely valuable to students of postmodern poetics.

Interestingly, in the few instances when Serres discusses actual lyric poems, he does not read them in terms of his own theory. Consider the discussion, in the third conversation ("Demonstration and Interpretation"), of the following Verlaine sonnet from *Sagesse* (1880):

L'Espoir luit comme un brin de paille dans l'étable.
Que crains-tu de la guêpe ivre de son vol fou?
Vois, le soleil toujours poudroie à quelque trou.
Que ne t'endormais-tu, le coude sur la table?

Pauvre âme pâle, au moins cette eau du puits glacé,
Bois-la. Puis dors après. Allons, tu vois, je reste,
Et je dorloterai les rêves de ta sieste,
Et tu chantonneras comme un enfant bercé.

Midi sonne. De grâce, éloignez-vous, madame.
Il dort. C'est étonnant comme les pas de femme
Résonnent au cerveau des pauvres malheureux.

Midi sonne. J'ai fait arroser dans la chambre.
Va, dors! L'espoir luit comme un caillou dans un creux.
Ah, quand refleuriront les roses de septembre!

[Hope shines like a wisp of hay in the stable,
What do you fear from the wasp, drunk from his crazy flight?
See, the sun is always powdering the dust through some crack.
Why weren't you falling asleep, elbow on the table?

Poor pale soul, at least this water from the frozen well,
Drink it. Then sleep. Come, you see, I'm staying,
And I will lull the dreams of your siesta,
And you will sing like a baby, rocked in the crib.

Noon strikes. Please take your leave, Madame.
He sleeps. It is amazing how a woman's steps
Resound in the brain of poor unhappy men.

Noon strikes. I have watered the room.
Go ahead, sleep! Hope shines like a flint in a cavern.
Ah, when will the roses of September bloom again?][1]

Serres cites this poem in a discussion about the inextricability of science, philosophy, and literature; for him, Verlaine's sonnet exemplifies the way a literary text can embody—indeed anticipate—an important scientific insight:

In the sonnet Verlaine describes someone who falls asleep, his elbow on the table, in the summer noontime heat, while hearing the hum of a wasp's flight. This is an ordinary coenesthetic experience: perceived by the body itself, or internally, in which the wandering sound, the noise perceived, comes both from the external world and from the organism itself. Now, in saying this, the poet comes close to contemporary theories on background noise. . . .

By observing his own intropathic experience with what I dare to call an unheard-of precision, Verlaine intuits the reality of background noise, which precedes all signals and is an obstacle to their perception—anterior to any language and either hindering or assisting its arrival. Inversely, the intense sound of language prevents us from hearing this sound.

As a result the observer provides a sort of genesis of language, or of everything that takes place, before its appearance. Now here's a subject that's truly poetic; at the same time it's a real, scientific object. The time lapse between these two propositions measures the historical distance between Verlaine and us. (*C*, 78–79)

Note that Serres's premise in this very interesting interpretation is that the function of Verlaine's poem—and, by implication, any poem—is to say something. Indeed, Serres tells Latour: "If you accept such a hypothesis, the enigma is resolved, and the sonnet becomes clear and transparent . . . what was inexplicable becomes illuminated" (*C*, 79). But in opting for such clarity and transparency, Serres is, ironically, forced to ignore the issue of "background noise" in the sonnet itself. For if the poem is taken to be about a particular coenesthetic experience (the inability to discriminate between those sounds that come from outside the body and those within) and hence "a sort of genesis of language, or of everything that takes place, before its appearance," it is hard to account for the sonnet's sestet, in which the focus is on the receding footsteps of the threatening "madame" (mother? landlady? estranged wife?) resonating in the poet's brain, followed by the tears that have watered his lonely vigil, and his hope, this time a little more substantial than at the poem's beginning, for the renewal of love (the flowering of the September roses).

Presumably, Serres has little interest in the imagery of love and loss that runs through the *Sagesse* sequence. But from a literary perspective, it would surely be important to know how and why the "intropathic" experience prompted by the wasp's buzz relates to the footsteps of Madame in line 9 and the tears of line 12. "To exclude the empirical," Serres insists in "Platonic Dialogue," "is to exclude differentiation, the plurality of others that mask the same" (*H*, 69). But he does exclude the empirical in putting so much weight on one image at the expense of the rest of the sonnet or, for that matter, the sonnet's place in the larger sequence.

One of the difficulties inherent in studies of science versus art, I would posit, is that different disciplines demand different methods of interpretation. The scientific philosopher who wants to "use" literary material tends to treat a given poem as a set of truth statements. Thus, elsewhere in the dialogue with Latour, Serres gently chides Apollinaire for the line "Sous le pont Mirabeau coule la Seine." The poet, Serres objects, "hadn't studied the Seine enough. He hadn't noticed the counter-currents or the turbulences. Yes, time flows like the Seine, if one observes it well. All the water that passes beneath the Mirabeau Bridge will not necessarily flow out into the English Channel; many little trickles turn back toward Charenton or upstream." And he goes on to discuss the evidence that "time flows in a turbulent and chaotic manner" (C, 58–59).

But, as Aristotle reminds us in what is still the best formulation of this problem, "a poet's object is not to tell what actually happened but what could and would happen either probably or inevitably" (Poetics IX, 1451b). And again, "The standard of what is correct is not the same in the art of poetry as it is in the art of social conduct or any other art. . . . It is less of an error not to know that a female stag has no horns than to make a picture that is unrecognizable" (1461). Apollinaire, by this reasoning, doesn't need to describe the flow of the Seine "correctly"; it is the relationship between river flow and other items in the poem that matters poetically.

And here Serres's theory of noise comes in. As early as 1972 in "Platonic Dialogue," Serres examined the complexity of communication in our technological age of "background noise, jamming, static, cut-offs, hyteresis, various interruptions" (H, 66). Following Norbert Wiener and others, Serres defines noise as "the set of these phenomena of interference that become obstacles to communication" (66). "To hold a dialogue," he argues, "is to suppose a third man and to seek to exclude him; a successful communication is the exclusion of the third man. . . . We might call this third man the demon, the prosopopeia of noise" (67). That demon becomes the subject of one of Serres's most important books, Le Parasite (1980), but in "Platonic Dialogue" the emphasis is less on the figure of the parasite as the demonic "guest" who destroys his "host" at the banquet table, than on the larger communication process, in which, as Serres says, "background noise is essential" (H, 66). Only in a mathematical formula—say, $x^2 + y^2 = z^2$—is noise wholly excluded; ordinary discourse is inevitably "noisy," and the further we move away from pure mathematical abstraction in the direction of empirical differentiation, the larger role noise plays:

> At the extreme limits of empiricism, meaning is totally plunged into noise, the space of communication is granular, dialogue is condemned to cacophony, the transmission of communication is chronic transformation. Thus, the empirical is strictly essential and accidental noise. . . . consequently, in order for dialogue to be possible one must close one's eyes and cover one's ears to the song and beauty of the sirens. (H, 70)

This last image reminds us that Serres is by no means suggesting that "successful" communication (the message received is identical to the message sent) is superior to the differentiation produced by the noise in the channel. Indeed, as Serres notes in his related essay "The Origin of Language," "Of course no one can call information fortunate and noise painful, for things are arranged in any number of chiasms."[2] In fact, "what was supposed to interfere begins constructing; obstacles combine to organize; noise becomes dialect" (*H,* 80). The Sirens' song, in other words, takes over.

In his study *The Noise of Culture,* William Paulson argues that the "noise" or "dialect" Serres speaks of is equivalent to what the Russian formalists called the poetic function:

> A language used as pure instrument of efficient communication should be as free from noise as possible; thus if literature is to deviate from the utilitarian task of communication, it must be an imperfect process of communication, an act of communication in which what is received is not exactly what was sent. Rather than attempting to reduce noise to a minimum, literary communication *assumes* its noise as a constitutive factor of itself.[3]

No doubt poetic language does function as "noise" in this large sense. But what neither Paulson nor Serres himself emphasizes is that the information theory in question, applicable though it may be to poetry—or indeed writing—in general, has special relevance in our own digital age. Even if, in other words, cacography has always been a factor in the transmission of the written word, even if "stammerings, mispronunciations, [and] regional accents" have always produced interference in the speech channel (*H,* 66), there can be no doubt that the technological environment of the present time from radio and TV, to cellular phones, to the new Internet technologies, creates a level of noise undreamed of even a few decades ago.

One of the prophetic texts, in this regard, is John Cage's "Experimental Music" (1957), reprinted in *Silence* (1962). As early as 1937, in "The Future of Music: Credo," Cage had declared:

> I BELIEVE THAT THE USE OF NOISE
> Wherever we are, what we hear is mostly noise. When we ignore it, it disturbs us. When we listen to it, we find it fascinating.[4]

And in "Experimental Music," Cage expands on this point in a now famous statement:

> There is no such thing as an empty space or an empty time. There is always something to see, something to hear. In fact, try as we may to make a silence we cannot. For certain engineering purposes it is desirable to have as silent a situation as possible. Such a room is called an ane-

choic chamber, its six walls made of special material, a room without
echoes. I entered one at Harvard University several years ago and heard
two sounds, one high and one low. When I described them to the engineer in charge, he informed me that the high one was my nervous system in operation, the low one my blood in circulation. Until I die there
will be sounds. And they will continue following my death. One need
not fear about the future of music.[5]

Cage's own work is committed to the incorporation of this inescapable
"noise."[6] But his own concern is with intentional and unintentional sounds
rather than with noise as the interference in the transmission of the message itself. For the latter, we will have to turn to more recent work, work
responding specifically to the dialectic of message and noise, communication and interference. I turn now to two recent but very different examples of this new "poeticity."

THE RECEIVER OFF THE HOOK

In his introduction to the "Language Sampler" (his selection of Language
poets) for the *Paris Review* (1982), Charles Bernstein writes:

> What we have here is an insistence to communicate. Not, perhaps,
> where communication is schematized as a two-way wire with the mes-
> sage shuttling back and forth in blissful ignorance of the (its) transom
> (read: ideology). There are no terminal points (me(you) in a sounding
> of language from the inside.[7]

Bernstein's own poetry has consistently positioned itself as a critique of
this "transom theory" of communication. The long opening poem of *Dark
City*, for example, is called "The Lives of the Toll Takers."[8] The title, with
its echo of *Lives of the Poets* or *Lives of the Rich and Famous*, immediately interjects an absurdist note into the discourse. Who, after all, has ever thought
of documenting the lives lived by those anonymous persons who operate
the toll booths at freeway entrances and bridges? Then too, the phrase "toll
takers" is a play on the idiom "to take a toll," a nice illustration of the complexity of language, for the mere inversion of noun and verb wholly
changes the meaning of the phrase: "toll takers" are those that collect the
toll, not those responsible for its existence, although, strictly speaking, we
could say with reference to someone old and ill, "The years have been terrible toll takers."

"Lives of the Toll Takers," in any case, begins as follows:

> There appears to be a receiver off the hook. Not that
> you care.

Beside the gloves resided a hat and two
pinky rings, for which no
finger was ever found.
                  Largesse
with no release became, after
not too long, atrophied, incendiary,
                stupefying. Difference or
differance: it's
the distinction between hauling junk and
removing rubbish, while
I, needless not to say, take
out the garbage
              (pragmatism)

Phone again, phone again jiggity jig.
I figured
they do good eggs here.
           Funny $: making a killing on
junk bonds and living to peddle the tale
          (victimless rime)

                                  (9–10)

The poem continues for another eighteen pages in this vein, creating an elaborate representation of contemporary "lives" at their most meaningless, so that, in a very indirect way, it really is "about" the lives of the toll takers. From the outset, Bernstein's world is one of miscommunication and missed opportunities: his toll takers speak at cross-purposes, fail to define their terms, and are everywhere defeated by an environment too hazardous to navigate, although failure and defeat are presented throughout in comic terms. The difficulty, as this poet sees it, is not some tragic circumstance—war, murder, treachery, illness—but an inability to find one's own place in an increasingly alien technospace. In the words of the poem's conclusion:

                                  not an operating system it
                     s'an

op

                  erating environm
                    ent.
          Besides.

                                    (28)

The last word points the discourse in the direction of recycling; "besides": the whole process will start all over again. Further recriminations, arguments, clichés, and malapropisms will be made as poet and reader continue down the freeways past those toll takers.

Now let's come back to the poem's first page, cited above. "The Lives of the Toll Takers" opens with a perfectly straightforward, if formal statement, "There appears to be a receiver off the hook." It could be the opening of a murder mystery or just a scene from an ordinary day at the office or at home. But the next sentence, "Not that you care," interjects a comic false note, for, in this situation, what can "not caring" mean? Either "you" would want the phone to function—in which case you will hang up the receiver—or you would want to avoid its functioning, in which case you will purposely leave it off the hook. But even if you were the window-washer or other transient who genuinely would not care, pro or con, whether somebody's phone is off the hook, it's hard to imagine a situation in which one would be reproached for not caring.

Bernstein's method here and throughout the poem is to take a normal or conventional speech paradigm and then skew it ever so slightly. In this case, the model is something like the reproach, "There appears to be something terribly wrong. Not that *you* care." A related deflation takes place in the next three lines where "no / finger was ever found" for the "two pinky rings." Again, note the reversal: we want to find missing rings for specific fingers, not vice versa. And this absurd "crime report" is followed by the hyperbole of "Largesse / with no release became, after / not too long, atrophied, incendiary, / stupefying." Here the rhyme ("Largesse" / "release") and flowery Victorian language are at odds with the context. Largesse with no release: one thinks of an overfond lover rebuffed by his mistress or a mad philanthropist whose riches no one wants. But the parenthetical "after / not too long" again injects a burlesque note. How long is not too long? And how does it affect the "atrophying" of largesse?

In line 8, "difference or *differance*"—a reference to the Derridean coinage designed to distinguish between the two contradictory meanings of the French word, "difference" and "deferral"—prepares the ground for some nice distinctions. Is "removing rubbish" the same thing as "hauling junk"? Not really, since removing doesn't necessarily lead to hauling, and rubbish needn't be junk. In everyday life, in any case, we just call it "tak[ing] / out the garbage," a phrase Bernstein nicely identifies as "pragmatism." And this elegant meditation on trash collection is followed by a sequence where noise gets into the channel in comic ways. "Phone again, phone again jiggity jig" sounds like the result of mishearing the second line of "To market, to market to buy a fat pig"/ "Home again, home again, jiggity jig." But wait a minute. The line also refers back to the opening of the poem: evidently that receiver has, after all, been put back on the hook.

Another common form of interference is ellipsis: the erasure of certain words and phrases that would make one's meanings clear. In the case of

"Phone again, phone again, jiggity jig," the missing first line ("To market . . .") leads metonymically to something like "To restaurant" or "To
café," and therefore makes sense of the next two lines, "I figured / they do
good eggs here." Such ellipsis is a common feature of everyday communication: we turn on the TV and hear the tail end of a crucial news story, or
our answering machine jumps so that we're not sure who it is that called.
So "phone again" leads to a breakfast date and, in turn, a conversation
about making a financial killing ("funny $"), in which "peddle," as in "ped-
dling junk bonds" is displaced so as to produce a variant of the cliché "living to tell the tale." What could be more appropriate for a tale about trad-
ing junk bonds than "living to peddle the tale"? Such "interference" begins
to sound perfectly natural. And so the poem is a "victimless rime" (and, in
terms of its effects, also a "crime") in that it doesn't seem to be hurting
anyone, and, anyway, the poem doesn't rhyme to begin with, except sporadically, so that even possible rhyming words are not its victims.

Here is the cacography Serres writes about in "Platonic Dialogue" and
"The Origin of Language." Once we understand that Bernstein's technique
is to represent not only a "message" he is sending the passive reader but the
noise that is endemic to it, the poem makes perfectly good sense. Indeed,
as a representation of the "Lives of the Toll Takers," Bernstein's text is
remarkably "realistic" and coherent, its metonymic structure highly
charged. The killing in junk bonds, for example, leads, in the next
sequence to the lines, "Laughing all the way to the Swiss bank where I put
my money / in gold bars / [the prison-house of language]" (10) and references to cost and price persist throughout the poem, as in "A picture /
[fixture] / is worth more than a thousand words" (10), which later modu-
lates into "A picture is worth 44.95 but no price can be put on words"
(15), "A depository of suppositories / give it me where it counts" (18),
"Catalogs are free, why not we?" (26), and so on.

To write this kind of poem is a high-wire act that has become a Bernstein trademark. My second example details a very different kind of "interference"—this time, not focused on everyday life and the media discourses
that now control it—but on autobiographical narrative—a genre where
noise in the form of jamming, interruption, or interference would seem to
be less appropriate. The work in question is "Split Infinites" from Rosmarie
Waldrop's book by that title[9]—a title that is itself a perfect example of
noise in the channel, an "error" in the enunciation of the term *split
infinitives*. And indeed, the first section of Waldrop's book, "Pre & Con,
Or Positions and Junctions" takes up the comic meanings that are made
when ordinary prepositions or conjunctions (*with, into, when, and of,* etc.)
are inserted into normal syntactic units, a situation that carries the "split
infinitive" to its logical extreme.

The title section is made up of eleven poems, written in short prose paragraphs, visually rendered as blocks of print with justified margins, framed by white space. Their "subject," or at least their occasion, is Waldrop's own childhood in World War II Nazi Germany, a subject Waldrop has generally avoided in her poetry, no doubt because it is too painful and because it would be too easy to sensationalize. Her solution, in Serresean terms, is to submit the message itself to the disruption of "extraneous" or "background" noise. Here is "Memory Tree":

AND SECONDLY, in German.

My first schoolday, September 1941, a cool day. Time did not pass, but was conducted to the brain. I was taught. The Nazi salute, the flute. How firmly entrenched, the ancient theories, Already using paper, pen and ink. Yes, I said, I'm here.

I was six or seven dwarfs, the snow was white, the prince at war. Hitler on the radio, followed by Lehár. Senses impinged on. Blackouts, sirens, mattress on the floor, furtive visitor or ghost.

And mother furious. Sirens. Hiss. The cat. My sister cried unseen. Her friend. Afraid to look. What did I know of labor (forced) or pregnant? The deep interiors of the body? I had learned to ride a bike.

The black cat. The white snow, the blue flower. A menace of a different color. Uniform movement with unsurpassed speed. Not fastidious. Not necessary for substance to be filled in deep inside.

Mother, I cried, extremely. And wolf. Exceeding the snow I was at home in, wool pulled over my eyes. O wolf. The boy who did not cry it also died. Twilight overtures.

Face fair. Black hair. Hands parsimoniously on knees. A Polish girl. In Germany? In the war? Moving along swiftly in the air between us, a continuous image. Enough of black cat panic, bells (hells, shells), of sirens, hiss of bombs.
*

A long life of learning the preceding chapter. That my soul in bluejeans, my mother in childbirth, my rabble of hopes in German, East of expectation, West of still waiting. In bed with an antidote.

Eating of the tree. Leaves falling before the fall. Through a hole in memory. The fruit puckers new problems, but doesn't quench. The orchard long-abandoned.

(58–59)

Like the other poems in the sequence, "Memory Tree" provides the reader with a skeleton of biographical fact. The poet's first school day took place in September 1941 when she was six or seven. She was taught the Nazi salute, penmanship, how to play the flute; in the same year, she learned to ride a bike. Meanwhile, the radio was broadcasting Hitler's speeches "followed by Lehár"—probably *The Merry Widow*. She remembers the sirens announcing air raids and their accompanying blackouts, even as the bombs hissed. In the midst of this turmoil, her mother went into labor and the poet's sister was born. Her father ("prince at war"?) seems to have been "in the field," as the next poem tells us. Evidently, he served in some capacity in the German army.

But as the title nicely puts it, this is a "memory tree" with many branches and ambiguous fruit. From its first line, Waldrop's poem derails what begins as one more "sensitive little girl" narrative, taking into account as much "noise" as possible so as to capture the complexity of such a moment. The very first line, "AND SECONDLY, in German," suggests that something else should have come first. But what? Does Waldrop mean that first she remembers these traumatic events in English, her adopted language, and only secondly, in German? That secondly, these things were part of a German world, not quite comprehensible to the English-speaking reader? Or that secondly, the German language is itself a vehicle tainted by the material it has been forced to relate, and hence secondary? And there are many other possibilities.

"Secondly," in any case, produces a sense of supplementarity that sets the stage for the seemingly irrelevant detail that follows. Why, for example, does the poet bother to mention that her first school day was "a cool day," a weather condition hardly unusual for a German September. Perhaps because the rhyme *school-cool,* like *flute-salute* in line 3 of the paragraph, and like the rhyming of "Face fair. Black hair," and "bells (hells, shells)," in the sixth paragraph, phonemically registers the marching and mechanization that plays so large a role in the poet's memory of the events in question. "Time," in this milieu, "did not pass, but was conducted to the brain." Everything is dictated, ordered, controlled. Not, as a normal narrative would have it, "I was taught x and y," but "I was taught," so as to make clear that the child has no volition, no choices: "How firmly entrenched, the ancient theories." The six-year-old child is already "using paper, pen and ink," and responding when her name is called out by the unnamed teacher: "Yes, I said, I'm here."

In the next paragraph, fact ("I was six or seven," "the snow was white") transforms into the shards of fairy tale ("six or seven dwarfs," Snow White, the prince). But here the prince is "at war," and what lives in the memory are the blackouts, the sirens, the "mattress on the floor." The child, hearing her mother scream, evidently in labor, assumes that "mother [is] furious" at something or someone. In this setting, childbirth seems more like death than the beginning of life. Sirens hiss, or is it the black cat that does so? The child is "afraid to look." And "labor" oddly merges with the "forced" labor of the prisoners of war, the "uniform movement" (note the pun on "uniform") of the troops moving (marching? Riding by on a train?) "with unsurpassed speed." No one explains to the child what "the deep interiors of the body" contain. Rather, "normality" prevails: she learns to ride a bike.

Paragraph 5 begins, "Mother, I cried, extremely. And wolf," the odd usage of the adverb "extremely" (where we would expect "violently" or "loudly") triggers a surreal identification with the notorious and ubiquitous boy who cried wolf. In the parable itself, the boy warns of danger when there is none and so no one listens to his cry and the wolf gets him. But in Waldrop's perspective on the story, "The boy who did not cry it also died." So hopeless is this wartime scene that it doesn't matter whether one is the boy who cried wolf or the boy who didn't. Death comes regardless. Yet at the time itself, the poet recalls, she had "wool pulled over my eyes." In using this idiom in apposition to "the snow," Waldrop gives it a Bernsteinian twist. One pulls the wool over the eyes of others; one doesn't report one's own victimization, for if the trick is successful, it remains unrecognized.

The war turmoil, in any case, comes to a head in paragraph 6 in the image of the Polish girl who may be a real person known in Germany, or may be an imaginary presence, perhaps a newspaper image, that takes the perceiver outside the "black cat panic," the "bells (hells, shells), of sirens, hiss of bombs." And now, in the section following the asterisk, narrative ceases and meditation begins. Here syntax unites what are in fact quite disparate items: "my soul in bluejeans," "My mother in childbirth," "my rabble of hopes in German." "East of expectation," "West of still waiting" relates the child's suspension during the war years to the situation in divided Germany after the war. Is there anything beyond the malaise produced by the Memory Tree? Yes, in that the poet finds herself "in bed," not with an aspirin, as the idiom demands, but "with an antidote." The orchard, in any case, has been "long-abandoned," and the "hole in memory" has become a kind of compost heap. For all we know, none of these things really happened to Rosmarie Waldrop, and she has invented what seemed like plausible "memories" for herself. As she puts it in "Association," "We swapped knives to peel off childhood like so many skins" (50).

"At the extreme limits of empiricism," Serres contends in a passage from "Platonic Dialogue" I have cited above, "meaning is totally plunged into noise, the space of communication is granular, dialogue is condemned to cacophony, the transmission of communication is chronic transformation. Thus the empirical is strictly essential and accidental *noise*" (H, 70).

And in a footnote he adds, "And, as has often been seen in any discussion between an empiricist and a rationalist—Locke and Leibniz, for example—*empiricism would always be correct if mathematics did not exist.* Empiricism is the *true* philosophy as soon as mathematics is bracketed" (*H,* 70 n. 12) Extreme as this may sound, it is in fact an excellent description of the turn that a cutting-edge poetics has taken at the turn of the twenty-first century. Certainly, both Waldrop and Bernstein present us with the "transmission of communication as chronic transformation," with "empiricism" as *"true* philosophy" in its rigorous interrogation of actual experience.

Would Serres himself like this kind of poetry? Ironically, the answer is probably no. As the Verlaine and Apollinaire examples with which I began illustrated, Serres's focus, when it comes to poetry, is more on the communication that occurs if we eliminate the "chronic transformation" of noise than if we let the noise in. Conditioned to think of poetry in a certain way, he continues to search for a nongranular, more comprehensive meaning. But a reconsideration of his own theoretical writing suggests that he understands the issues only too well. "Time," Serres tells Latour in their second conversation, "does not always flow according to a line . . . nor according to a plan but, rather, according to an extraordinarily complex mixture, as though it reflected stopping points, ruptures, deep wells, chimneys of thunderous acceleration, rendings, gaps—all sown at random, at least in a visible disorder" (*C,* 57). Indeed, "time can be schematized by a kind of crumpling, a multiple, foldable diversity. . . . An object, a circumstance, is thus polychronic, multitemporal, and reveals a time that is gathered together, with multiple pleats" (*C,* 59).

Multiple pleats are what we have just witnessed in Waldrop's "Split Infinites" and Bernstein's "Lives of the Toll Takers." And so I like to think that Serres will come to admire these poems (and others like them) that his theories have done so much to elucidate.

NOTES

1. Paul Verlaine, *Oeuvres poétiques complètes,* ed. Y.-G. Le Dantec, completed by Jacques Borel (Paris: Bibliothèque de la Pléiade, Gallimard, 1962), 278. The English translation is my own.

2. Serres, "The Origin of Language: Biology, Information Theory, and Thermodynamics" (1980), *H,* 78. For the original, see *LD,* 259–72.

3. William Paulson, *The Noise of Culture: Literary Texts in a World of Information* (Ithaca, N.Y.: Cornell University Press, 1988), 67.

4. John Cage, *Silence* (Middletown, Conn.: Wesleyan University Press, 1976), 3.

5. Ibid., 8. Cage has told this story again and again, for example, in the recording of *Indeterminancy* (1958).

6. See Marjorie Perloff, *Radical Artifice: Writing Poetry in the Age of Media* (Chicago: University of Chicago Press, 1992), chap. 1; Perloff and Charles Junkerman, eds., *John Cage: Composed in America* (Chicago: University of Chicago Press, 1995).

7. Charles Bernstein, *Content's Dream: Essays, 1975–1984* (Los Angeles: Sun and Moon Press, 1986), 239.

8. Charles Bernstein, *Dark City* (Los Angeles: Sun and Moon Press, 1994), 9–28. Subsequent citations are given in the text.

9. Rosmarie Waldrop, *Split Infinites* (Philadelphia: Singing Horse Press, 1998), 50–71. Subsequent citations are given in the text.

THE SMOOTH OPERATOR

Serres Prolongs Poe

PAUL HARRIS

TOO FASHIONABLE A STYLE?

Michel Serres's name evokes a certain brand of discourse. It designates a trademark style, a mode of fashioning words and concepts into a distinctive weave. The style has brought certain accusations and doubts, well documented in the *Conversations about Literature, Science and Time* with Bruno Latour. His extremely quick passes that thread various fields together have been taken as loosely fabricated, as if they would unravel under the wear of time. Simply put, he has been taken as something of a smooth operator, an overly fast mover always on shaky ground, one whose work will, under closer inspection, fold like a cheap suit. Oddly enough though, these attempts to dress down Serres, even if a bit too casual, a bit too plain, do carry some merit.

Serres is indeed a smooth operator, and his writing does fold up when read attentively. But to see the matter clearly, one should not hide behind and look through green spectacles. "Serres" is an operator, "a method or strategy working on formations different from itself" (*H,* 39). *In* Serres's writing, an operator is a term extracted from one discourse used to labor in other fields. The term is often simple—bridges and wells serve as well as vortices or clouds. *On* Serres writing, we may take him at his word and "be content with saying it's 'a general theory of relations'" (*C,* 127). In writing on Serres before, I have detailed how topology provides the means of understanding the operations that his writing enacts.[1] Topology suits Serres because his writing has a distinctly pleated texture: "The advantage that results from [topology] is a new organization of knowledge; the whole landscape is changed. . . . It brings together the most disparate things. People quickly criticized me for this. . . . But these critics and I no longer have the same landscape in view, the same overview of proximities and distances. With each profound transformation of knowledge come these upheavals in perception" (*C,* 71). Unruffled by off-the-cuff criticisms, Serres links disparate materials. This is the smooth quality of Serres's bumpy discourse—the way in which he makes continuous or proximate what had been discrete and distant. "Serres" the smooth operator: his writing a method of working on other texts or domains, stitching together various materials in an almost unnaturally synthetic manner. Ultimately, then, Serres is about dressing one thing up as another; he is the master of the makeover. His interest is not fixed identities but the *transformations* that are possible on a given set of materials.

FROM PSYCHOANALYSIS TO *ANALYSIS SITUS*

Or, stated differently: Serres deploys a mathematical method of analysis to establish a transdisciplinary synthesis. The operation involved is to map disparate discourses onto one another, by means of uncovering equivalent structures in them. The notion of "structure" here is not based on the rigid forms of Euclidean geometry, but the elastic ones of topology. Simultaneously, and more abstractly, Serres's notion of structure derives from the Bourbaki, the group of mathematicians bent on using set theory to systematize all mathematics into abstract syntactic relationships. In the first *Hermès* volume Serres defines structure as "an operational set of undefined meaning . . . bringing together a certain number of elements whose content is not specified, and a finite number of relations of unspecified nature, but whose function, and certain results concerning the elements, are specified" (*LC,* 32; translation mine). Topological mapping and set theory concepts of structure overlap in point set topology, where geometrical figures are treated as collections of points, with the whole collection often regarded as a space. Serres's deployment of topology as a privileged language or method for discovering rules and operations governing transformations between structures hearkens back to his very first work, the two-volume study of Leibniz. Leibniz sought to formulate basic geometric properties of figures and then to combine these properties through a series of operations to produce other figures. Leibniz called this study *analysis situs* because while coordinate geometry treated figures in terms of their magnitude, "we lack another analysis properly geometric or linear which expresses location [*situs*] directly as algebra expresses magnitude."[2] Such, then, are the underpinnings of what Serres calls his "mathematical method" (*C,* 66–73).

What does this mean concretely, though? In essence, Serres treats the text or discourse at hand as a set of elements bound together by some rule(s), which may be formulated in their purest form in spatial terms. In "Language and Space: From Oedipus to Zola," Serres demonstrates how the Oedipus myth "traces a graph upon space" (*H,* 47). The landscape through which Oedipus travels becomes a map of both human psychology and culture: the crossroads where he kills his father, Laius, is a catastrophe point conjoining the unconscious and unknown (Thebes, from whence Oedipus sets out to consult the Oracle) and knowledge and the word (Delphi). At this moment, Serres posits, "the text turns inside out like a glove and shows its function: the establishment of separations between spaces and their difficult junction." Serres believes that *analysis situs,* topology as invented by Leibniz, supersedes psychoanalysis as the privileged set of terms within which to understand the text: "One can say that Oedipus kills Laius at this place and miss the place, and thus repress the place of the repressed; or one can say instead that this place is such that Oedipus kills his father there, that it is a point so catastrophic and so confined that he must kill father and mother to go past it" (*H,* 47). The rule of thumb might be stated, then, that one should "draw an appropriate method from the very problem one has undertaken to resolve" (*C,* 91). One may take elements from the text, extract from them an underlying structure, and read the structure back into the text. Or turn the text inside out, to find in it a map of itself.

In the final analysis, Serres's project might be said to entail a mapping of conceptual space. This is not a game of epistemology, though: for Serres "spaces" or "structures" are surfaces onto which both mind and world may be mapped; they comprise a common ground where knowledge and nature mesh. The will to synthesis permeating Serres's work (*C,* 86–90) entails the work of analysis: to break down the elements of texts and topoi in order to uncover their underlying topology. Surveying the lay of Serres's oeuvre, it might seem that he has moved from the world of interpretation to interpretations of the world. In the 1993 *Conversations,* Serres announces that he has finished with commentary. Instead of texts and concepts, his writing will work with events and the world. Serres's books of the 1990s map the terrestrial (*The Natural Contract,* 1990; *Atlas,* 1994; and *Nouvelles du monde,* 1997) and the celestial (*La Légende des anges,* 1993). Typical topoi from tables of contents include, respectively, casting off; war, peace; global space, virtual space, distances and proximities; the forest, the river, the wind. The move from texts to world is marked by expanding out from learned knowledge to popular culture: Tin-Tin and Tarzan rather than Turner and Thales.

At the same time, however, this apparent shift from texts to world proves chimerical on further inspection. Indeed, such an opposition simply has never obtained for Serres. Thus we should not be surprised to find within the global concerns of *Atlas,* for instance, a textual interpretation that yields a conceptual spatial discourse. Serres sets out in *Atlas* to remap the subject's orientation in a world where familiar categories like the body and nature become imbricated in and changed by virtual spaces and new corporeal prostheses. The first section, "Prolongements," introduces the new demands on humans brought on by global space, the way in which the body is extended in space and time as global effects are felt in local places. The adjustment called for by such fundamental reconfigurations of the human in space is then exemplified in a chapter called "Être hors là." Here, Serres returns to the late nineteenth century to discover in Maupassant's story "The Horla" a shift in the cartography of the human subject. This shift hinges on a change from the subject as a stable, interior space to one located in multiple spaces while in one place. Serres maps this shift as a movement from the space of topography and Euclidean geometry to one of topology—a movement that is itself embedded in Maupassant's tale. Thus, tracing the narrator's movements through different spaces answers Serres's "need to connect intimate spaces to successive ones by a sort of analytic extension [*prolongement*]" (*A,* 67). The translation effected here within Maupassant's tale stands, then, for a transition from the world of inhabiting familiar places to the haunting of places by the uncanny. Serres's method of moving by "analytic *prolongement*" turns literary analysis into an exercise in projective geometry—in the sense that it maps the surface of fictional discourse onto topological surfaces.

A PROLONGED SERRES AS MAU-POE-SAVANT

The present essay continues along this same path, by giving it a further twist. I will prolong Serres's "analytic *prolongement*" of Maupassant into an analysis of Poe's "The Purloined Letter." The application of Serres's principles to Poe begs two questions: (1) why go down this well-trodden path again? (2) what light can be shed on the story by identifying our mind with that of Serres? A simple answer to the first question is, why not put Serres's analytic method to the test on a case made famous by other eminent French theorists? One detects an irony in using Serres to add a literary interpretation to a deeply imbricated hermeneutic palimpsest, for he abhors the game of going one up on others by citing them. Serres has always preferred to remain laconic rather than deride others. Yet to consult Serres in this case is also an appropriate gesture, since Serres has risen to the challenge before, producing in *L'Hermaphrodite* a book-length study of a text that had been submitted to an exhaustive analysis that raised the structuralist bar to a new level. And since Serres has never enjoyed the same success as these other theorists in North American sites of French theory, there is a sort of pleasure in prolonging Poe into Serres's encampment.

Now to the second issue raised: what does one see using Serres's analytic method that had remained hidden from view up to this point? In *Atlas,* Serres demonstrates how one may find a topology inscribed in literature. He traces in Maupassant's "The Horla" the contours of the topology, which was emerging when the story was written. For instance, in the story there is a closed water bottle that the narrator awakes from a nightmare to find empty. Rather than looking at this incident as a psychoanalytic symptom, Serres sees the object as a Klein bottle, a topological object Felix Klein introduced in 1882. (Imagine a higher-dimension version of a Möbius strip: a bottle's neck twisted back through the bottle and connected to its base.) Raiding Serres to read Poe, similar surfaces surface: the purloined letter is first opened (by the queen), then closed (she folds it). The letter is transformed by the minister in a topological operation: the letter is a surface that gets everted, "turned inside out, like a glove." Topology has become increasingly interested in problems of eversion, particularly the eversion of a sphere. In the story, we are witness to competing models of space: the prefect cannot solve this open-and-shut case because he treats the letter as an object that has "volume," while Dupin demonstrates his grasp of the minister's conceptual model—he replicates the everted letter, stamps it with an imitation of the minister's own seal, and inserts a signature that turns the tables on him.

What will prove interesting for our purposes is that in several ways Poe's story actually prefigures the topology Serres discovers in Maupassant nearly forty years later. "The Purloined Letter" thus exemplifies Serres's oft-made claim that literary texts anticipate subsequent developments in the history of mathematics and the hard sciences. The case of Poe also differs from most authors Serres examines, though, in that Poe was both poet and mathematician—he studied mathematics extensively, and the tale makes this interest explicit (even if only by hiding this theme in plain sight). Serres usually takes up cases of authors whose work has no mathematics "in" it, and so must be mapped onto the other domain. In fact, in tailoring Poe to fit our darker Serresean purpose, we will find them cut from the same cloth: Poe's tale combines fiction and mathematics to arrive at a model of "analysis," and in submitting the story to an analytic *prolongement* after Serres, we find both Poe and Serres preoccupied with the same *analysis situs.* In using Serres as an operator to work on Poe, we essentially are folding Serres into Poe, and in doing so, we replicate a splitting and doubling that comprises one of the essential operations at work in Poe: we split Serres and double his Maupassant with Poe. A model of analytic acumen one might name a Mau-Poe-*savant.*

FAR AWAY, SO CLOSE

Broadly speaking, for Serres topology connotes a "crumpled" concept of space and time. In *Conversations,* Serres explains the contrast between metrical geometry and topology by describing how points and distances between them on an ironed-out handkerchief change spatial relations when the handkerchief is crumpled up and put in one's pocket (*C,* 60). Previously distant points become close together or even superimposed, while close ones may now be far away from each other. For Serres, this simple topological image exemplifies concepts of time, space, and interdisciplinarity. Time is not a line; the past may be immediately in the present. Space is not flat and rigid; folds abound. And disciplines that seem far removed from one another may become proximate or even imbricated with one another (*C,* 57–62).

In *Atlas,* Serres's reading of Maupassant's "The Horla" demonstrates the topological underpinnings of relations played out in several spheres. The general pattern of the story Serres traces is how the remote and the immediate are brought into constant contact. In terms of geography, the ships that pass on the river bordering the narrator's property express the presence of things and places far away. In historical terms, these ships echo the narrator's Norman ancestry—they remind him of his roots, and of the sailors who burned their ships and remained. From a psychological standpoint, Maupassant's narrator destroys himself because of an invisible being. It manifests itself in forms like a shadow in the mirror; it is both nonbeing and a being; it is both here and absent—as expressed in the very name *horla: hor,* "outside," and *là,* "right there." The key term for Serres's reading is the preposition *hors,* because it instantiates the many different ways in which the outside or distant comes inside or close, while the inside moves out and the proximate becomes distant in the story. *Hors* thus denotes a movement rather than a location: *hors* is not a fixed place but "a careful displacement by analytic *prolongement*" (*A,* 69). As Serres shows, this dynamic revolves around the narrator's house: the story is comprised by a series of ventures out of the house, only to discover that the outside has entered. Etymologically, Serres informs us, *hors* has its roots in words for "door." Thus the *horla* is a hinge or passage between inside and outside. This makes the Maupassant's narrator's house a sort of POE in both senses: a port of embarkation (from here, out) and port of entry (the outside coming in).

In Poe's story, similar foldings between inside and outside are discernible from the outset. As it opens, the narrator and Dupin are cozily tucked in the library of their apartment. The narrator is contemplating the prior Dupin mysteries, hence stretching the edge of this story's border and enfolding the two previous tales into "The Purloined Letter." Suddenly, their peaceful meditations are disrupted: "the door of our apartment was thrown open," and the prefect enters.[3] He brings news of a letter that has been purloined. Etymology once again conjoins Poe and Maupassant: *purloin* is from the Norman French *purloigner,* to put far away. But here, distance and proximity are sewn together in a manner similar to Maupassant's tale. The mystery of the letter, from the prefect's viewpoint, is that while it seems distant (by virtue of its obscurity), its power depends on its being kept "close at hand." Simply put, it is hidden in plain sight—that is, is has been put far away by being kept within immediate reach. Poe, like Maupassant, gives the paradox a geographical spin: Dupin illustrates hiding things in plain sight with the example of a game where a person chooses a word on a map that another player must find. The most difficult to find, Dupin says, are "such words as stretch, in large characters, from one end of the chart to the other" (345). These cartographic words denoting distant places are associated with the central object in the tale by virtue of both being "purloined letters"—letters made far away by being too close at hand.

TOPOLOGY IN LINEAR HISTORY

Though to do so is slightly at odds with Serres's method and sense of "crumpled time," it is important to take an even-handed look at the historical backgrounds against which his reading of Maupassant unfolds. The brilliance of Serres's synthetic reading of Maupassant lies in the ways in which he uncovers within the story's materials a shift from one spatial order to another. Serres shows how Maupassant prolongs Euclidean space and an interior, unified subject of metaphysics into topological space and a multiple, distributed self. The narrator's sojourns from the fixed, metric interior of the house literally embody this shift: the boxlike house is overhung by a tree, which is in turn a shelter or house to the narrator's home. The natural outside replicates the cultural inside. And then the narrator moves into the forest, space of uncanny presences. Serres can thus pronounce the spatial inference in axiomatic terms: "I inhabit geometry even as topology haunts me" (*A,* 73).

Serres mentions the historical background to his interpretation of Maupassant, but only in passing. Part of Serres's reputation as a smooth operator, in fact, comes from not spelling out the historical contexts within which he operates. Serres reads texts with the eye of the historian of ideas, but he does not wish to plod the heavy tread of the historicist—the winged-sandaled Hermes has already taken off on a journey that joins distant bodies of knowledge in a speculative synthesis. In typical fashion, Serres's most specific, technical example to support the claim that Maupassant invents topology in his story is made via a teasing allusion: "the carafe on the night table is called, in this discipline [topology], a Klein bottle, without outside or inside, a Mobius strip in three dimensions. It is scarcely paradoxical that this volume dates from the same time as 'The Horla' (*A*, 77). Given the crumpled time underwriting his nonlinear transdisciplinary itineraries, it is curious that Serres looks on this image as something of a coincidence. But let us follow through on this suggestive observation, and examine the stories by Maupassant and Poe in the context of the development of mathematics in the nineteenth century.

Poe's detective stories were written in the early 1840s, about four decades before Maupassant wrote "The Horla." Mathematics in the first half of the nineteenth century was marked by a split between work in two fields: attempts to install rigor into analysis, on the one hand, and the development of descriptive, projective, and eventually non-Euclidean geometries on the other. At the turn of the century, analysis was a sprawling subdiscipline in which crucial terms (e.g., function, series) were not precisely defined. There was a pervasive "dissatisfaction with the logical status of analysis."[4] A critical movement began to rebuild analysis on solely arithmetic grounds. This attempt to reduce mathematical analysis to algebraic methods pushed the divergence between algebra and geometry even further. Analytic geometry, where the two parallel branches of analysis and geometry overlapped and could have fused, was dominated by algebraic and analytic methods rather synthetic geometric ones. Transformations on a space were applied by means of equations. Geometry only entered the process at the beginning in the formulation of the problem, and at the end, when the results obtained by algebraic transformations are translated back into geometric terms. While analytic geometry is practically by definition the application of algebra to geometry, then, in the early nineteenth century it essentially entailed applying the integral calculus to geometric problems.

Yet there was also a growing backlash to the dominance of analytic methods. Anxieties about the internal consistency of analysis were accompanied by the sense that its truths were purely formal, limited to the methodological application to numbers and functions. Geometry, by contrast, was still predominantly accepted as providing the true description of space and physical reality. Unlike analysis, Euclidean geometry rested on a firm axiomatic foundation—with the notable exception of the parallel postulate. And unlike the tangled methods of analysis, the geometric method proceeds in an intuitive manner where proofs and conclusions are demonstrable at every step. The geometric method did not, however, yield results with the general applicability of analytic methods—each proof or problem was true only for that instance, rather than obtaining for a class of such problems. The revival of synthetic geometry at the beginning of the century was initiated by Gaspard Monge, whose *Traité de géometrié descriptive* (1799) showed how three-dimensional figures could be projected into two-dimensional ones, so that from the representation it was possible to deduce mathematical properties of the object. Monge's book and lectures at the École Polytechnique from 1795 to 1809 inspired several students, among them Jean-Victor Poncelet. Poncelet went on to do essential work in projective geometry, a more general study of transformations between corresponding figures. Technically speaking, Poncelet sought to understand properties of geometrical figures unaltered by projection and section.[5] Informing this work was a search for geometric methods that would yield results with the general applicability of the analytic geometry dependent on algebraic methods. Monge's work, wrote Poncelet, showed that "it is sufficient . . . to introduce into our language and our geometrical conceptions these general principles and transformations analogous to those of Analysis, which will permit us to seize a truth in its pure and primitive state and in all its manifestations and therefore enable us to make fruitful deductions with ease."[6] Parallel to the development of projective geometry in midcentury, the foundations of non-Euclidean geometry were being laid in place by Gauss, Lobatchevsky, Bolyai, and others. We cannot treat non-Euclidean geometry in any detail here, though it is hailed as the most important conceptual revolution in nineteenth-century mathematics.

The two branches of projective and non-Euclidean geometries were finally brought together in the great synthetic work of Felix Klein's *Erlanger Programm.* "Klein's basic idea," Kline explains, "is that each geometry can be characterized by a group of transformations and that a geometry is really concerned with invariants under this group of transformations."[7] Klein's synthesis of geometry in terms of transformations is a landmark in the formation and formalization of topology, which investigates properties of figures that remain invariant under elastic motions. In topology, the size and to a certain extent the shape of an object are irrelevant. In particular, two objects or structures are considered topologically equivalent if one can be stretched, shrunk, or deformed in such a way that no new points are created or existing ones fused. Such a transformation is called "continuous," and continuity is the key property in topology. Klein's synthesis completes our brief historical review of the development of topology in the nineteenth century, in order to flesh out the background to Serres's reading of Maupassant's "The Horla."

ANALYZING POE'S SYNTHESIS

Given this sketch of the mathematical backgrounds, how might it illuminate our reading of Poe's tale and contribute to this labor of prolonging

Serres's treatment of Maupassant? What emerges from this sketch is the enigmatic split between analysis and geometry, specifically as their respective methods bear on the problem of transformations. According to Piaget and Garcia, the historian of mathematics must "explain why . . . almost two centuries went by before transformations were first used in geometry, while algebra, the science of transformations *par excellence,* had been applied to geometry from the seventeenth century on."[8] One reason that these opposing methods were not better integrated is simply that algebra and the integral calculus were seen to be a matter of numbers, which many mathematicians believe to be a creation of the human mind. By contrast, geometry was a matter of space, and inherently related to the nature of physical reality. Piaget and Garcia clarify the epistemological nature of the contrasting treatments of transformations: algebra, they point out, is an *endogenous* form of knowledge—it comprises "a system of forms which generate their own contents."[9] The algebraist is free to construct such transformations as are deemed useful. The geometric method, by contrast, is an *exogenous* mode of conceptualizing in that one must ask, given a figure, what transformations are possible or allowed. The long period during which analytic geometry developed as the application of algebraic methods and the calculus to geometry, then, "can in no way be reduced to a history of collaboration between two kinds of instruments that can readily be intercoordinated. Rather, it is characterized by difficult adjustments (given the duality of space as both a subjective and objective reality) between two heterogeneous types of truth, which require novel instruments in order to be reconciled."[10]

AN ANALYSIS OF POE'S MATHEMATICAL SITUATION

"The Purloined Letter" marks nothing less than such a "novel instrument," because it does in fact bring together analytic and geometric methods of treating space and transformations of figures. Grasping what Poe puts into play in "The Purloined Letter" entails exploring the full scope of his detective stories. From the outset, Poe's detective tales explicitly seek to construct a model of thinking under the name of "analysis." "The Murders in the Rue Morgue," the first in the detective series, opens, "The mental features discoursed of as the analytical, are, in themselves, but little susceptible of analysis" (189). This opening gambit snares analysis itself in a paradox of self-reference: one cannot oneself analyze the powers of analysis.[11] The resolvent power of the mind, Poe contends, "is much invigorated by mathematical study, and especially that highest branch of it which, unjustly, and merely on account of its retrograde operations, has been called, as if *par excellence,* analysis. But to calculate is not in itself to analyze"

(189). Poe here sets a course for appropriating mathematical analysis as a necessary but in itself insufficient condition for developing the analytic faculty, while also exposing its limits in developing his own concept of analysis. This first tale demands that the people possessing the "analytic ability" be "*truly* imaginative" (192). Poe's use of the term is predicated on a contrast between fancy and imagination, and hence beckons to Coleridge, and a notion of synthetic or creative imagination. Analysis must be accompanied by a synthetic impetus. Thus the narrator "amused [him]self with the fancy of a double Dupin—the creative and the resolvent" (194).

In "The Purloined Letter," the last of the detective series, Poe returns to the theme of mathematical analysis and its limitations. The minister, Dupin knows, can fool the prefect because he is "both poet and mathematician." Dupin is also both: he has written "certain doggerel" and demonstrates his mathematical acumen with a long speech that is central to Poe's assessment of analysis in the story. Here, as we will see, Poe takes a stand in mathematical debates of his day: through Dupin, he joins in a polemic against the champions of analytic methods, while inventing, implicitly or not, a geometric treatment of the transformation of a figure. This conscious, meticulously crafted intervention by Poe provides the grounds on which we may retrospectively read his story as a meditation on competing models of space. In particular, the tale treats space in the Leibnizian sense of *analysis situs*—the study of operations on figures in terms of location rather than magnitude.

Poe's mathematical training places him in the perfect situation for this turn from analytic to geometric methods. As a cadet at West Point in 1830, Poe would have concentrated on various fields of mathematics, including algebra, descriptive geometry, and plane analytic geometry. This geometric training was directly derived from Monge's seminal work, through the figure of Claude Crozet. Crozet was a student of Monge's at the Polytechnique, and his *Treatise of Descriptive Geometry for the Use of Cadets of the U.S.M.A.* would have been available to Poe at West Point.[12] The synthetic, intuitive methods of conceptualizing space and transformations would have thus been a major part of Poe's education. He was poised, then, to take up the question of "analysis" and give it a geometrical turn.

THE CHARACTER OF SPACE

In "Être hors là," Serres treats the psychology of character as an index to different models of space. In "The Horla," the breakdown of the narrator's mind takes the tale into new territory, and with this new territory comes not just another map but another type of cartography. In Maupassant's story, the rational mind "inhabits geometry"—the home as stable identity is a metric, Euclidean space. The journey into the irrational marks a move into topological space—"topology haunts me." Fear changes the narrator's perceptions, stretching the narrow window of vision and enabling him to see the proximity of the very distant to the very near. He feels the presence of forces of the invisible while in his garden. The narrator now moves through a patchwork of neighboring spaces without a common metric: his room, his house, the river, a narrow path between overarching trees in the forest (A, 70). Serres is suggesting that the tale should not simply be classified as "fantastic" literature, where the rational surface of a narrative conveys an irrational content. The fantastic genre trope of another being in my place, Serres contends, is displaced onto a different plane. Maupassant is reinventing a subject whose internal workings are not diagnosed by psychopathological means, but known through a spatial and temporal map (A, 80). Thus, for Serres the story's movement from the rational to the irrational on the level of the narrator's psychology also marks, on a completely different level of abstraction, the move from a Euclidean space of rigid metric to a topological space that stretches, folds up, inverts itself.

This interpretation of Maupassant also implies a different disciplinary configuration. Serres contends that Maupassant's writing invents a new form of knowledge, one that subverts scientific knowledge but without opposing it, for writing also comes to occupy science's role or place. Serres points out that the narrator takes different empirical, positivistic, or scientific approaches to investigating the Horla, only to discover their failure to explain anything. For instance, he wraps bottles of milk and water in white muslin, and rubs his lips, beard, and hands with pencil lead before going to sleep. Upon waking suddenly, though, he discovers that with no trace of lead on his sheets and no sign that the muslin has been opened, the bottles are empty. As we have seen, Serres treats this episode not as signaling the presence of the supernatural, but the truly imaginative invention of a Klein bottle in fiction. The milk and water bottles share with the subsequent séance of Dr. Parent a preeminent preoccupation of topology: tracing the border between the inside and outside. In all cases, Serres insists, we witness Maupassant conscientiously injecting his narrative with the positivism of the day, only to show its limits: "science is not certain of anything," Serres concludes, "even as artistic writing, precise, rigorous, takes a great deal on itself, preceding and directly entering into science: an implacable lesson of intellectual integrity" (A, 78).

Investigating Poe along similar lines, we also find the psychology of characters projected onto different models of space. And, like Maupassant, Poe reserves for writing (aka "poetry") a specific role in reconfiguring scientific/mathematical knowledge. "The Purloined Letter" sets up a contest between the minds of the prefect, the minister, and Dupin. Analytic acumen is attendant on the ability to locate the purloined letter. Each character's mind is expressed in a conception of space, and the power to locate and take possession of the letter hinges on the respective spatial models. Following Serres's diagnosis of the narrator's psychopathology as itself a means of mapping a new concept of space, we might posit that the mind-set of each character in Poe indicates a different method of mapping space—with a Leibnizian emphasis, once more, on location and transformations.

THE PREFECT AS PERFECT SQUARE

The prefect in Poe's story is portrayed as a square, the voice of official reason and the embodiment of a Cartesian positivism. The prefect conceives of space as empty, three-dimensional, and isotropic, and objects in that space as rigid figures. Mathematically speaking, the prefect lives in a world of Euclidean geometry governed by congruence. Here, the metric properties of "geometric structures are considered independent of their position; theorems about the square or the circle do not depend on where these figures lie in the plane or in space. If we restrict ourselves to plane geometry, then propositions are independent of translations and rotations in the plane; the square always remains the same square, the circle the same circle."[13] Translated into Poe's tale, this means simply that the prefect looks for a letter that remains the same object, independent of its position. He searches for a space that could contain the object, by dividing up the minister's furniture and apartment into a series of compartments. Poe conveys the conventional nature of the prefect's scientific mind-set through several punning allusions: when the prefect looks through the minister's papers, he searches in "volumes" that are treated not as a space of writing (where a "purloined letter" would inhere) but as objects with "thickness" that can be "probed, longitudinally" (336). Dupin ridicules the prefect for reflecting the ingenuity of "the *mass*," a pun linking the mechanics of mass and volume with a common intellectual ability. The prefect has no "variation of principle"; his fault is the "exaggeration of *the application* of the one principle" of a search in which "the reward is of magnitude" (341). In short, the prefect places the letter in a coordinate geometry where it has a certain magnitude; he holds to the generalizability of his analytic methods, unable to conceive of space and objects in terms of location and transformations.

THE MINISTER'S ANALYTIC METHOD

The minister acts as a transitional figure in the tale. He removes the letter from the Cartesian space inhabited by the prefect, and then subjects it to a transformation; in so doing, the minister changes the nature of the space in which the letter persists. The minister first demonstrates his mastery of Cartesian space when he purloins the letter from the queen's boudoir: he sees the open letter on the table, with the address uppermost. Here, the letter is a three-dimensional figure; the minister is quite easily able to "produce a letter somewhat similar to the one in question" (332–33). He feigns reading his own letter, leaves it lying next to the queen's epistle, and then takes both on leaving. To hide the letter from the prefect in plain sight, all the minister has to do is subject it to a transformation that makes it a different kind of spatial object. The minister works as a transitional figure in the story in terms of mathematical history, in an intriguing fashion. For he takes two different steps in transforming the letter, which correspond, as we shall now see, respectively to analytic and geometric methods.

The analytic method of the minister is alluded to when Dupin recounts how he first recognized the letter as his eyes made the circuit of the minister's apartment. The minister has identified his mind with that of the prefect, and so he has simply made the letter appear as different as possible in outward detail, and left it carelessly visible in a letter rack. As John T. Irwin discusses in some detail, the contrasts between the letter's original appearance and how the minister has made it look are described in terms that allude to the integral calculus. Poe establishes this link when he has the narrator comment that the minister "has written learnedly on the Differential Calculus" (342). The letter in view, Dupin says, is "to all appearances radically different" from the original as described by the prefect: "Here the seal was large and black, with the D- cipher; there it was small and red with the ducal arms of the S- family." It is precisely "the *radicalness* of these differences" that bears the traces of the method the minister uses here, contrary to his "methodical habits" (346–47). The elements of D, S, radical and differences all add up to an allusion to the analytic methods of the calculus. D designates changes: a lower case d stands for the differential of a variable, or an infinitesimal difference; the Greek capital letter delta, for a finite difference. S signals the integration of differences: the capital S resembles the sign for the integral in calculus, which signifies an infinite sum of infinite differences. The underlying conception informing the minister's hiding of the letter, then, is to utilize an analytic method— to calculate that the prefect cannot integrate the differences between the outward appearance of the letter to recognize that it is the one in question.

Embedded in this analytical method of the minister is a simple geometrical transformation. He simply everts the letter. The introduction of "differences" has already altered the nature of the letter as a spatial figure: it has ceased to be a flat pile of sheets, and is now "much soiled and crumpled" (346). Dupin tells the narrator that when he observes the letter closely, he sees something else:

In scrutinizing the edges of the paper, I observed them to be more *chafed* than seemed necessary. They presented the *broken* appearance which is manifested when a stiff paper, having been folded and pressed with a folder, is refolded in a reversed direction, in the same creases or edges which had formed the original fold. . . . It was clear to me that the letter had been turned, as a glove, inside out, re-directed, and re-sealed. (347)

The letter is in effect a map of its own space, insofar as its surface functions like a diagram that illustrates the folding operation it has undergone. The story repeatedly emphasizes that the mystery is "simple," that it is the "very simplicity" of how and where the minister has hidden the letter that prevents the prefect from seeing it. As Irwin points out, the word *simple* derives from the Latin *simplex,* meaning "single," "unmixed," "not compounded." But the roots of the Latin *simplex* are *semel,* meaning "once," and *plico,* meaning "to fold, fold together." In effect, then, the "simple" letter is a single thing that is folded once. This etymological game of Poe's, Irwin contends, "make[s] it clear that to be unmixed or uncompounded does not mean to be undifferentiated."[14]

The minister has turned the letter into a figure subject to elastic motions—topological transformations involving folding and eversion. The letter goes from being a figure with a clear outside (the address) and inside (the contents) to a single surface where inside and outside are reversible because of a fold. Figuratively speaking, the letter has become a Möbius strip—a single surface where inside and outside continuously turn into one another, without crossing an edge. Just as the one object (letter/Möbius strip) takes on a double or duplicitous quality in being folded, so too is the reverse true—when divided or cut, it remains itself. What a famed Parisian analyst spoke of as the "divisibility of the letter" finds its pleasing analogue in the Möbius strip:

A mathematician confided
That a Mobius band is one-sided
And you'll get quite a laugh
If you cut one in half,
For it stays in one piece
When divided.[15]

The folding of the letter in the tale, then, serves as an equivalent to putting a twist in the strip of paper when making a Möbius strip. Technically speaking, the eversion of the letter is a very basic transformation—the letter in question is presumably an old-fashioned four-page sheet, and so it was simply unfolded, and then refolded in the opposite direction.

DUPIN'S PSYCHOTOPOLOGY

For the minister, the un- and refolding of the letter is only an instrumental act, a pragmatic step taken as part of his encompassing analytic method that relies on manipulating differences. The minister performs a simple calculation of the prefect's methods, and deploys the differences of the calculus to hide the letter. "Yet to calculate," Poe stipulates in the first paragraph of "Rue Morgue," "is not in itself to analyze" (189). It is only with Dupin's comparison of the folding of the letter to turning a glove inside out that the conceptual aspect of the transformation becomes more interesting. For to evert a glove is geometrically more complex than merely un- and refolding a letter. To turn a glove inside out, one must essentially send it through itself—by pushing or pulling the fingers out through the wrist opening. Eversion and passing figures through themselves are essential aspects of many significant topological figures and problems. As we have noted, a Klein bottle is formed by a twisting a bottle's neck back through the surface of the bottle and connecting it to its base. One may also imagine this construction in terms of a reversal of outer and inner: take a torus composed of an outer and inner skin. Cut open the torus perpendicular to its axis, and then stick the outer skin on one side of the cut to the inner skin on the other side, and vice versa. There is now a one-sided surface without inside or outside. In a further twist to our geometrical tour, a Klein bottle can be cut into two Möbius strips—which calls for another limerick.

> A mathematician named Klein
> Thought the Mobius band was divine.
> Said he, "If you glue
> The edges of two
> You'll get a weird bottle like mine."[16]

Eversion has become an increasingly intricate subject of investigation in topology, a predominant example being the process of everting a sphere. In the very strictest terms, however, the eversion of the letter as depicted by Poe violates the criterion of topological transformations that holds that figures may pass through themselves, as long as this does not give rise to intermediate stages with sharp points or creases. Because the letter displays chafing at the creases, the eversion of the letter is not exactly a *continuous* function. Yet we still may argue that with the minister, we have moved from a Euclidean space of coordinate geometry and objects measured by magnitude to a topological space where objects undergo elastic transformations.

Dupin's analytic *prolongements* give this topological space a full conceptual expression. On one level, the model of analysis Dupin offers in the story is exceedingly simple: "an identification of the reasoner's intellect with that of his opponent" (340). Yet the ability to identify one's mind with another's also generates, at that very moment, the next viewpoint—from which one sees the other's mind. The dynamic is, in the terms of the story, that one "gets even by going one up" on the other. To do so demands a cognitive flexibility, an imaginative faculty that stretches one's own mind to replicate an other's. The operation in effect turns two opposing sides, where one's mind is felt as an "inside" and the opponent's as an "outside," into one continuous surface. Or, to put it differently, analysis in this respect is an exercise in projective psychology that unfolds as a topological operation. As if to underscore the connection between the psychological and spatial aspects of "analysis," Dupin provides two different illustrations of the analytic process, one a psychological exercise and one a spatiovisual one.

The psychological model of analysis is conveyed in Dupin's account of the game of even and odd. One player holds in his hand a number of marbles, and his opponent must guess whether the number is even or odd. If the guesser guesses correctly, he gets one marble. One boy wins all the marbles by thinking exactly what the other is thinking. His method of matching his thoughts to an other's is almost humorously naive: "When I wish to find out . . . what are his thoughts at the moment, I fashion the expression of my face, as accurately as possible, in accordance with the expression of his, and then wait to see what thoughts or sentiments arise in my mind or heart, as if to match or correspond with the expression" (340). The term "expression" as deployed by Poe here brings several convergent lines together: the facial expression becomes a single surface where outer appearance and inner thought or feeling become continuous. The transformation on the face here entails an elastic, and therefore topological, motion: you stretch your features to become continuous with the other person's. The prefect's erroneous psychological and spatial model is precisely the opposite of this surface-oriented one: "he perpetually errs by being too deep or too shallow" (339). Perhaps an oblique allusion lurks here to mathematical expressions as well—the most common form being an equation, itself another example where an equivalence is established between two distinct "sides." The mathematical terminology sprinkled throughout the paragraph would support this suspicion: the game is a counting game; the boy must contend with a second player "a degree above a first" (the problem of matching his expression thus being a second-degree equation, as it were); and in concluding, Dupin asks, "Now this mode of reasoning . . . what, in its last analysis, is it?" (340).

The spatial model of analysis is provided by the game of puzzles already alluded to, where one chooses a word that must be found on a map by another. The strategy of hiding something most effectively by leaving it plain sight is here directly associated with what is for Serres *the* topological property par excellence: a proximity between the very near and the very far, for the large letters on a map, even as they will appear to the eyes the "nearest," will actually indicate something that spans a great distance and hence is far away. The proximity of near and far occurs, in Serres's imagery, on a crumpled-up space like a handkerchief stuffed in a pocket. While the map Dupin refers to here would presumably be a flat surface, it is characterized by words that imply a kind of stretching and folding. Dupin refers to "the motley and perplexed surface of the chart" (345). By motley, Dupin likely means the heterogeneous nature of words found on a chart—different sizes and fonts of letters, designating different sorts of geographical features. At the same time though, "motley" immediately evokes the jester's patchwork garb, with the craziness of its quilted cloth being an index to the jester's role as a trickster—precisely the role that the player plays in the game. By "perplexed," Dupin of course means the confusing nature of the chart's surface—what makes it perplexing. Something perplexed is, more particularly though, a surface which is thoroughly (the Latin *per*) woven or entwined (*plectere,* past participle of *plexus,* to weave or entwine). The words on this intricately woven surface pass through themselves, in effect, in that small names are interspersed between letters of long ones—different scales inhering in the same plane being a version of inside and outside passing into one another.

In general, then, the contrast between the methods of the minister and of Dupin may be cast in mathematical terms. To hide the letter from the prefect, the minister deploys an analytic method based on the differential calculus, to get as much as possible out of minute differences. The geometrical element of his work comes only as a practical step. But to hide his purloining of the letter from the minister, Dupin relies on topological transformations. He forms a "fac-simile" of the letter by stretching out dough to form a seal like the minister's. (The image plays conveniently into Serres's love of stretching, folding, and kneading dough as an exemplary image of topology; it is only icing on the cake that there is in fact a topological operation known as the Baker transformation.) Other stretching operations unfold in altering facial expressions and distributing letters across a chart. Ultimately, both the minister and Dupin rely on operations that change sameness and differences into one another. The minister steals the letter by using a different one that loosely resembles the original, and then hides it by making the same letter look different. Dupin then steals the letter back by creating a different letter that looks the same. The contrast lies in the analytic predilection of the minister versus the geometric taste of Dupin; the former entails an approach to transformations based on the calculus, while the latter utilizes transformations based on topology. Poe forges a link between this mathematical component of "analysis" and

an analogous linguistic dimension by repeatedly referring to the "D—
cipher" on the letter. The minister has de-ciphered the prefect's concept of
space and hidden the letter in the space of differences from calculus. Dupin
has de ciphered the minister's concept of space and used topological methods to create a new cipher—a letter that is but an empty signifier, at least
as concerns the minister's political intrigues. On the personal level of
revenge, though, Dupin has of course carefully constructed his cipher in
the form of a coded allusion to the myth of Atreus and Thyestes.

This concluding allusion to myth provides grist for the baker who gets
his supplies from Serres's mill. One of Serres's best-known axioms is that
myth lies at the foundation of science. Here, as we prolong Poe along a trajectory modeled after Serres, we would posit that Poe's closing reference
discloses a mythic structure subtending the mathematical structures and
operations extracted from the tale. The purloined letter poses the problem
of insides and outside: when the minister has stolen it, it is hidden inside
his house, out in the open, on the surface, that is, on the outside of an
inside. This hiding has been accomplished by everting the letter, turning it
inside out. Then Dupin in turn steals the letter, and leaves behind a fac-
simile which is now "inside" the space of the minister's apartment but "outside" his vision. Dupin reveals to the narrator the "inside" of the letter he
left behind: Crebillon's aphoristic summation of the Atreus and Thyestes
myth, in which Thyestes seduces his brother Atreus's wife, to which
Atreus responds by killing Thyestes' sons and serving them to him at a banquet. The myth itself contains an image of inversion (a reversal of power
of priority between equals—the myth hinges on the struggle for the
throne between brothers) and eversion (eating one's sons is passing a family through itself, an internalizing of the outside). We are back to the
crossroads of Oedipus, only it has been turned inside out: in place of pat-
ricide and incest, we have fratricide and cannibalism. The taboos are
linked, though, in that one cannot mate with kin or eat of the same kind.
At the end of the story, then, Poe discovers the mythic structure of which
his own tale is simply another version. Inscribed in the story is the citation
of the myth of which the story is a version: the story contains a part of the
myth that contains it.

ANALYSIS   Poetry and Mathematics

Largely under the auspices of French theory, "The Purloined Letter" has
achieved the status of a paradigm of literary analysis. That is, the tale has
become itself a code for analyzing literature and language: the game of
analysis played out in the tale becomes a blueprint for a concept of interpretation or language. Irwin persuasively argues that on one level, the

game of analysis staged in the story constitutes Poe's model for the continual process of detection at the heart of the reading process. Taking eversion as an image of Poe's hermeneutics, Irwin argues that "the temporal movement from reading to rereading bears an implicit spatial vector pointing from surface to depth, and since rereading is imagined as the process of going deeper into a work, the temporal opposition earlier/later as applied to successive readings is coded as the spatial opposition outer/inner, that is, an earlier reading is experienced as an outer to a later reading's inner."[17] Irwin then extrapolates from this hermeneutic model a full-blown epistemology. The purloined letter, as the object of the mind's knowledge, embodies the mind itself—in the final analysis, the mind is itself its own ultimate object of knowledge. Playing on the "simple" and "odd" nature of the mystery and the letter, Irwin asks, "But what is that simple thing whose simplicity makes it so odd, so mysterious because so obvious. . . . What but self-consciousness, that condition of being at odds with oneself that constitutes the sameness, the simplicity of a rational being?"[18]

From an epistemological standpoint, "The Purloined Letter" exemplifies the recursive nature of the analytic process. Each first step the mind takes, each result or thought, then becomes an object subject to the next analytic act. Thinking does not occur in a vacuum; it demands context. Each recursive move is a reiteration: a reflection on existing or previous results. This analytic process is played out in the tale as the conflict between characters: each player in the game does this to the prior one. Furthermore, "The Purloined Letter" performs a similar operation on the two prior Dupin tales; it marks the synthesis of the detective series. Irwin has shown that this tale amounts to "a compendium of the oppositions and motifs" introduced throughout the three, including the complex interplay and reversals involving inner and outer.[19] Perhaps the most appropriate single synonym for analysis would be *reflection:* first, because to reflect on something is to take it as an object of scrutiny; and second, because "reflection" in the mirroring sense reverses right and left, as does turning a glove inside out.

In reading Poe's idea of analysis in terms of an interdisciplinary synthesis advocated by Serres, we have treated the tale as a nascent mathematical discourse. Taking a cue from Serres, we might now ask, what emerges when we examine the mathematical themes in "The Purloined Letter" from an epistemological standpoint? Here we find that the successive concepts of space associated with the prefect, minister, and Dupin provide an interesting model for the development of mathematical ideas. With only a bit of stretching and squeezing, we may graft these respective concepts of space onto the historical model Piaget and Garcia propose in *Psychogenesis and the History of Science.* The essential thesis informing their discussion of the history of mathematics is that "Abstract mathematical notions have, in many cases, first been used in an instrumental way, without giving rise to any reflection concerning their general significance or even any conscious awareness of the fact that they were being used."[20] The observation fits the Poe tale rather neatly: within the story, I have argued, the minister is depicted as a master of differential calculus but only incidentally and instrumentally turns to geometrical operations on space. From the outside, Poe's story itself could be seen as an "instrumental" discovery of what will become the abstract mathematical notion of topology.

In assessing the history of geometry, Piaget and Garcia distinguish three stages of epistemological development. The "intrafigural" stage is one of figural realism—it focuses on the relations within a given, rigid figure. This is the stage of Euclidean geometry, the study of the properties of solid figures. The prefect fits this category in that his notion of the letter depends directly on the physical description he has of it. He searches only for that one object, never thinking of it as something that could be transformed. Next, Piaget and Garcia posit an "interfigural" stage in which a given object is seen as a variable element within a system of transformations. Here one studies what transformations can be made on an object to create a corresponding object. This would be the stage of projective geometry, with operations such as translations from three- to two-dimensional spaces. The minister in essence makes a transformation in the letter that takes it out of one "space" and places it in another, without altering the object. Finally, Piaget and Garcia identify a "transfigural" stage, in which the object of study involves relationships that obtain at the level of systems of transformations. Klein's Erlanger Programm marked such an abstract synthesis in that he showed how different geometries may be understood as being different structures subtending systems of transformation. Topology provided something like a geometric lingua franca—a "space" in which one could translate among different spatial languages. Dupin provides an equivalent synthesis in the story by assimilating the prefect's and minister's respective concepts of space within a space with topological characteristics: a proximity of distant and near, in which figures are subjected to elastic motions, including eversion.

The elasticity definitive of topological space expresses figuratively the flexibility of mind demanded by Poe's analysis. The difficulty in picturing topological transformations finds its analogue in "The Purloined Letter" in its depiction of visual perception. The difficulty in seeing what is hidden in plain sight lies in a conceptual rather than a perceptual deficiency. Dupin tells the prefect that "any point requiring reflection we shall examine to better purpose in the dark"—which the prefect calls another of Dupin's "odd notions" (330). Reflection, as a paradigm of analysis, shifts the visual metaphor to a cognitive plane. Topology is replete with examples of visual thought's being an abstract matter. Bernard Morin, one of the first mathematicians to understand how a sphere can turn inside out, is blind. It bears reiterating, however, that topology is not explicitly formulated but instrumentally or metaphorically uncovered in Poe's tale. In hindsight, it is as if Poe reinvented "analysis" as a process of conceptual transformation precisely when algebraic "analysis" required a reformulation in terms of geometry.

REPOSITIONING PURLOINED LETTERS

A final remark about Poe and Serres. Poe's analysis and Serres's synthesis are both conceptual methods of transformation. Poe integrates several different allusive textures into his tales, while Serres's writings function as operators on other discourses. Eversion, we have seen, is a crucial conceptual or methodological figure in the writings of both men. Both also share a predilection for seeing some set of elements or group of materials as components in a structure that can be rearranged or mapped into some other structure. What emerges from encounters from each writer, not to mention taking the two together, is a distinct pleasure, a delight in playful machinations born of combinatoric manipulations. On this note, I end with a last operation on them, one that combines mathematical combinatorics with language—the anagram. The anagram resembles some aspects of point set topology, in that it both transforms elements into a corresponding structure, and reduces all versions of combining the same letters into possible configurations of an underlying structure. Poe's fondness for anagrams is evident in small facts—the tale "Isope," for instance, is an anagram of "is poe." Thinking about the ground we have covered here, we might think of the analytic game at play in "The Purloined Letter" as culminating in the exclamation, "Hell! out interpreted!" The trio of famed theoretical readers of the tale might be known ironically as the "rude, potent, ill three." Edgar Allan Poe, man of letters, could be transformed into a caricature of a character from his story (an old, large ape), subjected to constant reinterpretations in light of his transgressive behavior (on legal parade), who has to insist that he is really just a control freak (plead anal ogre). And finally, the theorist to whose work this article owes its genesis might well see such writings as mere "Hermes relics."

NOTES

1. See Paul A. Harris, "The Itinerant Theorist: Nature and Knowledge/Ecology and Topology in Michel Serres," *SubStance* 83 (fall 1997).

2. Leibniz, *Analysis Situs,* cited in Morris Kline, *Mathematical Thought: From Ancient to Modern Times,* vol. 3 (Oxford: Oxford University Press, 1972), 1163.

3. Edgar Allan Poe, *Selected Writings* (London: Penguin, 1967), 330. Subsequent citations of Poe's works are to this edition and are given in the text.

4. Kline, *Mathematical Thought,* 947.

5. Ibid., 842.

6. Poncelet, cited in Jean Piaget and Rolando Garcia, *Psychogenesis and the History of Science,* trans. Helga Feider (New York: Columbia University Press, 1989), 93.

7. Klein, *Mathematical Thought,* 917.

8. Piaget and Garcia, *Psychogenesis,* 137.

9. Ibid., 137.

10. Ibid., 138.

11. Or, as John Irwin characterizes Poe's sentence: "as an analytic statement about the nonsusceptibility of analysis to being analyzed, it is included in the class of things to which it refers, but what it says in effect is that analytic statements cannot wholly include themselves. In analyzing the act of analysis, self-conscious thought turns back upon itself to find that it cannot absolutely coincide with itself" (*The Mystery to a Solution: Poe, Borges, and the Analytic Detective Story* [Baltimore: Johns Hopkins University Press, 1994], 11).

12. Ibid., 347.

13. W. Lietzmann, *Visual Topology,* trans. M. Bruckheimer (New York: American Elsevier, 1965), 3.

14. Irwin, *Mystery to a Solution,* 28.

15. Lietzmann, *Visual Topology,* 111.

16. Ibid., 117.

17. Irwin, *Mystery to a Solution,* 21.

18. Ibid., 27.

19. Ibid., 412.

20. Piaget and Garcia, *Psychogenesis,* 105.

THE DESIRE FOR UNITY AND ITS FAILURE

Reading Henry Adams through Michel Serres

PHILIPP SCHWEIGHAUSER

In *McTeague: A Story of San Francisco* (1899) and *Sister Carrie* (1900), Henry Adams's younger contemporaries Frank Norris and Theodore Dreiser evoke a soundscape[1] of noise that captures the acoustic world of an America at the height of its industrial expansionism and in the midst of rapid urbanization that would change the quality of city life forever. In Dreiser's novel, the apprehensive narrator tells us that it is the noise of the city that lures the impressionable Sister Carrie from her quiet hometown Columbia City, Wisconsin, to the bustling city life of Chicago:

> A blare of sound, a roar of life, a vast array of human hives appeal to the astonished senses in equivocal terms. Without a counselor at hand to whisper cautious interpretations, what falsehoods may not these things breathe into the unguarded ear! Unrecognized for what they are, their beauty, like music, too often relaxes, then weakens, then perverts the simplest human perception.[2]

In Norris's *McTeague,* an acoustic onslaught of far greater proportions tears apart the "vast silence"[3] of the Californian desert, to which McTeague flees after he has killed his wife:

> Here and there at long distances upon the cañon sides rose the headgear of a mine, surrounded with its few unpainted houses, and topped by its never-failing feather of black smoke. On near approach one heard the prolonged thunder of the stamp-mill, the crusher, the insatiable monster, gnashing the rocks to powder with its long iron teeth, vomiting them out again in a thin stream of wet gray mud. Its enormous maw, fed day and night with the carboys' loads, gorged itself with gravel, and spat

out the gold, grinding the rocks between its jaws, glutted, as it were, with the very entrails of the earth, and growling over its endless meal, like some savage animal, some legendary dragon, some fabulous beast, symbol of inordinate and monstrous gluttony.[4]

Norris and Dreiser define the American landscape at the turn of the century as a site of ever-present noises. As Norris suggests, the noises of civilization have penetrated far into the western wilderness. By 1900, industrialization and urbanization and their attendant noises define the experience of an ever-larger portion of the U.S. population. It is in this historical as well as literary-historical context that the absence of representations of noise in Henry Adams's *The Education of Henry Adams* (1907/1918), first published in private seven years after Dreiser's *Sister Carrie,* must strike us as an anomaly.

Several explanations for this conspicuous absence suggest themselves. As the strongly autobiographical text[5] of a progeny of one of the richest and most powerful American families, *The Education of Henry Adams* registers a wholly different range of experiences than Dreiser's and Norris's texts, with their working-class or middle-class protagonists.[6] Even though he professes to stay away from such occasions as often as possible, Adams is more accustomed to the acoustics of society receptions, where "the tone was easy, the talk was good, and the standard of scholarship was high" (194), than to the bustling life of the poorer parts of cities, where "[o]ne heard the chanting of street cries, the shrill calling of children on their way to school, the merry rattle of a butcher's cart, the brisk noise of hammering, or the occasional prolonged roll of a cable car trundling heavily past, with a vibrant whirring of its jostled glass and the joyous clanging of its bells."[7]

Norris's evocation of the acoustic world of Polk Street, San Francisco, betrays his naturalist interest in the daily trials and tribulations of human lives. This suggests a second reason for the absence of noise in *The Education.* The far greater geographical, political, and historical scope of Adams's text—which covers some of the major geopolitical events between 1838 and 1905—largely excludes attention to these more mundane affairs. The worlds of experience Norris and Dreiser attend to are in more than one way the noise that remains at the margins of Adams's discourse. In this context, Adams's choice of a symbol for the increasingly accelerated process of modernity is significant. He chooses the "silent and infinite force" (361) of the dynamo, which he first encounters at the 1893 Chicago World Fair, rather than the steam-powered "clacking, rattling machines"[8] Sister Carrie works at in the din of a shoe factory.[9]

Still, as a narrative charting almost seventy years of turbulent American history, *The Education* remains surprisingly devoid of the noises that

accompanied the massive changes wrought by industrialization and urbanization. Adams traveled extensively and visited most American and European metropolises, witnessed the prodigious expansion of the railway system, and worked as a bearer of dispatches in Rome during the Italian
Risorgimento. But, even in his condemnation of the horrors of industrialization as he witnessed them in England's Black Country, Adams does not
give us any acoustic impressions. He lets us see its gloomy darkness but
does not make us participate in its auditory turmoil (73).

One of the few exceptions is Adams's description of New York, to
which he returns in 1905 after almost forty years of absence, and is con-
fronted with a cognitive, visual, and acoustic uproar of apocalyptic dimensions:

> The outline of the city became frantic in its effort to explain something
> that defied meaning. Power seemed to have outgrown its servitude and
> to have asserted its freedom. The cylinder had exploded, and thrown
> great masses of stone and steam against the sky. The city had the air and
> movement of hysteria, and the citizens were crying, in every accent of
> anger and alarm, that the new forces must at any cost be brought under
> control. Prosperity never before imagined, power never yet wielded by
> man, speed never reached by anything but a meteor, had made the
> world irritable, nervous, querulous, unreasonable and afraid. . . .
> Everyone saw it, and every municipal election shrieked chaos. . . . The
> two-thousand-years failure of Christianity roared upward from Broad-
> way, and no Constantine the Great was in sight. (471–72)

We may here catch a glimpse of the significance of noise in Adams's discourse. Even though this passage does capture something of the city's
soundscape, noise is here less a physical, acoustic phenomenon than a
trope for the fragmentary, uprooted, chaotic nature of human existence at
the beginning of the twentieth century. Adams is less interested in the
realist representation of the auditory manifestations of trains, city streets,
city crowds, and factories that writers like Dreiser and Norris execute
with such precision, than in using noise figuratively to evoke an atmosphere of disorder and disorientation:

> Every day nature violently revolted, causing so-called accidents with
> enormous destruction of property and life, while plainly laughing at
> man, who helplessly groaned and shrieked and shuddered, but never for
> a single instant could stop. The railways alone approached the carnage
> of war; automobiles and fire-arms ravaged society, until an earthquake
> became almost a nervous relaxation. (467)

In Adams's figurative use, noise is aligned with multiplicity, chaos, and the
dissolution of traditional values. While his patrician family background

certainly conditions his exposure to, as well as his perception of physical noise, it is this tropological association that accounts for the role of noise in Adams's system.

As a resigned critic of his times, Adams sought to tame the noise of modernity, to impose order on chaos and unity on multiplicity. In the editor's preface, Adams juxtaposes thirteenth-century unity, which he sees embodied in the Virgin as represented in the Cathedral of Notre Dame at Chartres, and twentieth-century multiplicity, with the dynamo as its symbol. Adams leaves no doubt about his allegiance to the principle of unity:

> Since monkeys first began to chatter in trees, neither man nor beast had ever denied or doubted Multiplicity, Diversity, Complexity, Anarchy, Chaos. . . . Chaos was a primary fact even in Paris—especially in Paris—as it was in the Book of Genesis; but every thinking being in Paris or out of it had exhausted thought in the effort to prove Unity, Continuity, Purpose, Order, Law, Truth, the Universe, God, after having begun by taking it for granted, and discovering, to their profound dismay, that some minds denied it. The direction of mind, as a single force of nature, had been constant since history began. Its own unity had created a universe the essence of which was abstract Truth; the Absolute, God! (431)

The text of *The Education* registers neither a denial of multiplicity nor a nostalgic longing for a unity that, Adams knows, has been irretrievably lost. Instead, it couples a profound sense of loss with a determined and fully conscious effort to establish unity in the face of multiplicity and chaos. In conceding that "Chaos was the law of nature, Order was the dream of man" (427), Adams betrays an awareness of the constructedness of ideals of unity in the age of "the new multiverse" (433). This awareness does not, however, deter him from attempting just that.

Adams's desire for unity is most clearly visible in his arguments for a dynamic theory of history. Expounded at length in the second half of *The Education* and in his "Letter to American Teachers of History," the dynamic theory of history is an attempt to construct a scientific theory of history on the basis of the second law of thermodynamics, which, in its simplest formulation, states that "the entropy of any closed system increases until it reaches a maximum at equilibrium."[10] In its recognition of the irreversibility of most physical processes, the second law of thermodynamics introduced a temporal dimension, an "arrow of time" into physics. The implications of this had reverberations far beyond physics. In 1854, Hermann von Helmholtz stated that the world, as a closed thermodynamic system, would continually move toward a state of maximal entropy, at which all energy is converted into heat and rendered unavailable for further work.[11] This idea of the "heat death" of the universe, of an irreversible increase in entropy, informs Adams's gloomy vision of the world as progressing toward a state of total disorder (or maximum entropy). What Adams attempts with his dynamic theory of history is therefore not to deny multiplicity and disorder, but to make it manageable, to cope with it by incorporating it into a unified scientific doctrine.[12]

Adams sees his own quest for unity safely embedded in a long line of philosophical thought:

> He got out his Descartes again; dipped into his Hume and Berkeley; wrested anew with his Kant; pondered solemnly over his Hegel and Schopenhauer and Hartmann; strayed gaily away with his Greeks—all merely to ask what Unity meant, and what happened when one denied it. Apparently one never denied it. Every philosopher, whether sane or insane, naturally affirmed it. (409)

Readers of Michel Serres's oeuvre will beg to differ. In his valorization of multiplicity over unity, Serres defines himself precisely against a tradition of rationalism that includes Adams's scientistic approach to historiography, and is dominated by reason and commands through reason. Like Adams's *The Education,* Serres's *Genesis* can be read as an extended reflection on the relationship between unity and multiplicity. But right down to the details of rhetoric, Serres differs on almost every single point Adams makes. Serres abandons Adams's pursuit of a unified scientific doctrine in favor of a "noisy philosophy" (*G,* 20) that accounts for background noise as "the basic element of the software of all our logic" (*G,* 7) and for which "the work is a confident chord" while "the masterwork trembles with noise" (*G,* 18). As is already hinted at in their contrary inscriptions of noise, the differences between the two thinkers are accentuated on the level of rhetoric. This becomes especially clear if we consider the range of tropes they share to sketch out the relationship between the one and the many.

One of Adams's preferred symbols for unity is "woman," not in the flesh-and-blood existence of individual women but as a female principle:

> She did not think of her universe as a raft to which the limpets stuck for life in the surge of a supernatural chaos; she conceived herself and her family as the centre and flower of an ordered universe which she knew to be unity because she had made it after the image of her own fecundity; and this creation of hers was surrounded by beauties and perfections which she knew to be real because she herself had imagined them. (434)

Adams continues by quoting from the beginning of Lucretius's *De rerum natura,* identifying the female principle with Lucretius's Venus: "Even the masculine philosopher admired and loved and celebrated her triumph, and the greatest of them sang it in the noblest of his verses" (434):

> O mother of the Roman race, delight
> Of men and gods, Venus most bountiful,
> You who beneath the gliding signs of heaven
> Fill with yourself the sea bedecked with ships
> And earth, great crop-bearer, since by your power
> Creatures of every kind are brought to birth
> And rising up behold the light of sun;
>
> . . . .
>
> Since you and only you are nature's guide
> And nothing to the glorious shores of light
> Rises without you, nor grows sweet and lovely,
> You I desire as partner in my verses.[13]

Serres in *Genesis* makes not a single reference to Adams's writings. But to Serres, Adams's reading of Lucretius's Venus as a symbol for unity would be a perfect example for "our regular misconstruals of Lucretius, and the road down which these misconstruals have misguided us right up to the present" (*G*, 107). The misconstruals of Lucretius were of at least two different kinds. On the one hand, *De rerum natura* was read as the work of a poet-philosopher whose combination of the two discourses was—considering its status as an Epicurean didactic poem and Epicurus's aversion to poetry—sometimes seen as problematic,[14] sometimes as congenial,[15] but whose findings bear little or no significance to contemporary science. Contrary to this tradition, Serres decides to read Lucretius literally, as "a treatise on physics" (*H*, 98).

On the other hand, *De rerum natura* was read as a justification of scientific rationalism. In the celebration of Bacon's ascendancy over "authority" and superstition in his ode "To the Royal Society," Abraham Cowley pictures the battle of reason (Bacon) against its/his adversaries (authority, superstition) in terms that betray his debt to Lucretius's lines on Epicurus's victory over *religio*.[16] In Lucretius, *religio* is painted as a giant who "from heaven's firmament / Displayed its face, its ghastly countenance / Lowering above mankind" and spread terror up to Epicurus, who was "the first to break apart / The bolts of nature's gates and throw them open."[17] In Cowley, authority is pictured as "some old giant's more gigantic ghost" who managed to "terrify the learned rout" until Bacon "broke that monstrous god," with the result that "[t]he orchard's open now, and free."[18] In Cowley's reading, Lucretius shares his celebration of reason over a more powerful adversary, whose dogmatic rigidity had prevented human access to the true knowledge of nature.[19]

It is to this second kind of reading that Adams's recourse to Lucretius belongs. In Serres's re-reading, *De rerum natura* is neither irrelevant to the natural sciences nor a harbinger of scientific rationalism. On the contrary, in Lucretius's vision of the clinamen, Serres finds a model alternative to the mechanistic and determinist worldview of scientific rationalism. Lucretius imagines the beginning of the world in the slightest atomic swerve from the straight line of atoms falling through space. In its departure from the uniformity of the fall of atoms, this swerve or clinamen provokes the collision of atoms, which initiates the birth of all things:

> Now here is another thing I want you to understand.
> While atoms move by their own weight straight down
> Through the empty void, at quite uncertain times
> And uncertain places they swerve slightly from their course.
> You might call it no more than a mere change of motion.
> If this did not occur, then all of them
> Would fall like drops of rain down through the void.
> There would be no collisions, no impacts
> Of atoms upon atom, so that nature
> Would never have created anything.[20]

With his notion of the clinamen, Lucretius not only departs from the Democritean model, which allows for no disturbance of the falling atoms,[21] but, as Serres argues convincingly in *La Naissance de la physique dans le texte de Lucrèce* and "Lucretius: Science and Religion,"[22] Lucretius also anticipates the twentieth-century movement in the natural sciences commonly known as "chaos theory"[23] rather than the rationalist tradition in science—precisely because it disturbs (in the most literal sense) the more rigid models proposed by rationalist thinkers like Descartes or Laplace:

> Without declination, there are only the laws of fate, that is to say, the chains of order. The new is born of the old; the new is only the repetition of the old. But the angle interrupts the stoic chain, breaks the *foedera fate,* the endless series of causes and reasons. It disturbs, in fact, the laws of nature. And from it, the arrival of life, of everything that breathes; and the leaping of horses. (*H,* 99)

More specifically, in Lucretius's vision of the turbulent beginning of all things in the slightest atomic swerve, Serres detects an anticipation of what "chaos" theorists call sensitive dependence on initial conditions and what has become popularly known as the "butterfly effect": "In this area, the least error as to the initial position makes for an immense uncertainty as to the final position" (*G,* 109). And indeed, contemporary Russian physicist

Ilya Prigogine and philosopher Isabelle Stengers (1984) explicitly take recourse to Lucretius, also reading him against a rationalist tradition:

> The clinamen, this spontaneous, unpredictable deviation, has often been criticised as one of the main weaknesses of Lucretian physics, as being something introduced adhoc. In fact, the contrary is true—the clinamen attempts to explain events such as laminar flow ceasing to be stable and spontaneously turning into turbulent flow. Today hydrodynamic experts test the stability of fluid flow by introducing a perturbation that expresses the effect of molecular disorder added to the average flow. We are not so far from the clinamen of Lucretius![24]

It is the image of the creation of things in an originary moment of turbulence and multiplicity that Serres also discerns in Lucretius's evocation of Venus at the beginning of *De rerum natura*. In Lucretius as well as Serres, Venus rises and is born from the noise of the sea. But to ally her with unity, as Henry Adams does, is to deny her turbulent origins, to appropriate her for a philosophical discourse of unity, in which "[w]e know only Aphrodite, if that. We turn away from the waves to admire the waveborn" (*G*, 25). Serres, however, wants to attend precisely to the noise of the sea and give multiplicity its due. In Serres's rereading of Lucretius, Venus does not stand for unity but for "Turbulence . . . born of the *noise*" (*G*, 121), turbulence conceived of as an intermittent state between unity and multiplicity, between order and chaos, forever oscillating between the two: "One must imagine Venus turbulent, above the noise of the sea" (*G*, 122).

In his preference of multiplicity over unity and chaos over order, Serres does not celebrate irrationality, and his passion is not aimed against the pursuit of rational unity as such,[25] but against the arrogance of a rationalist discourse whose desire for unity turns violent in its exclusion of everything that does not fit its rigid order. In his "Literature and the Exact Sciences" (1989), Serres speaks out against a science with hegemonic claims, against a science whose ascendancy over other forms of knowledge today "strongly resembles those divisions of territory at the end of great battles where the victor takes everything, leaving only vanquished miserable reserves and strange, savage speech."[26] It is this aspect of scientific rationalism that has allied itself with the bourgeois project of the mastery of nature, in which the desire to know is put in the service of the desire to dominate. We may return to Cowley's ode "To the Royal Society" to see this logic at work:

> From you, great champions, we expect to get
> These spacious countries but discover'd yet;

Countries where yet in stead of Nature, we
Her images and idols worshipp'd see:
These large and wealthy regions to subdue,
Though learning has whole armies at command,
Quarter'd about in every land,
A better troop she ne're together drew.[27]

Lines such as these lend weight to Serres's conviction that, in its inextrica-
ble conflation of an epistemophilic discourse and a discourse of power and
domination, the discourse of rationalism is ultimately a violent discourse,
a discourse of death:

> The stable chain of the rationalists only expresses, I think, their desire
> for domination. . . . This chain is a chain of reason, this chain is a chain
> of death. . . . My predecessors were fascinated by dominating reason,
> the clerical alliance of empire and ideas, of which the chain of reasons
> was the emblem and the tool. . . . They loved only the order fit to
> invade the world. . . . I have understood at last why the endeavor that
> was no doubt born in the classical era had to end in the Los Alamos
> desert, at the place where all the grains of sand look alike, where the
> work of men still vitrifies them. Rationalism is a vehicle of death. Sci-
> ence must dissociate itself from it. (G, 72–73)

The spatial metaphors both Cowley and Serres use ("spacious countries but
discover'd yet," "large and wealthy regions to subdue," "empire," "fit to
invade the world") gain a decidedly literal weight once we recognize that
rationalism's bid for unity is analogous to and reproduced in the violent
processes of unification that accompany the formation of empires. As Serres asks with regard to the Roman Empire: "There is the Roman mob, turbulent, restless, powerful, magnificent, there is the throng and the multitude, there is the population, what chain of circumstances made it glide
along its history?" In his answer, Serres draws attention to the violence
inherent in the unifying impulses of empire: "It is to forget the press of the
throng in fury, to repress the multitude and the population, that the furious hero and the orderly army are made ready, constructed, represented"
(G, 54). Serres's prime example is Rome, but examples drawn from the
books of history are legion, and the imposition of the Christian faith on the
multitude of Native American peoples and religions is only one of the
bloodier proofs of the dark underside of e pluribus unum.[28] Serres's valorization of multiplicity and noise therefore defines itself both positively,
in its celebration of the birth of things out of chaos and noise, and nega-
tively, in its dissociation from the death-dealing discourses of unity.

Adams, on the other hand, while clearly aware of the fragmentary
nature of human existence at the beginning of the twentieth century, never

renounces his quest for unity. This is evident in the details of his rhetoric. Maria L. Assad's discussion of the "tropological space"[29] Serres lays out in *Genesis* offers us a model to bring the two thinkers' differences into a dialogue. As Assad points out, a word like *noise* or the figure of *la belle noiseuse* functions in *Genesis* and later writings as tropes that do not "stand for" chaos but point in its direction, not unlike the word *time,* which points in the direction of something that cannot be defined and cannot ultimately be known.[30] If we follow Serres's assertion in the first chapter of *Genesis* that the object of his book is "the multiple as such" (*G,* 6) and consequently direct our attention to multiplicity rather than chaos, we realize that the tropological space of the multiple is even larger and includes noise, dancing, time, the clinamen, the parasite, the crowd, the sea, and the collapsed tower of Babel, all of which function as tropes gesturing toward the black box of the multiple. Serres uses these tropes in order to approach the idea of the multiple without ever ultimately "knowing" it and turning it into a concept. In his own reflections on multiplicity, Henry Adams opens up a similar tropological space. Adams shares many of Serres's tropes, but in Adams's text, these tropes all acquire decidedly negative connotations.

One of the more striking differences between Adams's and Serres's figural inscriptions of the same word concerns the sea. Adams repeatedly associates the turbulence of the sea with war. In Adams's discourse, the American Civil War becomes "the surf of a wild ocean" in which young soldiers of Adams's age are "beaten about for four years by the waves of war" (110). Likewise, the Franco-Prussian War of 1870–71 figures in Adams as a historical event that slips out of the hands of human actors and is abandoned to the vagaries of the sea: "Mr Gladstone was as much astounded as Adams; the Emperor Napoleon was nearly as stupefied as either, and Bismarck himself hardly knew how he did it. . . . Under one's eyes France cut herself adrift, and floated off, on an unknown stream, towards a less known ocean" (277). For Adams, the turbulence of the ocean serves as an appropriate metaphor for the chaotic nature and unruliness of war. Like the sea, war is a force that eludes and threatens human desires for control.

In Serres, the sea is turbulent, too, but, as in Lucretius, it is the source from which Venus and all life springs: "Aphrodite, beautiful goddess, invisible, standing up, is born of the chaotic sea, this nautical chaos, the *noise*" (*G,* 25). It is not for nothing that Serres's *Genesis* begins with "A Short Tall Tale," in which the shipwrecked narrator constructs a raft out of countless bottles, each with a little message inside, colliding noisily on the Sargasso Sea. The sea, the noise, and the multiple are not only at the beginning of things, they are also at the beginning of Serres's text: "Before language, before even the word, the noise" (*G,* 54). The chaotic, noisy sea is the originary space of a "chain of contingency" that "emerges from the sea noise, the nautical noise, the prebiotic soup" (*G, 72*). As in Adams, the turbulence of the sea gestures toward a lack of control, toward indeterminacy. But for Serres, this is precisely why the sea offers an alternative and a redemption to the stable chain of the rationalists, at the end of which he envisions nothing but "the tomb of an immense transparent and burning pyramid" (*G, 72*).

War, on the other hand, is for Serres a decidedly orderly affair. It is this conviction that enables him to state that Hobbes uses the wrong term when he describes the original state as one of war of all against all:

> War is decided, it is declared, ordered, prepared, institutionalized, made sacred, it is won, lost, concluded by treaty. War is a state of order, a classic state of lines and columns, maps and strategies, leaders and spectacle, it knows friends, enemies, neutrals, allies, it defines belligerence. . . . The primal state, the primitive state, before any contract, is a pre-ordered state, undecided, undeclared, unprepared for, not stabilized in institutions. No, it is not war, it is *noise*, no, it is not war, it is the multitude in a fury. (*G, 83*)

War and its attendant noises therefore do not provide Serres with a model to think about multiplicity. In Serres, it is much rather the crowd, "the multitude in a fury," that becomes, like Lucretius's clinamen, a trope for multiplicity beyond the historical specificity of the Roman mob: "The *turba* of Lucretius, a stormy mass of diverse elements in disorder, given over to shocks, to impacts, to the fray, a chaos given over to jostling, is a crowd, is a mob" (*G, 100*). Serres celebrates the fury and the noise of the crowd as an originary moment: "Background noise is the first object of metaphysics, the *noise* of the crowd is the first object of anthropology. The background noise made by the crowd is the first object of history" (*G, 54*).

The patrician Adams, on the other hand, remains detached not only from the carnage of war, but also from the noise of the crowd. The great temporal gap in the *Education* between 1871 and 1892 not only eclipses his wife's suicide in 1885,[31] but also extremely violent labor conflicts in 1876–77 and 1885–86.[32] *The Education* remains conspicuously silent on these noisy events. Even crowds of a more congenial nature are anathema to him. During his stay in London, Adams remains as far away from the madding crowd as possible: "He never felt himself in society, and he never knew definitely what was meant as society by those who were in it" (190). As a matter of principle, an Adams does not immerse himself in the noises of the multitude but remains detached and aloof from "the plainness of the crowd" (194).

In Serres, the crowd is always also a linguistic multitude, and the archetypal situation this many-tongued crowd evolves from is of course the story of the tower of Babel. In his reflections on Babel, we find the most striking of Serres's figural reinscriptions. As Aleida Assmann points out, Babel has become a signifier for the loss of an originary unity, the loss, that is, of an original language shared by all of humankind.[33] Before Babel, the one: "And the whole earth was of one language, and of one speech" (Gen. 11:1). As Assmann goes on to explain, Babel has traditionally been interpreted in terms of human hubris and sin, a fact that relates closely to the values Christian religion attaches to unity and multiplicity respectively: "You will find that wherever you encounter in Scripture terms like plurality, chasm, division, dissonance or the like, they are evaluated as evil [*kakias*]. Where you meet unity and unanimousness, however, such terms are synonymous with goodness [*aretes*]."[34]

This value-laden discourse on Babel informs literary works ranging from the realist to the postmodernist period (and probably beyond, in both directions). Adams's evocation of Babel in *The Education* is no exception. While not implying religious notions of sin, Babel in Adams gestures toward a decidedly undesirable state of affairs, namely the confusing multiplicity of ideas and exhibits he encounters at the 1893 Chicago World Exhibition: "[S]ince Noah's Ark, no such Babel of loose and ill-joined, such vague and ill-defined and unrelated thoughts and half-thoughts and experimental outcries as the Exposition, had ever ruffled the surface of the Lakes" (324). It is no coincidence that it is also here, at the exhibition, where Adams first encounters the dynamo, which would later, in the context of the 1900 Paris World Fair, become his symbol for twentieth-century multiplicity.[35]

Contrary to Adams, Serres inscribes Babel not as a site of loss (of unity, of an originary language), but celebrates it as a redemptive moment of multiplicity. In Serres, Babel becomes a trope for the collapse of a rationalist edifice of ideas that is closed in upon itself, immune to change, and that only speaks the language of death: "Babel is not a failure, it is at that very moment when the tower is dismantled that we begin to understand that one must understand without concepts. . . . Babel is an unintegrable multiplicity, a sort of intermittent aggregate, not closed upon its unity" (*G*, 123). As in his reading of Lucretius, Serres's thinking on Babel attempts to reappropriate something of that which has been buried beneath centuries of readings linking Babel to a discourse of (lost) unity. In Babel, Serres finds a possible countermodel to Leibniz's *Theodicy,* that most perfect edifice of rationalist thought. Again invoking the image of the pyramid, Serres asks, "Could the tower of Babel, uncrowned above by the haze of languages, be the very pyramid of the *Theodicy,* upside-down?" (*G*, 128). In his celebration of Babel, Serres disassociates himself from the erection of Leibnizian edifices of reason, for he is convinced that "we shall inhabit the great pyramid only when we are dead" (*G*, 126).

Like Serres's *Genesis,* the text of *The Education* time and again registers an awareness of the violence inherent in the imposition of unity: "True, the church alone has asserted unity with any conviction, and the historian alone knew what oceans of blood and treasure the assertion had cost" (408). But, contrary to Serres, this insight does not distract Adams from the steady pursuit of that unity. As he writes in the wake of the Civil War, "Law should be Evolution from lower to higher, aggregation of the atom in the mass, concentration of multiplicity in unity, compulsion of anarchy in order; and he would force himself to follow wherever it led, though he should sacrifice five thousand millions more in money, and a million more lives" (224). Even though he begins to understand that it is ultimately doomed to failure in a time of fully fledged multiplicity, Adams never abandons his quest for unity. Toward the end of his book and shortly after his evocation of Lucretius's Venus, Adams still maintains, "He [man] sacrificed millions of lives to acquire his unity, but he achieved it, and justly thought it a work of art" (434).[36]

As it turns out, it is precisely Adams's recognition of failure that must appear as a redemptive gesture. As Adams repeatedly insists, *The Education* reports a failure, "the shifting search for the education he never found" (180), an endeavor that leaves him "alone and uneducated" (340) at the age of sixty:

> All one's life one had struggled for unity, and unity had always won. The National Government and the national unity had overcome every resistance, and the Darwinian evolutionists were triumphant over all the curates; yet the greater the unity and the momentum, the worse became the complexity and the friction. One had in vain bowed one's neck to railways, banks, corporations, trusts, and even to the popular will as far as one could understand it—or even further—the multiplicity of unity had steadily increased, was increasing, and threatened to increase beyond reason. (377)

Many readers have been baffled and some shocked by the persistent sense of failure and futility characterizing the text of a progeny of the finest of all American families.[37] But as readers of Serres, we are aware of the violence that inheres in the move from multiplicity to unity and must therefore read Adams's admission of failure—particularly in the light of his own reflections on unity and violence—as a, however reluctant, step in the right direction. Henry Adams's resigned admission that "order was an accidental relation obnoxious to nature" (433) foreshadows Michel Serres's conviction that "[t]he multiple as such . . . is not an epistemological monster, but on the contrary the ordinary lot of situations" (*G, 5*). What Adams perceives as failure is what "chaos" theorists Prigogine and Stengers celebrate as a liberation from deterministic and reductionist conceptions of science. But what they found was essentially the same thing. Prigogine and Stengers's account of their encounters with multiplicity and chaos in *Order Out of Chaos* (1984) would suit Adams's voice equally well: "We were seeking general, all-embracing schemes that could be expressed in terms of 'eternal laws' but we have found time, events, evolving particles."[38]

It would therefore be too facile to reduce Adams's position to that of a nostalgic longing for unity. What distinguishes the historian Adams from a conservative historian like Arthur M. Schlesinger Jr. is not only his recognition that processes of unification are inherently violent, but also his admission of the failure of unity in the face of multiplicity. Even though the tropological spaces of Adams and Schlesinger converge in their negative inscription of Babel, the tone of Schlesinger's diatribe against multicultural politics in *The Disuniting of America* (1991) is far more nostalgic and disturbingly self-assured than anything we find in *The Education:* "The national ideal had once been *e pluribus unum.* Are we now to belittle *unum* and glorify *pluribus*? Will the center hold? or will the melting pot yield to the Tower of Babel?"[39] While Adams is certainly far from a Serrean celebration of multiplicity and would have been bewildered by Jay Clayton's manifesto for multiplicity and multiculturalism in *The Pleasures of Babel*,[40] a Serrean rereading of Adams allows us to tease out the redemptive moments in his argument. Reading Adams through Serres enables us to see Adams's exploration of an evolving "multiverse" (433) at the turn of the century as a first, hesitant and reluctant step toward Serres's headlong plunge into the rich world of what he calls the "diverse" (*G,* 111).

NOTES

1. The seminal text on soundscape studies is Murray R. Schafer, *The Tuning of the World* (New York: Knopf, 1977). Bruce R. Smith expands on the concept of the "soundscape" in *The Acoustic World of Early Modern England: Attending to the O-Factor* (Chicago: University of Chicago Press, 1999), where he defines it as an ecological system that includes all the sounds, human as well as nonhuman, the members of a given community may hear (44–48).

2. Theodore Dreiser, *Sister Carrie,* ed. James L. W. West III (London: Penguin, 1995), 4.

3. Frank Norris, *McTeague: A Story of San Francisco* (London: Penguin, 1994), 423.

4. Ibid., 380.

5. Henry Adams, *The Education of Henry Adams,* ed. Jean Gooder (London: Penguin, 1995). Subsequent references are given in the text. Even though Henry Adams insists that his text should be read as a treatise on education rather than an autobiography (8) and even though the subtitle "An Autobiography" was added for commercial reasons and against Adams's express wishes (Edward Chalfant, "Lies, Silence,

and Truth in the Writings of Henry Adams," in *Henry Adams and His World,* ed. David R. Contosta and Robert Muccigrosso [Philadelphia: American Philosophical Society, 1993], 20–22), *The Education* is a highly autobiographical text that cannot ultimately be disengaged from its author's life, the elevated social status of which goes a long way toward explaining the continuing appeal of the text.

6. Henry Adams's great-grandfather John Adams was the second president of the United States, his grandfather John Quincy Adams, the sixth. For an account of Adams's life and family history, see Ernest Samuels, *Henry Adams* (Cambridge: Harvard University Press, 1989).

7. Norris, *McTeague,* 250.

8. Ibid., 36.

9. Of course, Adams's choice is also historically the correct one, for the production of electricity enabled by the invention of the dynamo was the principle motor of the second wave of the Industrial Revolution in the second half of the nineteenth century, just as the invention of the steam engine had sparked off the first wave a century earlier. Manuel Castells, *The Rise of the Network Society* (Oxford: Blackwell, 1996), 38.

10. Henry Adams, "A Letter to American Teachers of History," in *The Degradation of the American Dogma* (New York: Capricorn, 1958), 133–259; Peter Freese, *From Apocalypse to Entropy and Beyond: The Second Law of Thermodynamics in Post-war American Fiction* (Essen: Die Blaue Eule, 1997), 105.

11. Freese, *From Apocalypse to Entropy,* 99–105.

12. This helps to explain an apparent contradiction in Adams's views on the nature of history. While he maintains that "[i]n essence incoherent and immoral, history had to be taught as such—or falsified" (287), he also stresses that "[h]istory had no use for multiplicity; it needed unity, it could study only motion, direction, attraction, relation. Everything must be made to move together" (359). What explains—though not quite defuses—the paradox is the fact that Adams is talking about historical events in the first passage and about historiography in the second. Historiography informed by the natural sciences is Adams's tool to impose unity on the irreducible multiplicity of history.

13. Titus Carus Lucretius, *On The Nature of the Universe,* trans. Sir Ronald Melville, with an introduction and explanatory notes by Don Fowler and Peta Fowler (Oxford: Clarendon Press, 1997), 1.1–7, 20–23. The Latin original is quoted in *The Education* on page 434.

14. M. Patin, "L'Anti-Lucrèce chez Lucrèce," in *Études sur la poésie latine,* vol. 1 (Paris: Librairie Hachette, 1868), 127.

15. Monica Gale, *Myth and Poetry in Lucretius* (Cambridge: Cambridge University Press, 1994), 1–2.

16. Abraham Cowley, "To the Royal Society," in *Poems of Abraham Cowley,* ed. A. R. Waller (Cambridge: Cambridge University Press, 1905), 140, 267. Cowley's familiarity with Lucretius's work is asserted by Arthur H. Nethercot, *Abraham Cowley: The Muse's Hannibal* (Oxford: Oxford University Press, 1931).

17. Lucretius, *Nature,* 1.62–73.

18. Cowley, *Poems,* 41–61.

19. Robert B. Hinman, who sees in Cowley "a kind of Christian Lucretius," like-

wise places Lucretius firmly in the rationalist camp: "*De Rerum Natura* draws upon the science of its day to describe a universe of order and law" (*Abraham Cowley's World of Order* [Cambridge: Harvard University Press, 1960], 32).

20. Lucretius, *Nature,* 2.216–225.

21. Warren F. Motte Jr., "Clinamen Redux," *Comparative Literature Studies* 23, no. 4 (1986): 263.

22. Michel Serres, *La Naissance de la physique dans le texte de Lucrèce: Fleuves et turbulences* (Paris: Minuit, 1977), and "Literature and the Exact Sciences," *SubStance* 18, no. 2 (1989): 3–34.

23. "Chaos theory" is actually a misnomer. Nonequilibrium thermodynamics as practiced by Prigogine and Stengers (1984) tries to trace the complex structures of order in what at first sight appears to be undifferentiated chaos. See David Porush, "Literature as Dissipative Structure: Prigogine's Theory and the Postmodern 'Chaos' Machine," in *Literature and Technology,* ed. Mark L. Greenberg and Lance Schachterle (London: Associated University Press, 1992), 289.

24. Ilya Prigogine and Isabelle Stengers, *Order Out of Chaos: Man's New Dialogue with Nature* (London: Heinemann, 1984), 141.

25. Maria L. Assad, "Michel Serres: In Search of a Tropography," in *Chaos and Order: Complex Dynamics in Literature and Science,* ed. Katherine N. Hayles (Chicago: University of Chicago Press, 1991), 291.

26. Serres, "Literature and Exact Sciences," 20.

27. Cowley, *Poems,* 109–16.

28. See also Aleida Assmann, who discusses the Christian idea of mission as an attempt to confer unity of faith in the face of linguistic and cultural multiplicity. Aleida Assmann, "The Curse and Blessing of Babel; or, Looking Back on Universalisms," in *The Translatability of Cultures: Figurations of the Space Between,* ed. Sanford Budick and Wolfgang Iser (Stanford: Stanford University Press, 1996), 89.

29. Assad, "Michel Serres," 278.

30. Ibid., 278, 294 n. 2.

31. Martha Banta, "Being a 'Begonia' in a Man's World," in *New Essays on "The Education of Henry Adams,"* ed. John Carlos Rowe (Cambridge: Cambridge University Press, 1996), 70–72.

32. Philip Jenkins, *A History of the United States* (London: Macmillan, 1997), 179–81.

33. Assmann, "Babel," 85.

34. Ibid., 88.

35. As has been argued above, Adams's attempts to come to grips with the bewildering multiplicity of modernity converge in his dynamic theory of history. In the biblical account, it is the miracle of Pentecost that reinstitutes (spiritual) unity without denying linguistic multiplicity (Assmann, "Babel," 86–90). Henry Adams's dynamic theory of history represents a secular version of this desire for unity in the face of multiplicity.

36. My reading of *The Education* therefore only partially agrees with John Carlos Rowe's in *Henry Adams and Henry James: The Emergence of a Modern Consciousness* (Ithaca, N.Y.: Cornell University Press 1976), which also registers Adams's failure but argues that Adams renounces his quest for unity in the second half of *The Educa-*

tion: "The general outlook of the *Education* repudiates Adams's own desire for historical coherence and suggests a tentative pluralism" (110). Rowe is certainly correct in likening Adams to the Lévi-Straussean *bricoleur,* who has to make do with what is available in a makeshift fashion, rather than the *engineer,* who authors his own designs (120–31), but Adams remains an extremely reluctant *bricoleur,* whose yearning for the role of engineer finds its most pronounced expression in his vision of a grand, unified, and unifying dynamic theory of history.

37. For a review of initial responses to Adams's *The Education,* see William Merrill Decker, *The Literary Vocation of Henry Adams* (Chapel Hill: University of North Carolina Press, 1990); and Samuels, *Henry Adams.*

38. Prigogine and Stengers, *Order,* 292.

39. Arthur M. Schlesinger Jr., *The Disuniting of America: Reflections on a Multicultural Society* (Knoxville: Whittle Direct, 1991), 2.

40. Jay Clayton, *The Pleasures of Babel: Contemporary American Literature and Theory* (Oxford: Oxford University Press, 1993).

MICHEL SERRES'S *LES CINQ SENS*

STEVEN CONNOR

Serres has spoken of his distaste for both the hermeneutics of critique and suspicion and the phenomenology of Heidegger and Merleau-Ponty, both of whom he finds risibly thin and bodiless. In his conversations with Bruno Latour, he suggests that *Les Cinq Sens*[1] actually had its origin in a kind of laughing revulsion from the emaciated nature of phenomenology:

> When I was young, I laughed a lot at Merleau-Ponty's *Phenomenology of Perception*. He opens it with these words: "At the outset of the study of perception, we find *in language the notion of sensation* . . ." Isn't this an exemplary introduction? A collection of examples in the same vein, so austere and meager, inspire the descriptions that follow. From his window the author sees some tree, always in bloom; he huddles over his desk; now and again a red blotch appears—it's a quote. What you can decipher in this book is a nice ethnology of city dwellers, who are hypertechnicalized, intellectualized, chained to their library chairs, and tragically stripped of any tangible experience. Lots of phenomenology and no sensation—everything via language . . . My book *Les cinq sens* cries out at the empire of signs. (*C*, 131–32)

Les Cinq Sens is part of the turn that Serres's work undertook during the 1980s from a certain kind of philosophically respectable and recognizable commentary to the work of invention, a work characterized by lightness, freedom, associativeness, caprice.

> There is a time for abstract science and then another one for things . . . the works of my youth . . . I henceforth find old, precisely because they are very learned or strictly under surveillance. Luckily, the more one writes, the younger one becomes. Finally, no more surveillance; finally, I can play truant—no more school at all. (*C*, 100)

Les Cinq Sens insists on the gymnastic possibility and need of the mind. It is the book in which Serres begins to stretch his limbs, to burst into flames, the book in which he first makes his scandalous approach to things. In it he declares that the world exists.

Les Cinq Sens marks a significant point in Serres's writing, but in marking a break, a breakout, an exit or an inclination, a rift in the fabric of Serres's work, it also folds itself back into that fabric, leading everywhere into it. A work that, we have begun to become accustomed to recognizing, consists of little else but these salutations, these leaps of faith, intuition, or inclination. After *Les Cinq Sens,* Serres's work would never be quite the same: "never the same after that never quite the same but that was nothing new . . . never the same but the same as what for God's sake," as we read in Beckett's *That Time.*[2] "Everything that you do is 'in the midst,'" suggests Bruno Latour to Serres, and wins his simple consent, glad, as it may be, or weary, in the words: "All right."

VEILS

No book on the senses can avoid evoking Condillac's famous, fabular statue, the thought-experiment at the beginning of the *Essay on the Faculties,* in which Condillac imagines a statue deprived, in turn, of every sense but one. But Condillac's statue, or the procedure that produces it, functions in Serres's text as a menace, or as a philosophical disgrace: it represents the threat of subtraction or abstraction, of analysis itself. Serres's aim is not to start with the statue and gradually to animate it, by draping it, one by one, in the separate senses, giving it interiority, movement. This action of clothing, one might imagine, is the exact equivalent of Descartes's sensory striptease, the action of systematic doubt in which he attempts to strip away from reason all the gorgeous, questionable habiliments of the senses, stripping away indeed the flesh itself, and then the bones, leaving finally, exposed to its own view, exposure itself, self-exposure itself.

In fact the book begins with a parody of the Cartesian question: where is the soul? Serres's answer is that the soul is not to be located in one solitary and invariant quasi position in the body, the pineal gland, but rather in the contingencies of the body with itself, and with its environment. The soul of the pilot of a ship extends coenesthetically into the whole of his vessel, just as the driver parking a car feels his fingertips extending all the way to his front bumper, and the amputee continues to occupy the empty space of their severed limb.

The soul is to be found also in the way in which the self touches itself.

I touch one lip with my middle finger. Consciousness dwells in this contact. I start to explore it. Often consciousness conceals itself in folds, lip resting on lip, palate closed on tongue, teeth against teeth, eyelids lowered, tightened sphincter, the hand closed into a fist, fingers pressed against each other, the rear surface of one thigh crossed on the front face of the other, or one foot resting on the other. I bet that the homunculus, tiny and monstrous, of which each part is proportional to the magnitude of sensation, swells in those automorphic places, when the skin tissue folds upon itself. By itself, the skin takes on consciousness. . . . Without this folding over, this contact of the self with itself, there would be no internal sense, no body of one's own, or even less coenesthesia, no body image, we would live without consciousness, featureless, on the point of vanishing. (*CS,* 20)

Commentators on the skin, such as Didier Anzieu, have frequently observed its duality, which allows us both to touch and be touched at once. But, for Serres, this self-touching is never merely symmetrical. At every touching of oneself, every contingence, soul or consciousness crowds disproportionately on one side or other of the transaction, and is relatively absent from the other. When I cut my fingernails, I am more in my right hand than in my left; but you cannot touch your hand with your shoulder, no matter which hand is in question (though another person's shoulder can touch your hand). Serres returns to this question in *Le Tiers-instruit* in 1991 (everything in Serres's writing crosses its own path sooner or later). There he argues that the world is sensible because it lists, because it has orientation or laterality; everything has a left hand or a right hand, leans in certain directions, pulled into shape, gait, or posture by gravity or conductivity or impulse, or lack or habit. There is no such thing as balanced indifference. There is no center or axis; it cannot be found, or is absent. Orientation can thus be said to be originary, invariable, irreducible, so constantly physical that it becomes metaphysical (*TK,* 15).

This means that all of us are lopsided, hemiplegic, carrying around with us a Siamese twin, an intimate stranger, who is and yet is not of our flesh. The condition of anosognosia, first described by Joseph Babinski in 1908, in which a patient denies ownership of a paralyzed limb or other portion of the body, is only the intensification of this split condition. Everything on our left is a not-self. But, in this sense, our sinister self, our gaucheness, is distributed unequally and intermittently across different portions of the body. Whether "self" resides, or is touched off, is our right hand, that which actively touches, and is therefore white, or transparent; wherever "not-self" or less-than-self, that which is touched, which cannot touch back (the shoulder, the foot) is found, is black, alien.

But these relations, though formalizable as a black-and-white dichotomy, in fact are mobile. For one thing, we have more than two hands. To some degree, whenever we touch, we grow a temporary hand. V. S. Ramachandran reported a neurological correlative for this effect in patients whose hands had been amputated but who reported intense sensation in their missing hands when their faces and upper arms were stroked. The reason for this seems to be the proximity of hands and face on the sensory map draped over the surface of the cerebellum, which allows a vacated or inactive area of hand sensation in the brain to be colonized by neighboring areas (the proximity of genitals and feet on the map accounts for the orgasmic sensations in the feet experienced during sex by those with leg amputations).[3]

Just as the map on the cerebellum is being shown to be much more plastic and revisable than we ever thought, so we are continually rewriting the map of inner and outer, self and not-self, on the surface of our skins. In *Genesis,* published in 1982, Serres had evoked the gymnastic condition of the body-become-hand as the image of a kind of blankness, an indetermination, and thus readiness to be absorbed in thought, contemplation, or experience; like the body of the dancer, like the thought of the inventive rather than merely critical thinker, the hand is a flight of forms from possible to possible:

> The hand is no longer a hand when it has taken hold of the hammer, it is the hand itself, it is no longer a hammer, it flies transparent, between the hammer and the nail, it disappears and dissolves, my own hand has long since taken flight in writing. The hand and thought, like one's tongue, disappear in their determinations.
>
> . . . Inventive thinking is unstable, it is undetermined, it is un-differentiated, it is as little singular in its function as is our hand. The latter can make itself into a pincer, it can be fist and hammer, cupped palm and goblet, tentacle and suction cup, claw and soft touch. So what is a hand? It is not an organ, it is a faculty, a capacity for doing, for becoming claw or paw, weapon or compendium. It is a naked faculty. A faculty is not special, it is never specific, it is the possibility of doing something in general. To talk about the faculties of the soul is a great misnomer, when we are differentiating between them: the soul is also a naked faculty. It is nakedness. We live by bare hands. Our hands are that nakedness I find in gymnastics, that pure faculty, cleared up by exercise, by the asceticism of un-differentiation. I think, un-differentiated. Thus I am anyone, animal, element, stone or wind, number, you and him, us. Nothing. Nobody. Blank. Bare. (*G,* 30, 34–35)

In *Les Cinq Sens,* the white or blank hand or body gives way to a more variegated form. Now, the soul is inscribed in the coming and going of subjectivity on the surface of the skin as the residue of its contingencies, the play of light and shadow, of the whiteness of subjectivity and the shade of objectivity.

> It remains to draw or paint. Isolate if possible, the secret little zones where the soul is always in residence, the corners or folds of contingency, isolate too, if possible the unstable zones where the soul knows how to play with another as though with a ball, mark out the spheres and slabs which become subjects only when face to face with objects, the dense and compact regions which remain objects always, alone or facing those which objectify them, deserts lacking in soul, black; this drawing rarely marks off compact zones, for these explode, fuse and flee in narrow strips of colour, forming hills, chimneys, passages, corridors, flames, zigzags and labyrinths, look at the changeable, wavelike and fugitive soul on the skin, on the surface, streaked, crowded, tiger-striped, zebra-striped, barred, troubled, constellated, gorgeous, torrential, and turbulent, incendiary. (*G,* 20)

Serres himself is what he calls a corrected, or completed left-hander, a natural left-hander who was compelled to write with his right hand. The result is the condition of the bicameral chimera or hermaphrodite, the one who can cross to the other side of himself, who can write two-handed (*TK,* 17–20). But this chimera-like condition can belong to us all. The crossing of the left hand and the right hand in the individual body is the condition for the meeting of the body and the world.

Skin is central to the "philosophy of mingled bodies" that Serres inaugurates here because of the principle of contingence:

> In the skin, through the skin, the world and the body touch, defining their common border. Contingency means mutual touching: world and body meet and caress in the skin. I do not like to speak of the place where my body exists as a milieu, preferring rather to say that things mingle among themselves and that I am no exception to this, that I mingle with the world that mingles itself in me. The skin intervenes in the things of the world and brings about their mingling. (*CS,* 97)

The skin and touch signify, finally, for Serres, a way of being amid rather than standing before the world, and are necessary for knowledge. Knowledge, which has previously and traditionally thought of itself as an unveiling or stripping bare, is offered here as a kind of efflorescence, an exploration amid veils, a threading together of tissues. "Tissue, textile, and fabric provide excellent models of knowledge, excellent quasi-abstract objects, primal varieties: the world is a mass of laundry" (*CS,* 100–101). Serres dreams of a one-to-one map of the world, reproducing all its fractal singularity, that would be its skin, in what he calls a "cosmic dream of an exquisite cosmetic on the skin of each thing" (*CS*, 36). For Serres, the cosmic and the cosmetic remain in intimate communication with each other: nothing is deeper than adornment.

We thus encounter what will be something like a principle of functioning of *Les Cinq Sens;* the effort to separate the senses out, displaying them adjacent to each other, like countries on a map, plan, or table of correspondences, will be gently and repeatedly precluded by the requirement to knot them together. It will emerge that each sense is in fact a nodal cluster, a clump, confection, or bouquet of all the other senses, a mingling of the modalities of mingling. Thus, in "Voiles," we hear of a sequence of six allegorical tapestries from the Chateau de Boussac in the Musée de Cluny known collectively as the *Lady with the Unicorn*. These tapestries depict the different senses in turn. There are six and not five of them since medieval philosophy decrees the existence of a sixth, unifying or common sense, the sense of selfhood, whereby the self apprehends itself as itself. This Serres identifies with the skin and the faculty of touch: the skin, he says, "carries the message of Hermes." Where topography is visual, "topology is tactile" (*CS*, 99). The skin encompasses, implies, pockets up all the other sense organs: but, in doing so, it stands as a model for the way in which all the senses in their turn also invaginate all the others.

BOXES

The second chapter, "Boîtes," concerns sound and hearing, sometimes thought of as the most libertine and promiscuously sociable of the senses. And yet in this chapter are to be found some of the most ill-tempered and unsociable things that Michel Serres has ever written. The setting or frame for the chapter is the ruined theater of Epidaurus, in which Serres sits in the early morning, seeking in its gathered silence a cure from the racket, not only of human noise, the immense exchange of communications, but also the interior noise of the body, its incessant exchange of messages to itself.

Surprisingly, the theater of Epidaurus, having the form of an immense ear or auditory pavilion marked out in the ground, visible from space, funneling sound to its center, comes to be a sinister image for Serres. He compares it to another remarkable theater at Pinara, in which an amphitheater opens onto a cliff occupied by the dead, buried standing up.

Hearing is understood in this chapter, in which the duality promised in the French word *entendre* is powerfully at work, in terms of a work of transformation. Hearing takes what Serres calls the hard, *le dur,* and converts it into information, *le doux,* or the soft (*CS*, 141–49). This exchange is effected by the senses, or by the work of sensation, which, in turning raw stimulus into sensory information, also makes sense of the senses, effecting a slight declination, or deflection within the word *sens* itself: sense becomes sense. These transformations are effected in every organism by a series of processes of transformation that Serres is wont to call "black boxes." By this be means processes whose initial conditions are known and whose outcomes are known, but whose actual processes of transformation remain inaccessible to view or understanding.

Performing the work of many black boxes, each receiving and reinte- grating the output from other black boxes, we are all of us therefore in the condition of Orpheus, who takes the inchoate cries and howls of the nat- ural world and turns them into music. But music, for Serres, is not the simple, once-and-for-all transformation of noise into information, of the natural into the cultural. Rather it is the looping, labyrinthine interchange of the hard and the soft. The labyrinth of the ear, with its complex invagi- nations of inner and outer, represents not a single diaphragm, or site of one-way transmission, but a complex, one might say fractal, landscape of transformations and recursions, which itself transmits as well as receives. Uncoil the cochlea, Serres suggests, and one finds a kind of piano, sound- ing out high and low frequencies: the ear receives vibrations, says Serres, but also broadcasts them, to a sensory apparatus, or third ear, which must in turn receive and integrate them (*CS,* 183). The ear is no more to be located in one place than the skin. For Serres, the body itself is caught up in a process of hearing, which implicates skin, bone, skull, feet, and mus- cle. Just when we thought hearing was going to be put in its place, Serres evokes its own mingled or implicated nature. Just as the ear consists in part of a skin, so the skin itself is a kind of ear, which both excludes and trans- mits exterior vibrations:

At the beginning, the whole body or organism raises up a sculpture or statue of tense skin, vibrating amid voluminous sound, open-closed like a box (or drum), capturing that by which it is captured. We hear by means of the skin and the feet. We hear with the cranial box, the abdomen, and the thorax. We hear by means of the muscles, nerves, and tendons. Our body-box, stretched with strings, veils itself within a global tympanum. We live amid sounds and cries, amid waves rather than spaces the organism molds and indents itself. . . . I am a house of sound, hearing and voice at once, black box and sounding board, ham- mer and anvil, a grotto of echoes, a musicassette, the ear's pavilion, a question mark, wandering in the space of messages filled or stripped of sense. . . . I am the resonance and the tone, I am altogether the mingling of the tone and its resonance. (*CS,* 180–81)

It is necessary for the body to form and retain itself in its complex and always transitory entirety, like the red spot on Jupiter, or the weather sys- tem formed out of pure movement, like the whorl of the ear itself, if it is not to be subjected to one of two fates: violent dissolution by and into pure materiality on the one hand, or rarefaction into the softness of information on the other. These two alternatives are embodied mythically for Serres in the persons of Orpheus and Eurydice. Orpheus, the originator of music, is finally torn apart, subjected to auditory extinction, in the *sparagmos* or dismembering effected by the howling Bacchantes. For Serres, analysis of this final moment of the Orpheus myth is supererogatory, since it represents the mutilating or dissective work of analysis itself, which leaves Orpheus a mere talking or singing head (*CS*, 173). Eurydice, on the other hand, is spectralized by the excess of information: for Serres, she is the body captured by language, and thereby rendered so soft and nebulous as to be no more than a shade, or a name. Between the two, in the musical condition of transition, there is the body, not an object, but a work of sensation, neither shade nor dismembered corpse, but a complex knot, niche, or enclave within flux. Orpheus, singing the name of Eurydice, attempts to harden or substantiate her form, bequeathing to death her numbness, redeeming her from the muteness of mere language into speaking embodiment.

The raising of Eurydice by Orpheus is precisely the work of cure and remaking that Serres sets out to effect in this work. Orpheus invokes: raises with the voice the body into speaking substance. It is important to distinguish Orpheus, who risks and eventually loses, from Ulysses, who is exposed to the disintegrative power of sound, but keeps himself immune from it, by binding himself to the mast, and thus wins. Orpheus visits the underworld, and loses: *visit* is a word that will become important later in *Les Cinq Sens*.

There are three kinds of hearing offered in this chapter. There is first of all proprioncentric hearing, the hearing of oneself, the gurgling of the viscera, the cracking of the bones, the thudding and pulsing of the blood, even the firing of the neurons, to which all of us are continuously exposed and that for most of the time, unless we are subjected to the rending tortures of tinnitus, we integrate unconsciously without effort. Then there is the hearing that constitutes the social contract: the blaring bedlam of the exchange of noise and signals, signals and noise. In fact, the first is the model for the second. In both of these cases, hearing attempts to close itself upon itself, in a circuit of self-hearing, tightening the coil of the ear. There is the hearing of oneself that forms the model increasingly for all communication: "We can neither speak nor sing without the feedback loop that ensures that we hear our own voices" (*CS*, 140). This is autistic acoustics, a hearing deafened by itself.

But there is also the hearing that puts one apart from oneself, the hearing that doubles or remakes the body, just as the hand extends and exceeds itself and the body to which it belongs and which it is.

> The I thinks only when it is beside itself. It feels really only when it is
> beside itself. The linguistic I is shrunk down to the large memory of lan-
> guage, the indefinite integral of others, the closure of its open group,
> freezing itself in habit. . . . I only really live beside myself; beside myself
> I think, meditate, know, beside myself I receive the given, vivacious, I
> invent beside myself. I exist beside myself, like the world. I am on the
> side of the world beside my talkative flesh.
>
> The ear knows this space. I can put the ear on the other side of the
> window, projecting it great distances, holding it at a great distance from
> the body.
>
> Lost, dissolved in the transparent air, fluctuating with its nuances,
> sensible of its smallest comas, shivering at the least derision, set free,
> mingled with the shocks of the world, I exist. (*CS*, 119)

This kind of exposed hearing, which breaks the circuit of hearing oneself,
constitutes the third form of audibility:

> In myriads, things cry out. Often deaf to alien emissions, hearing is
> astonished by that which cries out without a name in no language. The
> third cycle, initiated by the rarest of hearing, and which requires that
> one be deaf both to oneself and to the group, requires an interruption of
> the closed cycles of consciousness and the social contract, may already
> be called knowledge. (*CS*, 141)

There is no question of merely opening oneself to the inhuman, or the
natural, of bypassing the black box, not least because the exposure to
things in themselves is what forms the black box. (The senses are in things,
are in the self-sensing of things.) Our house of experience, which includes
not just each individual body, but also what Serres calls the "orthopedic
sensorium" (*CS*, 190) of our social structures, must remain sufficiently
open, the social ear sufficiently labyrinthine to allow the capture of the
unintegrated, or the disintegrative, and the rapture of the ear by what
forms and deforms it.

Hearing is finally the unlocalizable mediation, or labyrinthine knotting
together of these two kinds of process, or the two sides of the black box,
exposure and integration.

TABLES

Tables begins with a bottle of wine, a bottle of 1947 Yquem, shared with a
friend. This wine will flow throughout the rest of the chapter that follows
it, a chapter that is concerned to evoke and celebrate the most despised,
the least aesthetic of the senses, taste and smell combined. It is perhaps
unsurprising that Serres finds these senses the most refractory to, and
therefore the most despised by, language. French, Serres observes, has no

word, other than the specialized *anosmia,* for the lack of taste. The absence of the very word for the absence of taste redoubles, redoubles the authority of the language that has no need even to mark this deficiency (*CS,* 254). Taste and smell open what Serres calls the "second mouth," the mouth displaced and overtaken by the first, golden mouth, the *chrysostomos,* of language. This second mouth is characterized by gift, grace, dispensation, opening rather than accumulation. Smell and taste differentiate; though what they differentiate is always itself composite.

Odor is spirit, the work of transformation, or transubstantiation, which Serres prefers to read through the action of cooking rather than alchemy, therefore not as refinement or purification, but as the work of combination or alloying of substance.

Serres conjures up a grotesque primal scene, a mingling of different philosophical banquets that include Plato's Symposium, the Last Supper, and the banquet of *Don Giovanni.* In it, the petrified, linguistic body, reduced to the condition of a statue or robot or automaton, is no longer able to smell or taste. The statue, or mobile talking head, its limbs creaking, its tongue and nostrils parched with dialectic, dines off the menu: the women who do the cooking off-scene, also do the eating. But opposed to the statue is the body of Christ. The incarnational metaphor has two sides for Serres. Considered in its perfected form, the body of the Assumption, the raised or resurrected body, stands for the Word-Made-Flesh and the Flesh-Made-Word of the annunciation—in other words, the statue. "When it is saturated by the word, the body loses its antique graces: [grace] flees the body when the word becomes flesh."

Set against the body of the Assumption, the body raised up into language, is the body consumed at the Last Supper. This body, which circulates in the form of bread and wine, is not a fixed, but a mobile transubstantiation. It signifies the grace or gratuitousness or givenness of what Serres calls "le donné." The world abounds: "le monde abonde." How, Serres enquires, can the eye requite the sun for its light, how can the palate repay the vine? Set against the classical table of correspondences or equivalences, language as restricted economy, there is the table at which eating and drinking take place, which exceeds this economy, Serres claims. Smell and taste are apt carriers of this transformative mobility, this metabolic circulation of elements that transform as they circulate. Smell and taste, themselves an irreducible composite, form the body as what Serres beautifully calls a "bouquet of vicariances."

VISIT

It seems clear enough from the first three chapters how the book is going to be structured. They deal, in turn, and in series, with skin and touch;

with hearing; and with taste and smell conjoined. Between the third and fourth chapters of the book, something happens, a kind of lurch, or swerve, an inclination, or clinamen, in Lucretius's term. In one sense, things seem to be going too fast: there are two chapters left, and only one sense remains to be dealt with, that of sight. But there is also a slowing down: for in fact we wait in vain for an exposition of sight in either of the two last chapters, or not in any daylit, head-on kind of way. Neither chapter completes the formation of the homunculus undertaken through the other chapters.

In fact, vision has appeared throughout *Les Cinq Sens* as a negative reference point for the other senses. Where the other senses give us the mingled body, vision appears on the side of detachment, separation. Vision is a kind of dead zone, as the petrifying sense, the non-sense, which it is the role of the other senses to make good or redeem. Thus, we hear of the work of vision undertaken by Pierre Bonnard in paintings such as the *Nude in the Mirror* and *The Garden* in the chapter "Voiles":

> The eye loses its preeminence in the very domain of its dominance, painting. At its extremity, impressionism returns to its really originary sense, that of contact. The nude, ocellated like a peacock, recalls us to the weight and pressure of things, to the heaviness of the column of air above us and its variations. (*CS,* 35)

However, vision itself is at length redeemed in the chapter entitled "Visite." This chapter is concerned, to all appearances, not with looking, but with voyaging. In other words, Serres seems in this chapter to be deflecting the French *sens*—sense—into another direction, in fact, into direction, itself.

The sensible for Serres, means the changeable, that which is capable at any moment of a change of direction:

> Sensible has a sense comparable to that of adjectives with the same termination. It reveals the always-possible change of direction. The magnetized needle thus enacts sensibility. At the minute and ubiquitous solicitations of quality, dimension and intensity, sensibility trembles, fluctuates and scans with dancing excursions the spaces through which it is showered and summoned by things, by the world, and by others . . . Open like a star, or quasi-closed, like a knot to all directions, mobile in every dimension and scanning everywhere, sensibility gives itself, indefatigably, to this dancing excursion, a functional intersection until the very hour of its death. (*CS,* 404–5)

It is this that allows vision to make its appearance, or to speak its appearance, but obliquely, in the word *visit.* "The noun *visit* and the verb *to visit* mean at first looking and seeing; they add to it the idea of itinerary—the one who visits, *goes to see*" (*CS,* 334). Visiting is, so to speak, vectorial vision, itinerant or excursive vision, vision on the move.

> In general, the bearer of the look, in traditional philosophy, does not move: it sits down to look, through a window at the blossoming tree: a statue posed on affirmations and theses. But we see things rarely in a condition of arrest, our ecological niche incorporates innumerable movements. . . . The earth turns, our global position of vigil lost its stability long ago, even the sun, the giver of light, is in motion, en route to some other part of the universe. (*CS,* 405)

Looking as visiting is therefore the sense that involves deflection, displacement, and gathers into itself the redirection or deflective nature of all sense experience:

> Displacements for the purpose of seeing borrow pathways, crossings, intersections, in order that scrutiny may focus on the detail or pass into a global synthesis: changes of scale, sense, and direction. The sensible, in general, holds together all senses, all directions, like a knot or general intersection. . . . Visitation explores and details all the senses of the sensible implicated or compacted in its knot. How could one see the compacted capacity of the senses if one separates them? We have visited this capacity without dissociating the senses of the word *visit.* (*CS,* 406)

Visiting the senses, in the way that this book attempts to do, partakes of the action of the senses themselves, as they visit the world, in actions of excursion, or self-exceeding:

> Spirit sees, language sees, the body visits. It always exceeds its site, by displacement. The subject sees, the body visits, surpasses its own position, goes out from its role or word. . . . The body goes out from the body in all senses [*dans tous les sens*], the sensible knots up this knot, the sensible in which the body never persists in the same plane or content but plunges and lives in a perpetual exchange, turbulence, whirlwind, circumstance. The body exceeds the body, the I surpasses the I, identity delivers itself from belonging at every instant, I sense therefore I pass, chameleon, in a variegated multiplicity, become half-caste, quadroon, mulatto, octoroon, hybrid . . .
>
> We have visited the complicity of the given. (*CS,* 408–9)

JOY

The final chapter offers us yet another candidate for the sixth or common sense: this is the sense of bodily joy, or ecstasy. Here, Serres evokes astonishingly the seraphic pleasures of self-exceeding, to be found, for example, in the pleasures of swimming, of running, in the human fascination with the trampoline, or in the playing of rugby. Here, the body becomes itself in playing with, or transforming itself.

The body is the site of the nonsite: a teeming plurality that overruns and overrules every vicious and narrow dichotomy; but this is guaranteed by the most implacably dichotomous way of arguing that is imaginable. On one side language, science, and corporate rationality: on the other side the life of the body. On the one side the global, on the other, the play of locality. On the one side, the statue; on the other, the veil, the visit.

This book derives its demand and its joy from its refusal of language, its delirious flight beyond, or recoil backward from language. Language, we hear time and again, makes one into a statue, identified variously with the statue of Don Giovanni, with Condillac's senseless statue. It petrifies one's skin, it empties one's mouth of taste, it occupies the body.

> We have lost hopelessly the memory of a world heard, seen, perceived, experienced joyfully by a body naked of language. This forgotten, unknown animal has become speaking man, and the word has petrified his flesh, not merely his collective flesh of exchange, perception, custom, and power, but also and above all his corporeal flesh: thighs, feet, chest, and throat vibrate, dense with words. (*CS,* 455)

But Serres also comes bizarrely to depend upon a reified or statuary idea of language itself. Language abstracts, makes the things of the world insubstantial; it alienates us from sensation. Language, in the memorable metaphor that Serres supplies in the closing pages of the book, is like a vast sea in which the things of the world have been irretrievably drowned, like an Atlantis or *Titanic.* But this metaphor, which insists on language's inundation, on the deathliness or petrifaction of the living, joyful body effected by language, itself enforces such a petrifaction in its own monochromatic or reifying view of language. Language is here an essential, absolutely homogeneous principle: its nature and effects universal and unvarying. Like the ocean, language is all one thing as far as the eye can see and deeper than did ever plummet sound. Discourse is deluge; it is itself deluged in homogeneity.

Serres's own language denies in its use what his language maintains, namely the emptiness, abstraction, and rigor mortis of language. Language, for Serres, is nothing less, nor anything else, than logos (*technology,* Serres says in *Angels,* is *techne* become *logos,* just as *phenomenology* signifies appearance that speaks itself, which becomes the speaking of itself [*A,* 71]). But Serres's language is always more, and other, then this. It is a language full of device and address, brimming with undigested material, spiky with the kind of hardness that Serres finds in music. His is the effort to incarnate, with the very language that he insists is toxic or paralyzing. "Yes, I have lost my Eurydice: I want to create a body present here and now, but I have only pure abstraction, this vocal emission, soft: Eurydice, Eurydice, I wanted so much to give you life and all I could write was philosophy" (*A*, 171). It is possible, it insists against the current of what Serres insists, pushing upstream against the flow that converts the hard into the soft, for language as music, to remain open to the unintegrated: language can be a kind of tympanum between the human world of linguistic *addiction* and the world of the given, the *donné,* which can take the impress of the hardness of things (the howling of animals, the breaking of stones), even as it transmits and translates them.

In the end, the body is not merely the body: not mere mass, which must be subjected to a work of transformation, or analysis, or understanding. Despite the insistence upon incarnation, and the recurrence of Christian images of resurrection in the book (the book begins with a passage describing Serres's escape from a burning vessel that is a violent kind of parturition, and ends with the words "resurrection, or renaissance"), the body does not rise again in Serres's work. This is because the body, or more particularly the senses, is never a mere object, but itself a kind of work. The body is the work of transforming mere sensitiveness into sense and sensibility both: the body is its work of transformation. There is no chance of getting back to the body, since it is the nature of the human body to be self-organizing and therefore self-surpassing. In the end, Serres's work is founded upon the unreachable continuity of this work as self-transformation and self-organization that the body conducts through sensation, and the work of organization undertaken by Serres's own writing about the body: the body forms itself, he writes, like a book. In folding sense over sense, translating flesh into word, Serres mimics and participates in the work of self-translation, self-complication, undertaken by sensation itself.

In the final section of the chapter entitled "Joy," Serres suddenly relaxes the severity of his denunciation of language. For our epoch, he says, is no longer the epoch of language. What dominates now are the code, the algorithm, information. Where language sought to fix and petrify its objects, distributing them in patterns of invariant conversion and exchange, information dissolves the object, by operationalizing it. The body that has become a series of genetic codes is no longer a linguistic body, but a source of production; no longer locked in place, but rather disseminated and multiplied. Language loses its three dimensions of power: the referential (taken over by science), the seductive (taken over by media and advertising), and the performative (taken over by the power of technoscience).

The era of the linguistic animal has come to a close. It is this death, or supersession of language that Serres wants to claim has made this book, this way of seizing the body in language, repeatedly said to be impossible, suddenly, though perhaps only for the time being, possible. *Les Cinq Sens,* says Serres, "celebrates the death of the word" (*CS, 455*). It is this death that makes possible, indeed imperative a new way of knowing. It seems to pardon language. Language has become redundant in the era of information and technoscience. This redundance, this ragged spectrality, makes possible a return to the primal adventure of philosophy, faced with and able to start out once again from the bottomless mystery of the givenness of things, now, and perhaps just for now, apprehensible otherwise than as the mere task or antagonist of the linguistic subject-protagonist: "Forgetful, detached, the subject plunges into the unforgettable world" (*CS, 461*), language is subsumed in the body's powers of self-invention. "Every time an organ—or a function—is freed from a previous obligation, it invents" (*CS, 460–61*), Serres observes: the hands, freed from the work of locomotion in *homo erectus,* occupy themselves in making tools; the mouth, freed from the need to grip and seize, invents speech. Freed from the function of naming, categorizing, and distributing, language-memory becomes available for a similar self-reinvention.

SANS

It seems incongruous that *Les Cinq Sens* should end with such an account of epochal loss and inauguration. For the book *Les Cinq Sens,* perhaps like the five senses themselves, seems to have no memory, no sense of temporal progression. Like so many other Serres texts, the time of the text forms a kind of climate, or weather system, shifting, recoiling, gathering, intensifying, diffusing: time, in French *temps,* as Serres frequently observes, is already available to be thought of as a kind of weather. Serres proposes no chronology of sense development, for example, as others working on these questions have sometimes been tempted to do. It is unclear whether or not the senses are merely before time—primordial, before reason, language, and the categories of linguistic time—or multitemporal, belonging to the crumpled or folded time, the temporal complexion, that Serres evokes in his discussions with Bruno Latour.

Serres celebrates abundance, increase, invention: the body is, repeatedly and in the end, the principle of propagation. Serres will have it no other way. The senses are the body forming and reforming itself. As such the body is a miraculous nook in the flux, a negentropic eddy or swirl in the current that traverses it yet which it delays.

Les Cinq Sens moves: in moving through its material, the senses, it also moves through itself. It begins and ends with this autocontingency, this self-touching, that faces outward and inward, backward and forward, at the same time. In doing so, it disobeys the fundamental law of time, the law of entropy or going out. Its vitalism refuses limit, suffering, degradation, exhaustion. In the celebration of grace, gratuity, giving, expenditure, and abundance over equivalence and conservation, and therefore also dying out or depletion, *Les Cinq Sens* denies the equivalence of the first and second laws of thermodynamics, the law of conservation and the law of decay. Serres ignores the mortality of the body, the fact that the body is the carrier or amplifier of entropy as well as its temporary remission.

In the "Boîtes" chapter, Serres imagines with a kind of horrified amusement Socrates heroically speaking right up to the instant of his death. Serres cannot believe that the *imperium* of language should seek to abut so closely upon death, suffuse every last atom of existence, leaving open no chink of grace, no space of animal existence before death. It is for this reason that language, for Serres, is death. But Serres proposes here another kind of exceptionalness plenitude, a plenitude that allows no exteriority, nothing that cannot be gathered up and redeemed in the self-renewing abundance of time. Where Socrates encroaches upon death, Serres incorporates it. In both cases, death is denied. Serres is bitterly opposed to the warlike Hegelian dialectic that, in its way of subduing time to a line, actually denies time, canceling its contradictions. But Serres's own ironic, peace-loving testimony to abundance and redemption works as a kind of atemporal or multitemporal dialectic, and exhibits its own stalling effect. Despite his homage to the pleasures of company, literally the breaking of bread together, and of conversation, the world of Serres's senses is a unsociable world; where are the others in all of this contingency of self with self? The answer is, perhaps, that Serres refuses the anthropomorphism of alterity, refuses to close the system of relations off with the claustrophobic or finally autistic calamity or catastrophe of the self in its relations to the human other.

Something is omitted in Serres's abundant and all-inclusive celebration of the senses. That something is loss, depletion, mortality, omission. There is an abhorrence in Serres's senses, a hole where negativity should be. If the sensitive body is excursive, if its nature is to list or lean into the wind, to go out from itself, this advance is into the condition of its own mortality, into its own slow going or going out, against a background of finally invariant and unremissable degradation. Serres makes us aware of the direction or itinerary of the senses, of the *sens* in the *sens*. But we may hear another variant in this transformation of the senses into themselves. The word *sens* is after all only the merest modulation of the mouth away from *sans*. The senses acquaint us and themselves with the condition of their own decay that will leave us sans eyes, sans ears, sans teeth, sans everything. French would allow us to say it in the following motto: *Les sens ont le sens du sans.* The senses have the sense of the less. The senses move toward lessness. They list to the leastmost. The senses take lessening's course. The lessons of the senses, like those of the Mock Turtle, are aptly enough so-called, for they get less and less.

Serres celebrates the ceaseless unraveling and reknitting of the body, in the principle of giving out, *dépense,* that is always itself renewed, that can never give out. There is no place, no time for this in Serres's five senses, which, in their ceaseless coming and going, are always, as we have seen, on the increase, rather than come and gone in no time. This intolerance of the exteriority represented by death and degradation makes for a certain paradoxical claustration in Serres's work, makes it a monism of the manifold. There is nothing Serres can do with it, because there is nothing anyone can do with it, this slow going, this ungraspable, unknowable, unignorable squandering of energy that in the end is what we will have amounted to. There is nothing we can do with it, though it has everything to do with us.

NOTES

1. *Les Cinq Sens* consists of five chapters, entitled "Voiles" (Veils), "Boîtes" (Boxes), "Tables" (Tables), "Visite" (Visit), and "Joie" (Joy). Unless otherwise indicated, all translations of Serres are my own.

2. Samuel Beckett, *Collected Dramatic Works* (London: Faber and Faber, 1986), 390.

3. V. S. Ramachandran and Sandra Blakeslee, *Phantoms of the Brain: Human Nature and the Architecture of the Mind* (London: Fourth Estate, 1999), 25–38.

OF STONES, ANGELS, AND HUMANS

Michel Serres and the Global City

MARCEL HÉNAFF

The cover of *Atlas* reproduces a Winkel projection of a planisphere; it shows a nocturnal view of the *orbis terrarum* (fictive since night is not simultaneous around the planet), where the ecumene appears, like an upside down sky, as an immense galaxy made of all the lights of the cities of the world.

The inhabited space is now dominated by urban megalopolises; increasingly, the human species seems to be concentrated in cities. Global space appears as the archipelago of the cities of the earth. The planet becomes a city. Arnold Toynbee already had a foreboding that this was the major event of current civilization since what has been called the "industrial revolution." He called this planetary megalopolis *Oecumenopolis.*[1] However, Toynbee's vision still belonged to the nineteenth century in as far as he saw this extension as a proliferation of the industrial city and its metamorphoses, and of the infinite and boring suburbs that today surround these metropolises everywhere or indeed actually constitute most of them.

In reality, in this invasion of the urban form, there is more at stake than the city; this transformation of the ways of inhabiting the city is not simply about the extension of the built environment and population management. Something very different is happening on multiple levels. This is what Michel Serres helps us to understand. He does so without having written explicitly about the urban question, not even in *Rome, the Book of Foundations.* Nevertheless, it is present in his work everywhere, but in the context of numerous other questions. One of the chapters of *Angels, a Modern Myth* is called "Los Angeles." It contains no analysis of the urban problems of the Californian metropolis; rather it is the extension of a reflection on global space as a worldwide network of messages, as a space filled with angels, figures of a plural Hermes.

The journey from Rome to Los Angeles is in fact a journey that goes from questions of foundations to questions of relations, both being intertwined. Those are important questions that include many others and pervade all of Serres's work: the relations between local and global, between narrative and concept, science and philosophy, history and myth, solids and fluids. One would have to retrace the steps of Serres's own journey, which would be just as presumptuous as to undertake the journey he proposes. Because of its incidental position as a theme but its centrality as a problem, the question of the city will allow us to approach laterally a whole *nebulae* of other questions. Our destiny itself is at stake with the creative and destructive means at our disposal that have become worldwide.

DOUBTS ABOUT THE CITY

On many occasions Serres shows reservations about the privileged status accorded to the urban site, about its invasiveness, its arrogance, its misdeeds: "I have always imagined that the city invented separateness. Why is it that those living in cities, the city dwellers, travel. To have a change of surroundings, they say. As soon as they leave, they are disoriented: a confession of their situation. . . . The farmer is never really in foreign lands. He never feels the need to roam the earth because he lives there" (*LT,* 245). Here the critic frowns: is this preference for the farmer not just nostalgia still attached to the days of country life? Where does Serres's suspicion come from? He gives us an additional explanation in another text ("Soup, Cyclone, Woman"), where right away the question becomes: what remains of the very substance of the world, of its physical, lively, resistant exteriority. "Have we become monsters? Our last relation to the world, air, water, land, and fire, goes through the imagination, dreams, and speech. The universe is a dream, a discourse. . . . Here we are, interiorized, inside *politope* cities and *gnoseotope* schools and in the intimacy of the private self that thinks and the small group that speaks" (*LD,* 145–46). Here a crisis emerges, linked to the hegemony of those who know, who govern messages and can decide the fate of others without seeing them, without feeling them or meeting them. The urban anthropoid is a zombie. "Having become abstract and inexperienced, developed humanity takes off toward signs, frequents images and codes, and flying in their midst, no longer has any relation, in cities, either to life or to the things of the world. Lolling about in the soft, humanity has lost the hard. Gadabout and garrulous, informed. We are no longer *there*. We wander, outside all places" (*NC,* 17).

These words may surprise us: the philosopher who puts the figure of Hermes at the center of his thinking, who has most profoundly reflected on the world of communication, denounces the city as the hegemonic space of signs, of relations and representations. Again, one has to ask: isn't this a timid, regressive position? We know that modernity is urban, the daughter of large metropolises, and that they have generated styles, works, narratives, and knowledge constituting the culture in which we live today, precisely the one we call global.

However, Serres is very much aware of the beauty and power of the urban site and wonders about them incessantly: the Paris of Balzac or Zola, the furnace city imbued with the representations of thermodynamics, Musil's Vienna, which is contemporary with Boltzman, the city of the Brownian movement of characters and events; finally, all the cities visited by angels, those ancient and modern figures of messages and relations that outline a virtual space as the global site of our experience. This is precisely what interests Serres and not what he ironically calls a return to "farm ontologies" (*NC,* 17).

How can we understand this double discourse? The doubt Serres has about the city can be explained as follows: immersed in the collective, we only talk about the collective; the social blinds us, and we ask it to explain the origins of things; we consider the world as its effect and reflection. Thus history incessantly refers back to history (for we can make everything into history) just as signs only refer back to signs (for we can make a semiology of everything as well).

> Immersed in the exclusively social contract, the politician has been countersigning it up until today, rewriting it, and having it observed: he is solely the expert in public relations and social sciences. . . . None of his speeches spoke of the world: instead they endlessly discussed men . . . closed up in the social collectivity, he could be splendidly ignorant of the things of the world. (*NC,* 74–75)

The urban site is the privileged space of narcissistic sociality. However, the problem is not so much the city as such, but the forgetting of the world. To think the city, one must leave it and see it as part of the world, *extra-muros.* What is at stake for our epoch is that the planet is being urbanized globally. Will we think about the entire world as a swelling city that invades space by homeothesis? In other words, will we see the world as the outgrowth of the ecumene only? Or will we think the city as part of the world, that is, think of the built environment inhabited by humans in its relation to the totality of the landscape, including the spaces of the other species, the mineral elements, the continents and climates, not to mention its relation to older traditions, various ways of life—whether urban or not—and the arts and sensitivities that make for the extraordinary cultural diversity of the world.

The globalization of the urban form forces us to face this question and to think in terms of the world as a whole. We must go from the Oecumenopolis to the cosmopolis. The issue here is less about the city becoming the world, than about the world asserting itself as the pedestal, the horizon and the environment of urban space and all inhabited space. The problem of the city is but a sign of the event talked about in *The Natural Contract* and *Atlas*.

The problem thus becomes global and not simply sociological or urbanistic. The city is an example of what Serres calls "world objects," that is artifacts that have the power to intervene globally (satellites, nuclear weapons, banking, etc.). It so happens that now the human population weighs on the planet as such, especially in urban concentrations. There is a kind of tectonics of the plates of populations: "When it is unevenly distributed, skyrocketing demographic growth becomes concentrated and stuck together in giant units, colossal banks of humanity as powerful as oceans, deserts, or icecaps, themselves stockpiles of ice, heat, dryness, or water" (*NC*, 17). For Serres, such is the scale of the problem of the city. The planetary archipelago of megalopolises forces us to consider the human collective on the same level as climates or continents. The social order is reaching the dimensions of geophysical units: "Global history enters nature; global nature enters history: this is something utterly new in philosophy" (*NC*, 4).

BABEL AND THE ARCHITECTONIC MODEL

At this point a question arises: when thus replaced in its planetary environment, the city as such almost seems to disappear, that is to say, the city in the sense that has always presupposed an architectural project and a number of religious, technical, and aesthetic gestures that can be summarized in verbs such as *to found, to dig, to measure, to divide,* and *to build.* This produces buildings such as ramparts, temples, palaces, houses, streets, squares, and neighborhoods. What does the emergence of this "built space" mean? This question needs to be linked immediately to the original emergence of the collective: how does a community become urban? why the city form? what is the relation between stones and humans? what does this shaping of space mean? There are historical, sociological, and aesthetic answers to these questions that occupy entire sections of libraries.

In his own way, Serres gives an answer that moves away from established disciplines. What the city has become obliges us to rethink its origins. The question of the city goes far beyond the urban question. It concerns simultaneously the emergence of the collective, of foundation and relations, forms of multiplicity, representations of the world, religion and science. That is quite a lot, but it is even more than that. To get a glimpse of the problem posed by Serres we must reread the last pages of *Genesis* (*G,* 199–222). This book takes up and elaborates on a whole set of earlier reflections on the relations between chaos and order, between background noise and sign, between the indeterminate and the conceptual, turbulence and stability, and finally on the passage from pure multiplicities to ordered multiplicities. Among other things, this means that what we call the universe as a rational totality is a rare stable state amid a larger turbulence; moreover, the concept is a cross-section with clearly defined borders in the middle of fuzzy sets.

The emergence of physics in Greece consisted in isolating by and through geometric science, an ordered cosmos to the detriment of its cloud of noise (see *Les Origines de la géometrie* and *Lucrèce*). It gave birth to a paradigm that has dominated our representations until the dawn of the twentieth century, that of the "architectonic order": the cosmos is the work of the divine architect; the city repeats in its constructions the well-ordered system of the world. Similarly, to philosophize will then be to found, organize, and build. And thus finally, to construct systems. But systems, by pretending to enclose the universal, repeat the failure of Babel. In what did that consist? In believing that a local model would be able to reach the global by the direct expansion of its forms; in other words, universalization by homeothetic projection—enlargement by scale drawing. The result: the confusion of languages, the collapse of the tower, and the return to fragmented multiplicity ensuing from the breakdown of the totalizing architectonic program. Architecture as such cannot organize humans. When it pretends to do so, the collective is shattered, and skillfully carved stones become again piles of rubble. To build, to organize, and to found always and simultaneously concern both the collective and space. The failure of Babel is thus the revenge of the multiple.

> We draw up plans, blueprints and graphs, flow charts, we construct a system, we even conceive a general theory of systems, a kind of general, universal system for reaching the sky. Let us call this whole endeavor the constructivist model. Now then, it ends in noise, in the foreign noise of external languages, soon spoken by the enemy. War, fury, the system lies in ruins. Upon these rocks no one has ever built anything but Babel. Babel is not a failure, it is at that very moment when the tower is dismantled that we begin to understand that one must understand without concepts. (*G,* 123)

Stones and humans, the system and pure multiplicity, have to be thought together: "The collective is not an architectonic, or, rather, it is an unfinished architectonic surrounded by noise" (*G,* 124). Serres wants to reconstitute precisely that genealogy in *Rome: The Book of Foundations.*

THE FIGURE OF ROME   Foundations, Multiplicities, Mixture

The West usually acknowledges two sources: Athens and Jerusalem (this is incidentally the title of a great book by Shestov). Rome is usually forgotten. One does not see Rome. Rome remains obscure. And probably for the simple reason that we are still in Rome. Rome built the aqueducts through which the double Greco-Judaic source flows to us; Rome paved the ways by which the two cities of our origins penetrated to the extremities of Europe. It is said that Rome was born of mixtures, did not innovate much, and was conquered by its conquests. Nevertheless, as a black body absorbs light from elsewhere, Rome has made us what we are; it gave a destiny of earth and stone to Greek transparency and biblical spirituality. Rome has administered, organized, ordered. Rome, Serres tells us, is "incarnation." Rome has indeed invented something decisive, something around which our entire culture was organized; it invented the "object."

> Rome does not speculate, does not speak, never converses about the latest refinement. Rome fights, Rome prays; it is pious, it humbly accepts the dark sense of a repeated gesture. It builds, extends itself, preserves. It is not the negative—the destructive work that seems to advance things. No—it does not progress by means of a NO; it progresses in the dark. . . . It gives flesh to the word; it builds. Rome incarnates itself; it is construction. Rome is not of the word, like Athens; it is not of the book, of breath, or of writing, like Jerusalem . . . Rome is hard and dumb as stone, black as the depths of stone . . . Rome is heavy . . . It is of ritual, not of myth. It is hardware. Rome can never be outside of Rome, as Athens was outside itself, as Jerusalem has never ceased to be. Rome is in Rome completely, always inside its walls. Athens is mind, Jerusalem sign, and Rome object. (*R,* 57–58)

Object? What does that mean? precisely this: "That's what it is to be an object, a thing of this world; it is the flesh of incarnation, a light captured, seized, and barred within walls" (*R,* 59). Thus hidden, the object is removed from human rivalries and ceases to be the stake or fetish for conflicting desires either of power or exchange. Thus does knowledge become possible: "It is because there was never any god of gravity that gravity became an object" (*G,* 90). The Greeks did have some premonition of this, but their solution was to protect the object of knowledge by exiling it from the world and constituting it as ideality. On the contrary, Rome restores it to earth, sinks it into the flesh of the world and from the

Platonic world brings it home to the black box of matter. This is the authentic birth of physics from Lucretius to Galileo. The object, the neutral thing, asserts itself beyond the scene of human relations: religion, war, politics. "Suddenly, a thing, something, appears outside the network. The exchanged messages no longer say: I, you, he, we, etc., but this, here is. Here is the thing itself" (N, 163). This question runs through Serres's entire work; as we noted in the beginning, it sustained his doubts about the city. Obsessed by interpersonal relations, we become and remain oblivious of our foundational link to the world. Rome is precisely this obstinate relation to the obscure, this acceptance of profound powerlessness in the face of the secret of the world; it is this almost oblique, lateral approach of a clarity that is incessantly restored to an earlier night. How did this happen? or rather, how was this original figure outlined in very ancient narratives before it became a legacy that we also ignored?

There are several converging stories that all tell about the same gesture, the one that constantly brings light to shadow. Livy's text, in which Serres chooses to read these stories, is itself a black box: "With Livy, nobody understands anything; we have to understand Livy first" (R, 59). This text tells us over and over again: Rome is moving toward darkness; it engulfs and buries, first of all the mother, *mater, materia,* as for instance Rhea Sylvia, the vestal raped by Mars, who gave birth to the twins Romulus and Remus. She is buried alive, ritually lynched as every vestal must be who looses her virginity. The vestal is the remote, intransitive body that makes exchanges possible everywhere else. The vestal embodies the secret of the object and of the nonknowledge it nestles; she is its guardian. She is the one who watches over the city's sacred fire that itself is immured in the temple. It is the radical opposite of the Greek center that is public, open and full of light. Here the light is surrounded by night and the object is removed from transparency, from view and from control. What is known never goes without its double, the nonknown, like the two sacred jars kept in the shadow of the temple. One of them is empty and open, while the other is full but closed. There is nothing in the one that exposes; there is something in the one that conceals. We are dealing here with a protoepistemology that subtly describes the relation between knowledge and the object. "Theory is empty and white; and the object is black and sealed" (R, 70). Rome exists only in order to establish itself, to sink its roots and to renew the obscurity of its origins, to maintain this black box and reconstitute it incessantly, not to interpret or deconstruct it, but to renew it persistently through ritual.

What interests Serres about Roman stone is not the architectural gesture so fascinating for art historians, which is more related to geometry—so Greek, so ordered—but the stone itself, the thickness of the monument sinking into the ground. The book of foundations does not talk about the base of the bright temple but about the obscurity of its pedestal, the night of the sanctuary, the veil of the vestal and the secret of the cult objects, in other words, all that is hidden from view, not what is exposed.

FOUNDATIONS

The underlying thought is that the object is not the reverse of the subject; even less is it constituted by the subject in the act of knowing, as a limited and definitive thing. The object remains in the black box, in the night; it remains indeterminate, that is, fraught with infinite possibilities. It keeps time in reserve, involuted and folded time before any branching off, ichnography—the integral of profiles and horizons—before scenography—the construction of a centered perspective. This folded time is the knot of multiplicities, the world itself that begins incessantly. However much of a geometer Plato was, however much he thirsted for bright sunlight, even he had intuited this fundamental indetermination in the *Timaeus,* this *chora* that precedes and underlies clearly delineated and differentiated things. Thus foundation is first of all the recognition of this incommensurable relation (even and especially for the architect) to the obscurity of the world, to its noise, its reserve of possibles, that is to say, to its ever renewed birth (even and especially for an already constructed world).

However—and this is the paradox of knowledge—we must admit, "I never have a rapport solely with an object. My attention, my perception, my knowledge are immersed in a social and cultural ensemble. A theory of knowledge in which the monadic subject has a relation with an object, passive or active, is a vain utopia. The object is instituted in and by the relations of the group" (R, 102). The multiplicity harbored by the object of knowledge calls for the multiplicity of the subjects of knowledge. But what binds the collective together is precisely an object that is not primarily the object of knowledge. Serres calls it a "quasi object": a token, a thing that circulates, an exchanged gift, the peace pipe, the team ball. As the mediating object, it fixes relations on itself or around itself. Such an object became the focal point for the foundation of Rome, becomes the point around which the collective takes hold and around which a relation to the world is constituted, including the world as object of knowledge. It is only then that the foundation can take place, can begin, over and over again. When did this happen in Rome? When was the empire born and when did it emerge? Do not look for dates: the empire is there right from the beginning. At the Marsh of Capra where the masses have been summoned, Romulus disappears in the middle of a violent storm as the dark night suddenly descends on broad daylight. The throne remains empty: absent, he became a god. But, says Livy, the rumor goes that while the mob was fleeing, the Fathers rushed to the throne and dismembered the king, each taking a part of his body. *Im-perium:* the shared thing. From now on, Rome is this unique body in pieces. Everywhere it spreads, this impossible body is repeated: "Empire, in one word, speaks of the unintegrable multiple. Romulus cannot be remade from his separated limbs . . . What then is *we,* this ensemble? No one in particular; everyone as a collective . . . No one in particular, nowhere, *imperium.* And it denies its locality; thus it rises to the universal" (*R,* 99–100).

The universal of knowledge increases with that of territory, just as the object of knowledge grows with the universality of power; the object is simultaneously that which evades, circulates, and unifies. However, in order to designate an object, a subject must be sacrificed; at least one must be glorified and annihilated in order for others to be freed from the imposture of this posture and for the group to cohere around the object through the ritual lynching that eliminates the subject. Then the work of knowledge can begin and peace can come to the knowing community. Serres intersects Girard here in order to go elsewhere, toward the questions he has been asking tirelessly, since the first *Hermès,* about those very ancient articulations and logics that subsist in the most recent forms of knowledge in which the understanding of the world and the relations between humans are indissociably linked. The lesson of Babel already showed that multiplicity shatters beautiful constructions. How does Rome embody this constantly reaffirmed relation between stone and multiplicity?

MULTIPLICITIES

At the origins of Rome there is the mob, *turba,* disorder, and in its middle the Fathers who flee with the pieces of the royal body. This is the social moment of the foundation, the moment when the collective constitutes itself. What else but the state of multiplicity is described here, asks Serres. Livy's entire narrative is full of it. The mob here echoes Lucretius's rain of atoms. It is pure multiplicity before the clinamen, before a gap or rupture introduces a nucleus of form and congeals atoms around a point.

This reflection on the multiple has been one of the major strands in Serres's thought since *Genesis.* For a moment it looked as if structural research, by privileging series and groups, differences and distribution, would open the way to a thought of the multiple. It soon became apparent that only standard multiplicities were dealt with, those that appear in an already constituted order and are immediately available for combinatory work. Serres invites us to a prior thought of the appearance of the pure multiple. "This pure multiple is the ground of order, but it is also, I think, its birth, or at least its power in the sense of potentiality" (*G,* 106). Before order, and making it possible, there is the background noise, the cloud, the jumble, the indeterminate. Order is rare, Serres repeats; it is exceptional, miraculous, both real and highly improbable. This is true at the level of physical phenomena and also at the level of the human collective. To understand this passage, in the case of Rome, is to understand the birth of the city and at the same time the organization of the group; it means understanding the gesture of the foundation. The latter is the passage from pure multiplicity (the dispersed and panicked mob) to standard multiplicity. This operation always takes place around a quasi object (the piece of the royal body) that circulates and is exchanged. Without this emergence of the collective, there is no foundation in stone. To presuppose an order at the origin—*cosmos* or *architectonia*—is to prepare Babel. It means starting with standard multiplicities and failing to hear the growling of the noise below the clear sound, failing to see the jumble among the rectilinear spaces. It is because the pure multiple keeps insisting and the crowd keeps returning that "Rome keeps on being founded." This is also why the writing of the book of foundations parallels Rome's becoming as Serres describes it.

MIXTURES: ROME BEYOND ROME

In its ritual and judicial practices, in its political and military institutions, Rome reveals how the gesture of construction that organizes the world seeks the geometric plan and the cadastral order capable of mastering space and submitting it to a previously promulgated law. But at the same time, as it stubbornly builds, the very gesture of construction shows that this mastery tacitly expresses that the earth is the essential base, and that foundation belongs to the night. Order then grows only out of this indetermination, and clear reason can prevail only by drawing on this obscurity; in short, knowledge is nourished by nonknowledge.

What is more, Rome has forever been carrying around the noise, the jumble, and the multiple layers from which it was born. It emerges from the mixture of Latins, Etruscans, Albans, Troyans and grows by absorbing Greeks, Syrians, Phoenicians, Africans, and so on. Its borders are always subverted by the multiple that sustains it. "Rome is a collection . . . Rome has no unity . . . Rome is a fabric of others; it does not strictly exist as a subject . . . I seriously believe that its history, its growth, and its power came from this inexistence" (R, 149–51). Because it is a mixture, it can be divided or grow without changing. This is the flexibility of time itself. "Time does not know the excluded third; Rome did not know it" (R, 151).

Here we can extend Serres's thought and suppose that Rome reveals something else as well: that the foundation site—the mythical point—cannot be imagined without its elsewhere, without its *limes,* its furthest border, where Rome risks losing itself by expatriating itself, by rushing toward foreign lands, toward the non-Roman. Ever since it was founded, Rome has no longer been in Rome, in a very different way from Athens and Jerusalem.

Rome only exists between those two poles: *urbs* and *orbs,* the city and the universe. The universe is the city. How? Probably by way of the road. The empire is a network. The architectural space of the city, the built, closed, delimited environment, rushes via all its roads into the landscape, embraces its hazards (valleys, hills, gorges, coasts, and rivers) as it comes across obstacles, various terrains and climates. The pavement of the roads, the splendor of the viaducts, the aqueducts and the bridges proclaim geometric and architectural mastery, while the adaptation to the curvature of the lines and to the unevenness of the terrain shows the perpetual negotiation with contingency. But Rome does not say it; it does it. Here, the engineers know more than the philosophers.

THE LOCAL AND THE GLOBAL

There is a yet more fundamental reason why Rome launched out of Rome, and successfully so. Rome tells us how a site becomes the universe, which kind of thought conceived this project and this projection, and with what successes and failures. Rome wanted to be universal and finally understood that it was mortal, like all civilizations. Like so many others, it learned that "every empire will perish," according to the prophecy. Nevertheless, Rome has survived in death itself. Through the ruins of its cities, its temples, theaters, viaducts, paved roads, something else has filtered through and resisted: first of all, the language, directly in Latin or laterally in the Romance languages, and even more, all the Latin and Greek texts that have nourished European culture until today, but still more profoundly, in its forms of civil, criminal, and constitutional law. Indeed, Rome has given birth to Europe and thus to the entire Western culture that is now globalizing itself. The center has collapsed and the monuments have become beautiful ruins, but the lightest, immaterial aspects have survived: the language, the texts, and the legal codes. Hugo was right: "This will kill off that, the written word will conquer the stone."[2] The solid—hardware—breaks and disintegrates, while the software—the program—resists and goes on. No stone rampart protects against irreversible time. Rome looked for the universal from the center and failed, but it reached the global from its periphery almost without realizing it.

Thus Rome teaches us the way from foundations to relations. Today, however, the common experience is that the universal, as it relates to the geometric model (homogeneous, isotropic, and stable space), only appears to us as a particular case or a limit in the midst of a global space consisting of connected local multiplicities. According to the most ancient tradition, the global merged with the universal. The universal was defined as the escape from contingency. Since Aristotle this has been known formally: the universal is that for which there exists a law verifiable every-where (such as the course of the planets). The local—a figure above all of the contingent—could never hope to attain the universal (and thus the truth of a law) except in as far as it can be recognized as having character-istics subsumable under the law. The universal confers its dignity on the local as part of the whole; outside the whole there is no salvation. The local as such, the singular, remains meaningless, at most an exotic particularity, the object of sterile surprise or else a comic object (the singular is laugh-able because it both persists in existing and has no reason to do so). It either takes place in a totality that assigns its place or only has an absurd, unthinkable place.

Global thought reverses these terms: the global does not precede the local but is the totality of its relations, as in a network. We will see later the importance of such thought to understanding the contemporary metropolis, but already we get closer to a more comforting truth about the contingency of our place in the universe. "Why be here rather than else-where": that question may refer to the initial absurdity of fate that has thrown us in a given spot on Earth or even to the fact of occupying any place at all. In the framework of a theory of the abstract universal, there is no sufficient reason for such an assignment. Therein lies its contingency. That is why geography, the knowledge of the contingent, could not attain the dignity of the classical sciences, since description does not equal expla-nation.

But as soon as the center/periphery model is abandoned, as soon as the center is everywhere and the circumference nowhere, the status of the local settlement changes: every point is a center in the multiple intersec-tions of the network; every site is in real or virtual communication with all other sites. Each local point implies the global network, and the latter is nothing without the multiplicity of the individual sites. But how can we define the process that determines the passage from the local to the global? It is important to understand it to conceive of the new space that opens up beyond the old architectonic paradigm and invites us to think very differ-ently about the city. What has changed about our knowledge?

THE DECLARATIVE AND THE PROCEDURAL

In *Eloge de la philosophie en langue française,* two concepts appear, the impli-cations of which have long been present in Serres but which are formulated in a new way. It is the distinction between the *declarative* and the *procedural:* "The whole revolution of this century is contained in those two terms" (*EF,* 159). What does this mean? Philosophy since the Greeks (that is since there is "philosophy") saw as its mission the discovery of the universal. It called on the science that was most successful in that project: geometry. When Plato inscribes in the pediment of the Academy, "No one but geometers can enter here," he not only wants to indicate that knowledge of the sciences of his time is indispensable for a philosopher—no one doubted that then—but he essentially wants to signify that the very processes of geometry must inspire the philosopher's quest (cf. *Republic* 7.526c and ff.). Now, geometry was an exercise in deduction par excellence, a science of the declarative type.

Declarative: Serres reminds us that this word comes from *declaro:* to clarify, that is to proclaim publicly—to decree what all should know without ambiguity, such as the theorems of geometry or the axioms of logic or the principles of metaphysics. The declarative posits truths that are not demonstrable in themselves but can be verified in their consequences; it makes deduction possible ("if this is posited, it follows that" etc.). The declarative order presupposes the universal as the homogeneous space of forms, those of geometry or physics. It is the universe of the greatest generality (hence of the science recognized as the truest) where the particularities of sites, events, individuals, customs, and traditions necessarily disappear because they are accidental and cannot be subsumed under a law.

Procedural: this term has its origins in *procedo,* the act of walking, or rather moving forward, step by step. This also means to advance among the particularity of sites and conditions. Can one define a way of thinking based on such a model? Is it not precisely what proper philosophy denounces as empiricism? Not even that, for at the end of its journey, empiricism intends to rejoin the universal it did not posit at the beginning. We are dealing here with something very different, that is, to take seriously the particularities of sites, the unpredictability of circumstances, the uneven patterns of the landscape and the hazardous nature of becoming. In short, again: How to think the local? Which means: Is there a science of the particular?

The answer has existed for a long time, but has only been understood recently, and according to Serres, it represents an exalted opportunity for our epoch. There is indeed an art of formulating cases and theorizing circumstances, that is, the *algorithm.* What is an algorithm? It is an elementary rule that intervenes in the operations of arithmetic (such as division, multiplication, etc). More generally, an algorithm is a set of rules or instructions making it possible to complete an operation mechanically. It is sequence of procedures. This is the case with different intellectual techniques such as "infinitesimal calculation; combinatory art; Pascal's triangle and harmonic triangle; calculators; various numerations; coding theory, etc., the models of which promise and sometimes allow the step-by-step construction of proposed or existing objects in their individuality" (*EF,* 229).

What Pascal and Leibniz discover anew and theorize in the seventeenth century were in fact very ancient practices of the Assyro-Babylonians and the Arabs (the word *algorithm* comes from them) or the merchants of the Middle Ages. Those are the procedures that come back forcefully with computer calculations and programs. This novelty is in fact but "the most ancient example of our forgetfulness."[3] So there is a fast, practical, flexible type of mathematics, capable of formulating local cases and situations, that corresponds well to what Pascal describes as *esprit de finesse,* while the other type is abstract, deductive, and rigid, stemming from *esprit de geométrie.* However, it is the latter that Plato praises as the correct one in the *Meno* when he rejects the empirical endeavors of the ignorant young slave and introduces him to deductive operations, supposedly the only ones capable of leading to the pure space of the Idea. This was the last obstacle to over-throwing Platonism. It was done without philosophers noticing it.

The difference between the declarative and the procedural shows in a surprising way that there is a double history of reason, which for centuries was defined and recognized only in the domain of the declarative. Reason had opted for the abstract universal, as seen triumphantly in the great geometric and mechanical models of the universe, or more recently in the age of thermodynamics, in totalizing and ratiocinating visions of history that were just the abstract universal provided with a motor (cf. "Moteurs," *LT*), a mobile element thrown into the homogeneous space of classical geometry.

On the other hand, there is more humble and more subservient reason, which calculates, organizes, adjusts, and goes from local model to circum-stantial solution. This is precisely the reason that succeeds in the new mathematics emerging from the theory of fractals, chaos theory, or that of strange attractors. No, there is no war of reason against irrationalism, no clash of categorical thought with empiricism. There is a classical, canonical figure of geometrical and mechanical reason, of solids with clearly circum-scribed borders, of the homogeneous universal, of abstract deduction that yields before a flexible and subtle reason capable of welcoming the partic-ular and providing formulas for the heterogeneous. Reason, Serres tells us, has been identified too long with what is hard, deductive, and homoge-neous. From now on, it can offer another figure: what is flexible, woven, and circumstantial. Diagrams, maps, landscapes are no longer unworthy of the most sophisticated knowledge; they are knowledge itself. Indeed, it is to this type of knowledge that disciplines like cartography or meteorology, so long considered minor, should be connected (see *Lucrèce, Atlas*).

Henceforth, it is possible to elaborate rigorously a transition from the local to the global by algorithmical procedures. The network is the geom-etry of these transitions and the virtual its mode of existence. This remains to be examined; perhaps this is how we could outline an entirely different way of thinking about the city, following Serres.

THE NETWORK AND THE VIRTUAL

Network thought has existed for a long time. Leibniz is certainly its most remarkable and most profound representative in the tradition of Western philosophy. Only recently, however, has it taken on an importance that is exactly proportional to the transformations that have occurred in information and communication techniques in the last decades.

The peculiarity of centerless networks is that any entry will work because every point, by its multiple relation to several others, is very quickly in contact with all the others through successive linkages. Today we experience these operations as banal characteristics of the means of transportation and communication. The network transforms various aspects of the relation of the local to the global. We will talk about three of them: stocks, the fold, and ubiquity.

Power in ancient civilizations (this ancient is still recent) was linked to concentrations in one spot of all the instruments of domination, influence, or organization (arms, money, freight companies, postal services, administration, universities, industries, etc.). He who had stocks held the world. This idea of monumentality has become obsolete. "Today, the relation of support to transport is reversed, the latter becoming essential, as always. It does not matter where the storage sites are since our networks connect them; they might as well be just as much dispersed as the stations that exchange information" (A, 152–53). From now on, stock is flux. Flux goes through singular sites and raises them to the level of the global.

However, there is not simply the dispersion of ancient elements; at the same time, there is above all their miniaturization; in other words, stocks themselves tend to lose in volume what they gain in information. This is precisely the passage from the solid to the fluid and then to the gaseous, just as we go from hardware to software. Thus the electronic chip is an interlacing of folds, that is, a bundle of coded molecules. Every local point is like those molecules. The local is a point of transit and relation only because it is a center of information.

Thus everyone in his place is virtually in every place. The old dream of ubiquity is beginning to take shape; more exactly it is materialized in multiple ways. There is the ubiquity of the bodies themselves that can now, in a few hours, change continents in travels that before took weeks or months. Even better, without moving, communication techniques allow us to intervene in real time and simultaneously in different places on the planet. That is why Serres calls one of the characters in *Angels: A Modern Myth* Pantope.

This is the situation of the virtual world. The virtual, as Serres reminds us, has a long history. Language, the imagination, fiction are modes of dealing with the virtual. However, even confining ourselves to the question of so-called virtual space, we experience the latter constantly. Thus when two people exchange letters or telephone calls, an invisible site is created that belongs to neither the one nor the other person (the same thing could be said of a simple conversation): more than a between two sites, it is a half-site or even a nonsite, an elsewhere with respect to each site, a space where our messages cross. Serres calls this elsewhere *hors-là,* outside-of-there, which is not a superfluous addition to our experience but a part of our condition itself. (He develops this in his writing about *Horla,* by Maupassant, in *Atlas,* chap. 2).

Thus contemporary communication technologies do not alter our belonging to a site, or disturb a niche destined to remain local, because we have always been living elsewhere; nor do they only prolong our sensory or motor organs. They do better: they actualize and realize our represen-tations: the imagination into images, the voice into messages and the *hors-là* into networks of connected sites. ("We populate our old *hors-là* with machines" [*A,* 187].)

This virtual space is not a simple space precisely because it contradicts the laws of place assignment and subverts the principle of the excluded middle. I am at the same time *here* and *away.* Thus the passage from the local to the global is verified. Can such a space be mapped? Yes and no, for it is a space that moves and changes. One can have maps, but they will be like those of streams and clouds. Here we leave the earth of solids for the earth of fluids and gases: "Earth with fluctuating forms in an open ocean, this is the archipelago of utopia" (*A,* 199). Utopia is undoubtedly the appropriate word, but paradoxically so: the site of nowhere has become reality.

RETURN TO THE CITY

These questions seem to have moved us away from the city. In fact, we have not left it. Indeed, the urban question today concerns above all the articulation between the local and the global.

As cosmopolis spreads, as the archipelago of the cities of the earth brings forth a global city where the population of the globe is increasingly concentrated in formations as powerful as geological masses (oceans, deserts, icecaps), the specificity of sites and their unique qualities assert themselves. The local can exist precisely because it is no longer defined by its relation to an all-powerful center that swallows it up or drains it of its lifeblood. The metropolitan city belongs to the age of the constitution of kingdoms and empires, an age where power was defined by the centrality of political, military, or administrative authority. This epoch is dying under our very eyes. The city of the Industrial Revolution, of vast concentrations of factories and workers, often grafted on ancient metropolises, more often born on sites disposing of energy and raw materials, is also disappearing. What remains are the population concentrations they provoked. Amid these demographic stocks is born the city of angels, the city that is no longer necessarily linked to the monumental space of palaces, temples, administrative buildings, knowledge institutions, theaters, offices, or industrial complexes. Each urban mass crumbles into an archipelago with islands awash in flows of messages; the cities of the planet form an immense and capricious galaxy surrounded by the ether of information.

This global becoming and this virtual becoming of the new metropolis require us to rethink a whole range of aspects of the city such as architecture, power, multiplicity. The city is not only defined by its architecture, but without it there is no city. However, we must admit that the very idea of architecture was obviously linked to the triumph of Euclidian geometry and the physics of solids. Until the age of Enlightenment, the ideal city was conceived as the *imago coeli* and the *compendium mundi,* a model of a universe ordered according to the laws of heavenly mechanics. Architecture refers to classical rationality, confirms it, reproduces it, and inscribes it in stone. It is this geometric city struggling against time that disperses or compounds (thus Paris had become an anthill, which Haussman straightened out with rectilinear avenues and large boulevards). Architecture wished to construct human space in the image of divine space, the space of the stable universe of the planets and canonical geometric forms. In this way, architecture provided philosophy with the vocabulary of its operations: to found, to construct, to support. Thought had to develop like a building and, if necessary the better to assert itself, erase the entire ancient city or at least its oldest buildings, or establish a new city, as Descartes proposes in his *Discourse on Method.*

Thought about the contemporary city (some will say the postmodern city) escapes this paradigm in as far as the new sciences radically redefine the relation between the local and the global, order and disorder, stocks and fluids, information and networks. So if the city spreads out and loses its nice architectonic organization and its monumental majesty, it is not because of some regrettable decadence or the sole negligence of urban planners. It is because all our relations to natural space and to the built environment are changing. Urban architecture is obliged to think about the residence of humans, the visible and collective forms of their presence on Earth, in the context of relations with the natural world and in changes in the conditions of the relations of humans among themselves. The city will no longer be this well-circumscribed monumental formation, this islet of order in an uncertain landscape. It is already a landscape itself, the archipelago of constructions in the variety of the spaces of the world.

This leads to a reflection on changes in the forms of power. The latter is no longer linked (except here and there in a regressive mode) to large administrative machines, nor to the spectacular majesty of public buildings and spaces, nor to the solemnity of ceremonies. It now lies in the hands of those who control networks. This new power is at the same time also a new danger:

> He who holds this network, who goes from the local to the global, replaces the judiciary since he has every right; because he knows everything, he replaces the scholar; since he operates the machine that makes gods, finally he possesses the sacred; he chooses the sites of violence and fires up or squelches trade and exchange. (*A*, 203)

On the planet of the angels, the old walls have crumbled. But bad angels also fly and follow in the wake of the good ones. Therefore what is urgent is not finding out how to save the disappearing order, but how to face the questions posed by the emergence of the cosmopolis of the networks.

DAWN ON TELEPOLIS

The city of messages, the virtual community (*telepolis*, as some already call it), the city of angels, becomes our common condition, our way of living in the *hors-là*. Serres is not complaining. But what happened to his doubts about the triumph of the world of signs, of discourse and discoursers? Where did the Roman stone go? What remains of the object and the incarnation? What has become of the landscape? Serres has not forgotten them: read or reread *Les Cinq Sens*. Are we then dealing with two strands of parallel and apparently incompatible statements? Are we still dealing here with the cultural arrogance of the city dweller faced with the peasant's clumsiness, that of impeccable bureaucrats faced with those who have dirty feet and calloused hands? In fact, new species of fine talkers have hatched, new masks for parasites and the new arrogance of those who manage, decide, and expatiate, far away from those who act. This is the privileged world of Villeneuve—Newcity (as the global city of the new masters is called in *Angels*), opposed to the poor of the fourth world, those ignored by technoscience and triumphant finance. There is still and always a division that Serres finds unacceptable, and rightly so.

What he helps us understand is precisely that the terms of the problem have changed. The imperious and imperial discourse of the orators or even that of "great speakers" or the "loudmouths" came from the center, closest to the governmental palaces even when they pretended to be in the opposition. Between the traditional power structure and the organic intellectual the relation was twinlike and specular. That era is finished; the last ones to play that role look histrionic. To paraphrase Pascal, burlesque is nothing more than operating in a genre outside its order, or worse, outside its time.

What has changed? Precisely that the local has been given a new lease on life. For it has become not only useless, but irrational and even criminal to erase landscapes in order to insert them in mass production, to create industrial conglomerates where work is Taylorized and dwellings are stupidly uniform, to destroy ancient cultures in the name of a technical and centralizing modernity. Local spaces and cultures can easily find the way to become global by means of the network. This is our new and wonderful opportunity, even if as always the parasite watches and is busy playing the sign against the thing, the software against the hardware, light against heavy energies. Since Aesop, Serres likes to remind us, language has remained the best and worst of things, but no longer in the same way. The question is no longer a matter of attitude; it concerns what is at stake for the universe. By the means of encoding, informational power—language, theory, programs—has equaled and gone beyond the threshold of energetic power (*LT,* 86–93); codes hold and direct matter, and humanity dominates nature. But in the name of what do the masters act? Who does the programming? How to master the masters? Those are the questions of the new age. They carry along in the same destiny our cognitive disciplines, our techniques, our economic operations, our forms of community, our modes of occupying space, our relations between cultures, and our relation to other natural species.

One age of humanity is ending, and we remain humans on Earth, men and women, sentient bodies, loving, suffering, unchanged since the emergence of our species. Urban civilization seemed to distance us for ever not only from our soil, from our lands, but even from the old ways of socializing in the cities. This was supposedly the price we had to pay for the too hasty and oppressive techno-science of the leaden years of hard rationalism and heavy industrialization. The new sciences and technologies take us back to a new starting point. The cards have been redistributed, but at the planetary level.

We now know that we can find the landscape again without giving up the urban community. Indeed, today, the problem has taken on a dimension that confounds the old oppositions. The city dweller and the peasant are no more; there are humans in a habitat where built environments and natural spaces alternate, zones of heavy human density and those of open cultivated areas or free landscapes. The city is everywhere and so is the natural world. Or rather, the cosmopolis itself takes on the dimension of a natural world. The history of the city is ending and that of the global landscape begins, where the built and the natural, the cultivated and the wild alternate.

The earth has finally become round. Here or elsewhere every one is now locally connected to the global. There is no more exile; the elsewhere is our abode. We are everywhere locally sedentary and globally nomadic. Who is my neighbor? You are the neighbor in my street, and you are my neighbor in the antipodes. Another day is breaking in a world that is being born. This dawn offers a new opportunity for every landscape: for this rice field in Tonkin, just as for that neighborhood in Marseilles, for the villages of the Amazon as for the temples of Kyoto, for the hills of Chiapas, as for the streets of Montreal, for the old stones of Rome as for the glass towers or the freeways of Los Angeles.

Translated by Anne-Marie Feenberg

NOTES

1. Arnold Toynbee, *Cities on the Move* (Oxford: Oxford University Press, 1970).

2. Victor Hugo, "Ceci tuera cela," in *Notre Dame de Paris,* bk. 5, chap. 2.

3. *EF,* 234; cf. *Les Origines de la geometrie: Tiers livre des fondations* (Paris: Flammarion, 1993), 240ff.

"THE GIFT IS A GIVEN"

On the Errant Ethic of Michel Serres

JULIAN YATES

> BRUNO LATOUR: *It's impossible to simply ask,*
> *"What is Serres' ethic? what are his politics, his*
> *metaphysics?"*
>
> MICHEL SERRES: *"Where are you?"* *"What*
> *place are you talking about?" I don't know,*
> *since Hermes is continually moving on. Rather,*
> *ask him, "What roadmap are you in the process*
> *of drawing up, what networks are you weaving*
> *together?" No single word, neither substantive*
> *nor verb, no domain or specialty alone charac-*
> *terizes, at least for the moment, the nature of*
> *my work. I only describe relationships. For the*
> *moment, let's be content with saying it's "a*
> *general theory of relations." Or "a philosophy*
> *of prepositions."*
>
> *As for my ethic, I trust we will have the*
> *opportunity to speak of it another time. I don't*
> *want to die without having written it. The*
> *same for my politics.*
>
> BRUNO LATOUR: *All of this is very enlighten-*
> *ing, at least for me.*

On the face of it, Bruno Latour would already seem to have asked the
question I wish to pose in this essay and learned all that Michel Serres has
to say on the matter of his ethic. "Where are you?"; "What place are you
talking about?"; "Ask Hermes" are his riddling replies. In the course of this
short exchange, Serres's ethic fails to appear. Instead, it becomes a matter
of trust, something that he and Latour agree to "speak of . . . another time"
(C, 127). At the same time, Serres introduces the alarming worry that it
may already be too late, that his death may cut short his work and so
infinitely postpone the revelation that is to come. Serres's ethic remains of

the future, then, even as it threatens to become a thing of the past. We must trust to luck, hope that he lives long enough to write it down. None of this bodes well.

It is tempting to feel that Latour's "All of this is very enlightening" is tinged with irony, but Serres's refusal to speak directly to his questions constitutes a truly instructive response. He registers that the categories Latour offers (ethics, politics, metaphysics) represent a philosophical geography that makes no sense to him—or worse, threatens to make non-sense of him. His work exceeds these categories, he tells us, or falls between them. "Hermes," he says "is continually moving on," "drawing up roadmaps," "weaving networks," constituting relations. It has been Serres's project to travel with him. And so, his work makes no sense according to the logic of nouns and verbs or according to the usual divisions of philosophy. His philosophy—and his ethic—takes shape in the spaces between substantives. "I only describe relationships," he says, traveling alongside Hermes, charting his progress, his appearances, the knots he ties. And it is according to these terms, according to these shifting land-marks, that Serres agrees to be represented. "Let's be content with saying it's a general theory of relations" or "a philosophy of prepositions" (*C*, 127), he suggests. Serres's ethic remains imminent to the road maps he draws. It is prepositional in mode and matter, a question of vectors, directions, ways of moving, rather than a singular position or a final orientation. One may not ask of it directly, but must search in the between-spaces that his writings occupy, for it is his way of constituting knowledge that represents, finally, a kind of ethic.

My aim in this essay is to chart a course through these spaces, describing the way an ethic or the ethical takes shape in Serres's road maps. What interests me is the way in which his "general theory of relations" or "philosophy of prepositions" already implies an ethic, already presupposes the necessity, and so ubiquity, of ethics as a first philosophy, and so might be said already to respond to what Simon Critchley has called the implicit "ethical demand" of a different critical household: "the textual practice of deconstruction"[1] and the "ethical turn" that, according to a recent issue of *PMLA*, has "gained new resonance" if not "paradigm-defining" hegemony in literary studies.[2] It is in this sense that my title may be understood: "The Gift Is a Given" refers to the core problematic of the gift that drives Jacques Derrida's double mediation on giving and ethics in *Given Time* and *The Gift of Death*. As the shift from noun to past participle in my title signals, I see in Serres's writings a different kind of response to questions of economy, of the *oikos,* "home, property, the hearth, the fire indoors,"[3] the household, and *nomos,* "the law of sharing or partition"—questions that, for Serres, light upon the gift at a different moment than they do for Derrida, a moment later in the game, so to speak.

Where Derrida proceeds from a philosophical tradition that derives from Heidegger and Nietzsche, Serres issues from a different, scientific home and derives his inspiration from mathematics, information theory, and chaos theory. This alternative philosophical "home" leads Serres to frame the questions differently. While each of his models (the mythical Hermes, the parasite, the Lucretian clinamen) represents ways of "outlining" a "unified discourse" that reveals the parallel workings of scientific and cultural systems,[4] each represents also an ongoing attempt to understand the collective, to address the ways in which communities are constituted, households built, how "living together" plays out as cycles of order and violence. Serres's horror of the violence of exclusion, which he represents most frequently as "a strong disinclination to 'belong' to any group, because it has always seemed to require excluding and killing those who don't belong" (C, 20), leads him to imagine different ways of configuring our households that are not founded on partition. Where Derrida remains invested in the problematic of the gift with the aim of enlarging or proroguing the rituals by which we constitute the *oikos,* Serres's writings seek to abolish the *oikos* entirely, traveling ever outward, creating a terrain in which "the Same is the Other," and "the gift is a given." It is this terrain that his writing seeks to maintain, eschewing the parasitic textual relations of deconstruction for the multiple, diverging paths and shifting turns of Hermes, Harlequin, and angels. Billed as an attempt to represent Serres alongside Derrida, to decode his project in relation to the gift, this essay continues the invaluable work of critics such as William Paulson and Maria Assad, among others, who have done so much to make Serres available to Anglo-American audiences. His erring or errant ethic represents a mode of reading and writing but also a way of moving between and among different ways of knowing, different configurations of knowledge, that, at present, are frequently organized as different, or even opposed, disciplines. Ultimately, however, Serres's way of broaching the question of the collective calls for a systematic examination and renegotiation of social relations and geopolitical spaces. And it is for this reason that I should like to frame this essay further by reading a moment from an institutional history very different from the one to which Serres belongs—the Anglo-American world of cultural studies. The questions it raises, however, are exactly those that I am interested in tracing in Serres's writings: questions about the home, the household, tradition, and the collective. My hope is that by placing Serres in terms of these different fields, we can begin to appreciate more fully the kinds of work, material and discursive, ethical and political, it may make possible.

My point of departure is an essay by Stuart Hall titled "Cultural Studies and its Theoretical Legacies," which Lawrence Grossberg reprints in his *Cultural Studies* volume from 1992, and which has again been anthologized in *Critical Dialogues in Cultural Studies* (1996). The serial reprinting of this address signals its importance both as a piece of writing and as a crucial, perhaps iconic, moment in the development of cultural studies.

CULTURAL STUDIES AND THE POLICE

Asked to imagine the "Future" of cultural studies, to map the discipline, to sort out where it should be headed, who's doing it well, who's getting it wrong, Stuart Hall pauses. He is unhappy with the project. He doesn't like the sound of what seems to him an exercise in border control, a mode of speaking that will simply reinforce his identity as a "tableau vivant"[5] as "a spirit of the past, resurrected" and made to speak the truth of cultural studies in order to "police us back into line." Hall is alive to the dangers of this moment, to the risk he runs in responding to this particular invitation, to acting as the voice of the institution of cultural studies. He counters this invitation paradoxically by speaking autobiographically. Hall takes a moment to insist that he is Stuart Hall, a singular, historical being, who will speak a kind of truth. "I'm going to tell you about my own take on certain theoretical legacies and moments in cultural studies," he says, "not because it is the truth or the only way of telling the history. I myself have told it many other ways before." He expects people to disagree. Indeed, he warns us that he may tell a different story himself the next time he's asked.

Hall's insistence that his account is the product of an individual perspective is no humanist nicety: his use of autobiography forces us to think about who is speaking, and so about the place from which history is spoken. It enables him also to draw attention to the problem of disciplinary borders, of group membership, of the collective, and to speak singly, as one whose voice will be heard as that of the corpus but which, nevertheless, tells only one kind of truth. Cultural studies, he observes, has multiple discourses—how can he speak for them all? The problem he faces, then, is precisely that of the collective, of the household, of how and where to draw the lines, to site the threshold of membership. It is precisely this focus on the place of enunciation that leads him to define the central wager of cultural studies—what he calls its "worldliness" (264). He dwells on "the dirtiness of it": on the dirtiness of the semiotic game. It's difficult to overestimate the seriousness of his use of the word *dirt* here, for it refers to cultural studies' hard, political edge—its aspiration to constitute an intellectual discourse that makes a difference, that produces change. Dirt for him is what resists—what matters—it is politics. It is for this reason that he is so unhappy at the prospect of polarizing the field—of deploying "dirt" as a disciplinary category—and singling out and expelling the unclean from those who walk collectively under the banner of cultural studies. He resists the urge to say, "I am clean and you are dirty." Cultural studies, he argues, focuses on the dirt, runs toward and not away from danger.

And yet, even as Hall resists the urge to deploy the language of pollution, the timing of the address and way it is configured as a question of "theoretical legacies," of what cultural studies both owes to theory and so bequeaths to its present practitioners, lead him to mark a boundary, to insist upon a code of membership. He does so in order to stem what he characterizes as "what one can only call the deconstructive deluge as opposed to the deconstructive turn" (274) and so to redress the "incredible theoretical fluency of American Cultural Studies." The truth he tells is hauntingly direct: theory is not our home, it is a way station on the route—it must be fought off. And, in a strangely Serresean moment, Hall speaks of angels—angels that must be wrestled with, mastered, kept at bay lest they make connections and lead one astray. Hall tells us that he has "wrestled with some of these Angels" (266) wrestled with Louis Althusser, in particular, and decided that "he has gone as far in this book as it is proper to go," gone as far as it is moral to do so, gone as far as he can without getting dirty.

At the same time, Hall is "extremely anxious that we should not decode what [he's] saying as an anti-theoretical discourse" (268). "It's not anti-theory," he writes; rather it is about the "problems of developing intellectual and theoretical work as a political practice." And it is here that he comes to the moral, to the truth he wants to tell and which he feels the theoretical fluency of American cultural studies threatens. For him it is a symptom of the dangers of institutionalization. "I do think," he writes, that "there is all the difference in the world between understanding the politics of intellectual work and substituting intellectual work for politics" (275). Perhaps the "I do" is merely manipulative, a rhetorical ploy so that we rush to agree with him, to make up for his apologetic tone by reassuring him, "We do, too." It doesn't really matter. What interests me is his dis-ease with the whole business and the way his language comes to resonate with questions of dirt, cleanliness, and the proper—with all that Derrida sees at stake in the question of the gift and also with all that Serres's fear of belonging, his horror of exclusion, conjures.

SAME AND OTHER

Michel Serres makes two crucial appearances in Vincent Descombes's introduction to modern French philosophy that appeared originally in French under the title *Le Même et l'autre* (1979), and which maps postwar French philosophy in terms of this core question of Same or Self and

Other. In both cases, Serres appears as a soul set apart from the fray, not so much a maverick as an observer, he who labors in a field altogether separate from that of his contemporaries, a field that is less a discipline than a conjunction, the intersection between philosophy and science. Serres appears as one of those thinkers who belongs "to the French tradition for which philosophy can only constitute itself in relation to science."[6]

Given that he does not speak of Marx or Heidegger but of mathematics, it is difficult to place Serres in relation to his contemporaries or to the key concepts of "same" and "other" that Descombes uses to title his book. There are no joint projects, no conversations between Michel Serres and Jacques Derrida, no engagement on either side. When Latour asks Serres about "projects like Derrida's, for the humanities" (C, 38), Serres replies with the absolute, "I never participated in the Heideggerian tradition. I only read his *Being and Time* much later. I've already said why." Immediately conflating Derrida with Heidegger—the two are apparently synonymous—Serres recalls his earlier comment that "when I read *Sein und Zeit* I feel the years before the war emanating from it—not through understanding or memory but physically—I irresistibly breathe the smell of it" (C, 3). Heidegger wreaks. Serres is revolted. And this smell turns into a general "nausea in certain situations," a nausea that led him to take the nearest exit ramp off the "superhighways" of Parisian intellectual life (phenomenology and Marxism) and forge his own alternative routes (C, 7).

Likewise, Derrida rarely speaks of Serres. There is a moment, however, a good way into Derrida's *Given Time (Donner le temps)*, when Serres makes a brief appearance in the text. Derrida is reading Baudelaire's short story "Counterfeit Money," and has been thinking hard about the fact that the action unfolds in a tobacconist's shop. He is approaching the association Marcel Mauss makes between figures of exchange and eating together in his essay *The Gift* by taking a moment to consider the co-incidence of this organic, and yet so thoroughly semiotized, object (tobacco) and an instance of faulty or counterfeit giving, of a particularly overdetermined instance of exchange. "Tobacco symbolizes the symbolic," he observes; "it seems to consist at once in a consumption (ingestion) and a purely sumptuary expenditure of which nothing natural remains. But the fact that nothing natural remains does not mean, on the contrary, that nothing symbolic remains."[7] This meditation on the symbolic aspect of tobacco leads him to the beginning of Molière's *Dom Juan* when Sganarelle holds up a tobacco pouch and extols the virtues of tobacco. "Whatever Aristotle and all of Philosophy might say, there is nothing to equal tobacco," proclaims Sganarelle, making tobacco the chief inspiration for honor and virtue. It is here, in *Dom Juan,* or, more specifically, in the conjunction between Molière and Mauss, that Derrida finds Serres waiting for him.

"So as to register his disappointment," Derrida writes, "Michel Serres briefly links this motif of tobacco in *Dom Juan* with Mauss's essay. One should also note, and Serres does not, that beyond generalities on the gift, Mauss explicitly takes account of the offering of tobacco."[8] The "disappointment" to which Derrida refers derives from an early essay of Serres titled "Le Don de Dom Juan où la naissance de la comédie," which appeared in *Critique* in 1968 and later as the conclusion of "L'Apparition d'Hermès: Dom Juan," in *Hermès I: La communication* (1969).[9] Derrida quotes the passage that draws his ire in a footnote:

> Now open *The Gift* and you will not fail to be disappointed. You will find there interest and compensation, alms and banquet, the supreme law that dictates the circulation of goods in the same way as that of women and promises, feasts, rites, dances and ceremonies, representations, insults and *jokes;* you will find there law and religion, esthetics and economy, magic and death, trade fair and market, in sum: *comedy.* Was it necessary to wander for three centuries over the dull azure eye of the Pacific to learn slowly from others what we already knew of ourselves, to go overseas to witness archaic scenes, the same that we represent everyday on the banks of the Seine, at the Comédie Française, or at the Bistro across the street. [But could we ever have read Molière without Mauss?][10]

Serres the homebody, Serres the killjoy—"unless it is faked," adds a slightly discomposed Derrida, a Derrida who cannot quite read Serres's response, who is uncertain of his sincerity—does not wish to travel, or finds it unnecessary to do so: Serres already comprehends the gift (apparently), already knows that story only too well. And all of this from the man whose patronym is Hermes; all of this from the writer who cruises in the stratosphere, who travels constantly and unpredictably from Lucretius to La Fontaine, to Egypt, Babylonia, Rome, and out into space. What's one short trip to the Pacific for he who is so well traveled?

"If we had to speak of disappointment," Derrida continues, "(which we don't believe we do), ours would not concern the fact that someone or other, at home or elsewhere, had been the first to discover what there is to be said about the gift, but rather that neither Molière nor Mauss, at bottom, has ever said anything about the gift *itself.* And what we are trying to explain here is why there is no *fault* in that."[11] Derrida reads Serres's "disappointment" with Mauss as ingratitude, as an inattentive reading, as an instance of someone who moves on too fast. Serres departs too early from a text upon which Derrida has just arrived, or has not yet left. And Derrida asserts his ownership of Mauss, seeing off Serres, deploying a communal "we" against Serres's singular disappointment. What interests me, however, is the way Serres's disappointment may signal not an

ill-spirited ingratitude or disappointment, so much as it figures a denial
that there is a strategic difference between the Pacific and Paris. Serres
does not rule Mauss out of bounds so much as he elides the distance that
must be traveled in order to understand the gift. It is not that this stay-at-
home Serres does not wish to move, but rather that something happens in
the course of Serres's reading of Molière and Mauss that transforms his
relation to both texts, that elides the temporal and geographical divides
that separate the kinds of knowledge each offers. What we see in this
momentary failure to converse, then, in Derrida's frustrated disappointment with a disappointed Serres, is a hint at Serres's own relation to
ethics, to the home, to the "proper," and so to the boundaries of the
household.

As William Paulson observes, Serres reads *Dom Juan* not as an object for
critique but as a "source of knowledge."[12] He reads the text not as an
object from which one must deduce the logic of exchange or the gift, but
as "a complete treatise on giving and counter-giving" (*H,* 12) that unfolds
"in the collectivity as it is lived, the structures of exchange are only dramatized, representable and represented, in the course of a festive meal"
(*H,* 12–13). Serres reads Dom Juan's succession of gambles, his false
exchanges, as already a meditation on the law of exchange, on the general
rules of living together. "What does one do at a feast if not exchange?" Serres asks. "Whoever will not come to a banquet refuses the law of the gift
and declares war" (*H,* 6). Dom Juan, however, "short-circuits the law of
exchange" by never "return[ing] tobacco for tobacco, that is goods for
goods, words for words, love for love" (*H,* 5). Instead, he gives "words for
goods and love for money." Monitoring this succession of unequal or
derailed exchanges leads Serres to conclude that "the reversal here is universal" (*H,* 11). Dom Juan is not the outsider everyone has taken him to
be, the criminal agent who sabotages society and reproduction: "the false
exchange generates the protective social cell."

It is this move that brought Serres so much attention. As Descombes
reminds us, Serres is the "only philosopher in France to abide by the structuralist method as defined" by Bourbaki, "the collective pseudonym of a
group of French mathematicians working, since 1939, on a definitive sur-
vey of Mathematics."[13] Serres understands "structure neither in the architectural sense (an arrangement of parts whereby 'everything holds
together'), nor in the organic sense ('everything is linked with everything
else' in living forms), but in the mathematical sense." Following his com-
parativist method, "there is no value in the separation of literary genres.
Learning should not be filed on one side (capable of being true or false) and
fiction on the other (neither true or false)."[14] The distinctions themselves
are artificial—the product of a particular historical settlement that disciplines the world into a series of discrete objects of knowledge. "A virtuoso

of the isomorph," Serres instead "brings Descartes' *Meditations* out of a La Fontaine fable or a locomotive out of the work of a nineteenth-century thinker, a theorem out of a narrative, a legend out of a demonstration."[15] "Fable is not a stammering prefiguration of science"; it is science by other means. Myth is already mythology.

Serres operates without metalanguage, then, and "it is impossible," observes Latour, "to distinguish who is providing the explanation; is it the commented text or the commentary?"[16] He aligns two texts (here Mauss and Molière), but, by the end, it is difficult to know which has dominance, which text pre-cedes the other. For example, just as Serres delivers his conclusion, Dom Juan begins to speak for himself:

> Dom Juan says: I am not the one who is breaking the promise; it is you who have failed to live up to your vows. And the extreme conclusion follows: I am not the hypocrite; the whole of society is an imposture. If it is enough to offer tobacco, let us smoke and continue our caprices. The dog, the Turk, the madman, the heretic, the devil dubs the society of reasonable men and Spanish Christians a cabal of heretics, of demons, of mad dogs. *The Other designates the Same as Other:* you follow my law and threaten me for not following it. Hypocrisy implies a distance which is the best criterion for making visible, for representing society as it is. What does one do to be a Turk? At this distance, one gives an objective description of morals and customs. No, Dom Juan does not become devout; he remains a sociologist, specializing in Ottoman customs and archaic rituals of exchange . . .The hero of modernity designates contemporary society as a tribe of primitives. (*H,* 11–12)

Here Molière's language becomes twinned with that of Mauss. Dom Juan becomes a sociologist, becomes Mauss, an ethnographer at home. Serres's essay stages an absorptive meeting that fuses Molière and Mauss, text and critique, an isomorphism so powerful that the one becomes the other: same and other mutually reflect their own conditions of possibility.

As *Dom Juan* ends, so Hermes appears.

> Must it be said of Hermes, the god of commerce, that he is the father of Comedy, by describing the circulation of all things, the inter-individual communication in the feast of exchanged tobacco? Is he the god of crossroads, of thieves and of secrets, this god sculpted on milestones and adorned with such conspicuous virile organs who, like Psychopomp, accompanies Don Juan to hell? (*H,* 13–14)

The crucial point here is that Serres's isomorphic structuralism leads him to understand the co-incidence of tobacco and the gift, of Molière and Mauss, differently than Derrida. His objection is not, as Derrida assumes, that Mauss says nothing about the gift. Serres's does not find "fault" with Mauss. His "disappointment" derives instead from the fact that he no longer operates according to the division of knowledge that insists on an absolute demarcation between Molière and Mauss. With the revelation of sameness—of the gift as an invariant structure of exchange, a general rule, whose ruptures are not true ruptures, but disorder within a self-organizing system—the gift ceases to be a determining absence.

Why then remain within the organization of exchange that the gift grounds? It is Dom Juan–Hermes, the agent of transformation, the figure who permits connections, the conjunction, the prepositional figure whose turns enable exchange, who demands attention.

It is possible, then, to begin to understand and even sympathize with Derrida's frustration. Serres's reading of Molière with Mauss serves as a point of departure rather than an engagement with the gift. It marks a decision to move in a new direction, to find a new set of metaphors, a new mode of transport between and among discourses. While there are clear affinities between Serres's and Derrida's modes of reading—Assad, for example, finds that Serres's "methodological tools are similar to, and at times identical with, deconstructive reasoning"[17]—there remains this fundamental difference. Derrida's commentaries remain within the turn of the texts they read. His readings are parasitic, "draw[ing] their sustenance from within the flesh of the host."[18] "A deconstructive reading must," continues Critchley, "therefore, remain within the limits of textuality, hatching its eggs within the flesh of its host."[19] And, following Critchley, we might say that these "eggs" represent a kind of "Levinasian hermeneutics," the act of revealing the "ethical saying at work within the Said of the text," of opening "the text up to the blind spots or ellipses within the dominant interpretation."[20] This mode of reading is the "ethico-political duty"[21] to which deconstruction enjoins us.

In thinking the gift, then, Derrida does not aim to exit the circle of exchange. Exiting might prove dangerous, perhaps even fatal. It might, quite literally, lead to our unmaking, to so radical a transformation that we would quite simply lose our way, leaving forever the circle of exchange that maintains the boundaries of the *oikos,* of the home, and also of the self. Thinking the gift, however, attenuating the circle of exchange, might enable us to relax the boundaries of the *oikos,* to expand our definition of the "proper" (the household) to include as broad a definition of the "human" as possible. For Serres, however, the gift becomes a given, a closed, self-regulating system. The discovery of sameness, of an overall system or structure, indicates the presence of another set of questions. The terms change. Just as the chronological distance between Molière and Mauss disappears, so also does the opposition between Same and Other, system of exchange and its disruption. Dom Juan is not an outsider, an agent who must be excluded, an agent of pollution, but he who reveals the weave of relations that constitute the total system.

As Paulson notes, in the course of *Conversations on Science, Culture, and Time,* Serres comes to admit that "this is a decidedly non-modern perspective, one that denies any superiority or even specificity to the discourses of modernity, and thus calls into question the status of modernity itself."[22] This point is crucial. For, where poststructuralist thought wrestles with the problems of the so-called Great Divide of the modern, which, as Bruno Latour shows us, insists upon absolute, ontologically distinct zones or dichotomies (nature/culture, world/language, nonhuman/human, same/other), insisting on the gap between the two poles (their purity), Serres behaves as if the poles did not exist.[23] Derrida remains within the terms of these oppositions, parasitically reading their ellipses. Serres, on the other hand, ignores these boundaries, proceeding inductively, empirically, calling things as he sees them, refusing completely to accept oppositions between ideas or concepts that otherwise appear to be the same. It is this "naiveté," as Latour puts it, that enables him to "see things from the point of view of the *known,* not of the knowing."[24] It is not that Serres's thought is in opposition to Derridean modes of reading (he finds no fault with the gift); Serres has simply moved on to frame the questions differently.

His inverted epistemology asks us to forgo subject and object in favor of "uncover[ing] the pre-phenomenological movement in which object, subject and language meet and blend before they separate into their phenomenologically respective domains."[25] Subject and Object, same and other, are part and parcel of a narcissistic narrative in which we humans find ourselves at the center of the world. The revelation of Dom Juan as parasite, however, and of parasitism as the elementary structure of relations, demands different questions and a different way of reading. It produces also a different understanding of the household or the collective as an ensemble of relations founded not on exchange but on the figure of Dom Juan, himself, of the parasite as a relation that precedes exchange.

FROM PARASITE TO SYMBIONT

The Parasite begins with a reading of a fable from La Fontaine: "The city rat invites the country rat on to the Persian rug" (*P,* 3). A meal is made of leftovers among the dirty dishes left on a table. It is a "royal feast." But a noise startles the rats, and they scurry away. Here, Mauss's scene of "eating together" falls prey to a noise, to the "ultimate parasite" (*P,* 4), which chases out the rats. By the end of the first page of Serres's text, there are only parasites in this fable. And Serres discovers in a meal shared by rats on a Persian rug in the home of a tax farmer the parasitic chain.

"Strictly speaking, they [rats, tax farmer, noise] all interrupt," he observes. Neither rat produces nor pays for their meal. The tax farmer has produced none of the food they eat. And the noise too counts as static, "a parasite who has the last word."[26] In this chain, "the last to come tries to supplant his predecessor" (*P*, 4): the arrow only goes one way, though the players may change positions. Serres has nothing to say here about production. Production (food) is a given. There are only parasites. And "to parasite means to eat next to" (7). He expands this definition later in the text, noting that to parasite means "to play the position or to play the location is to [and] dominate the relation . . . that is the meaning of the prefix *para-* in the word *parasite*: it is on the side, next to, shifted; it is not on the thing, but on its relation" (38). The *sitos* is the food; but, sometimes, it is also dirt.

Serres is alive to the fact that he is speaking a strange language. The subtitle to this opening chapter is "Cascades," a term derived from cybernetics. He is crucially aware, also, that all he is doing so far is describing La Fontaine's story, representing each player and each move as it occurs. "The system constructed here [in the fable]," he tells us, "beginning with a production, temporarily placed in a black box, is parasitic in a cascade. But the cascade orders knowledge itself, of man and of life, making us change our terminology without changing the subject" (*P*, 5). In the course of his description of this cascade, the players change positions, passing from parasite to host, as successive interruptions produce the narrative line. In the course of the cascade, "our main object is decentered; the subject is decentered in turn, three times" (8). "Philosophy," however, "is still caught in the relation between subject and object." In the story Serres is reading subject and object keep moving around, crossing lines, weaving together all the players: rats, farmer, noise. It's hard to keep things straight according to the usual rules. By the end of his reading, no differences will remain between rats, humans, microbes, breaks in the message, static. Ontology collapses. Hospitality reigns. The world of fable accommodates them all. But all the guests are abusive.

Tracing the relations between hosts and parasites, the turns by which positions are exchanged, by which subject and object switch places, Serres posits this law: "there is no system without parasites. This constant is a law" (*P*, 12). As soon as one parasite installs itself as king, another chases it out. This law leads him to doubt the wisdom of chasing out the parasite at all, of policing a discipline perhaps. "Someone once compared the undertaking of Descartes," he adds playfully, "to the action of a man who sets his house on fire in order to hear the noise the rats make in the attic at night.

These noises of running, scurrying, chewing and gnawing that interrupt his sleep." But what is the point, finally, of insisting, "I want to sleep peacefully . . . I want to think without an error, communicate without a parasite?" For "mistakes, wavy lines, confusion, obscurity are part of knowledge; noise is part of communication, part of the house." "But is it," he asks, "the house itself?" (12).

What is the rest of *The Parasite* if not an attempt to come to terms with this question, to discover if an ethical relation is possible or whether the parasite as primary relation precludes the possibility of symbiosis, of the gift as that which appears? In the succession of interrupted meals, diminishing returns, disputed portions, and unpaid rents that follow, Serres traces the shape of this irreversible arrow that is the elementary relation of the parasitic chain. Information theory permits him to talk of collectives, households, and communities. Whereas for Derrida *oikos* and *nomos* are mutually implicating categories, a double articulation, if you like—"as soon as there is law there is partition: as soon as there is nomy there is economy"[27]—and economy is circular, a figure of exchange, of the circulation of goods, for Serres the household ceases to be an entity founded on exchange. As *The Troubadour of Knowledge* makes explicit, his formulation supplies a new anthropology, dethroning the sovereign premise of exchange in favor of what in he calls "the straight, asymmetrical, more elementary arrow" (*TK*, 46). The parasite comes first; exchange comes second.

It all costs him dearly, though. Serres has his salad bowl spat in repeatedly; marked as someone else's property—their food—and so rendered inedible to him. And all the while he encounters players who would happily kill their hosts or chase out the parasite, declare it an infection, declare war on what is unclean, improper, dirty. Faced with the dubious conclusion that he has written a book of evil, faced with the knowledge, in the end, that there are only parasites, that all he can do is describe the chain, that he cannot delimit a space of ethical action, Serres pushes off into the ocean—an ocean that, as Eric White notes, seems to figure as "[an] image of absolute dissolution,"[28] an ecstatic embrace of the sea as that which will dissolve the evil that he sees everywhere. But is pushing off into the ocean after discovering the parasitic structure of home really a figure of unmaking, of complete dissolution, what Stuart Hall might see as flight from danger, dirt, or "worldliness"?

The Parasite ends with what Serres calls the "worst of definitions": the end of *The Odyssey*. "Ulysses won the contest," writes Serres, "making a simple arrow, the relation, irreversible, with no possible return, through the lined-up axes, iron that separates" (*P, 252*). And so, both texts end at home, "amidst corpses"—an ending that Serres finds unbearable. "Thus," he goes on, "the horrible insect left my room . . . Something had begun. Quiet, serene, no anxiety. The high seas" (*P, 253*). Could not this image of the sea serve just as well as a figure of possibility, as a beginning rather than an end? Ulysses arrives home: Serres departs. Ulysses comes home, as he must, completing the circle, marking out the space of the home, the archetypal figure of economy, "going away," as Derrida observes, "only in view of repatriating himself, in order to return to the home from which the signal for departure is given and the part assigned, the side chosen, the lot divided, the destiny commanded"[29] and so, by Derrida's logic, the gift—that which suspends economic calculation, which interrupts the circle—fails to appear. But, for Serres, this knowledge marks a beginning.

Accepting the parasitic chain as home, as *the* definition of home itself, and not as a perverse aberration, suspends the logic of pollution that characterizes Hall's response to the invitation he receives and that haunts *The Parasite*. "Home" ceases to be a place that one may speak of in terms of belonging. The household ceases to be marked by a boundary and instead becomes a permanent act of turning, a permanent movement—what Assad teaches us to understand as a "'Ulyssean meandering' *(randonné)*, with no fixed destination to cut short its inventive course,"[30] and what Levinas represents by "oppos[ing] the nomadic wanderings of Abraham to the well-rounded narrative of the *Odyssey*."[31] The word *randonné* derives from an Old French noun that expresses also the quality of randomness, an erring, errant, disordered course, but it also embraces the gift *(le don)*, presenting it as a state, a permanent relation.

This acceptance begins an ethical project, a project that requires a thinking through and beyond the fixed categories of the modern, and that, in *The Natural Contract*, Serres casts in terms resonant of Derrida's exploration of responsibility and gift giving via the notion of the contract. "I am deliberately playing on a single word of exchange, *give*," writes Serres; "we receive gifts from the world and we inflict upon it damage that returns to us in the form of givens" *(NC, 43)*. The shift in tenses is, I think, crucial to understanding the ways in which Serres is playing here with both the gift and the parasitic chain. These past-tense gifts, the nominal results of an unequal exchange, signal to us our parasitic identity—they constitute a call from the Other, an address, a call to responsibility, a call to make a contract with the world itself, and to reject the irreversible, single arrow of the parasitic chain. For, if Derrida remains interested in the gift, Serres takes on the matter of the given, of the *préposé*, of the tare, the gifts we have received, but which we have forgotten, and so take for granted. We are finally, according to Serres, growing up—"irresponsibility only lasts through childhood" *(NC, 39)*. We're finally, paying attention to the givens.

And so we come to the question of the collective, of the ways in which we may begin to constitute this responsibility as a practice. Crucially, the penultimate section of *The Parasite* raises this very question—"what living together is. What is the collective?" "How do we make the common proper?" (P, 224)—the same questions that made Stuart Hall so very uneasy. The answer Serres comes up with is initially rather disappointing. "I don't know," he admits, "and I doubt that anyone does. I have never read anything that taught it to me. This black category of the collective, group, class, caste, whatever, is it a being in turn, or a cluster of relations?" (P, 224–25). Proceeding from this confession of inadequacy that sounds a little like Hall's desire to speak singly, autobiographically, Serres lights on the figure of the quasi object as a constructor of intersubjectivity, "the object that is not an object but a quasi-subject since it marks or designates a subject who, without it, would not be a subject." In the shifting pronouns that the quasi object weaves together, Serres finds the collective, a model of the household different from that of economy, of which Ulysses and the *oikos* represent only one possible variation—the worst definition. *The Natural Contract* marks an attempt to make the network of relations that Serres finds in the quasi object a reality, to force the issue, so to speak.

Here, Serres returns to the sea, to the ending of *The Parasite,* but this time he "casts off," in a boat, his favorite trope of government, and also of the global. For on a boat, he observes, "there is no refuge," no leftover space to make one's own, to capitalize upon. There is only a "sea-going pact," a precursor to the natural contract, "because here the collectivity, if sundered, immediately exposes itself to the destruction of its fragile niche, with no possible recourse or retreat" (NC, 40). As "contemporary society" becomes worldwide, he adds, "occupying all of the earth, solid as a block through its tightly woven interrelations, it has nothing left in reserve, no external place of withdrawal or recourse" (NC, 41). The earth becomes a boat; host and parasite are forced into a symbiotic relationship in order to keep from drowning, from a literal unmaking. Casting off then would mean not immersion in the sea, not a sublime or ecstatic irruption of the system, the arrival of the gift, but an acceptance of the givens, of the symptoms that return to us as evidence that "we have acted irresponsibly."

But how to effect this "casting off?" "How," to reprise Hall's accusations concerning intellectual and political work, do you get from "the personal to the political"? Here, Serres speaks of ligatures, of cords that bind us together, and also of the elision of leftover spaces beyond the boundaries of what we each call "home," an elision of the "proper" as we all become members of a "home" that occupies the surface of the entire planet—we are becoming collective whether we like it or not. I could say also that if Serres is always at home, if in all of his travels, from Hermes to Harlequin, he insists that "everywhere everything is the same," then it is perhaps, as he says, because,

> the body [that travels] assimilates and retains the various differences
> experienced during travel and returns home a half-breed of new ges-

tures and other customs, dissolved in the body's attitudes and functions, to the point that it believes that as far as it is concerned nothing has changed. (*TK*, xvii)

To travel, already comprehending the gift, having already understood the logic of the parasitic chain, to travel already knowing Levinas's observation that to have a home is to deprive the other of a place, knowing that every declaration of a gift is predicated on a violent sacrifice, is to understand that wherever one goes, the risks that pertain to constructing a household, of constituting a collective, remain urgently present. The question is not therefore of doing away with the parasitic chain but rather of finding a modality that will not turn deadly; returning home to the law of the proper, to the law that excludes the other, is only the worst outcome—it is not the only outcome. Casting off requires an attention to the ligatures that bind the crew together, the roped part or crew as collective in which the "subject is not you or I or he, but the roped party, that is the cord. You may be an anchorite who has emigrated to the remotest dens of high silent valleys, but now you have cast off doubtless in spite of yourself, for something collective" (*NC*, 103).

In the final sections of his conversation with Bruno Latour, titled "Wisdom," Serres begins to speak in a different way about this becoming global, about the fate of morality for us. "So, then, science and technology remove the distinction upon which morals are based?" Latour asks (*C*, 170). And Serres responds by noting that now we no longer have to ask "the Cartesian question: How can we dominate the world?" We are forced to answer a different question: "How can we dominate our dominion; how can we master our own mastery?" (172). The issue is not a limitless freedom, however, so much as an increasingly obligated course of action. "In dominating the planet," Serres observes, "we become accountable for it . . . *We are going to have to decide about every thing, and even Everything*" (173). And this obligation leads to what he calls an "objective morality." The issue is this: "When necessity decamps from the objective world and moves towards people, morality, in turn, moves from individual people towards the natural world" (175). Suddenly, the reasons for our behavior become global, "so the Earth can continue, so that the air remains breathable, so that the sea remains the sea." The party is over. The West may no longer stuff itself at the expense of the world. The stakes are too high.

This knowledge will come individually; however, it will be felt locally. And what Serres discovers at the end of *The Natural Contract* is the logic of irreplaceability—the logic that Derrida locates in the "gift of death" and that he represents through the *mysterium tremendum* or "frightful mystery, the secret that makes you tremble involuntarily,"[32] the moment at which you are brought face to face with your own objecthood, and which Hall approaches through his redefinition of autobiography as a provisional way of speaking "here and now." It is with just such an involuntary trembling—an earthquake—that Serres ends *The Natural Contract:* he calls it his signature. "In distress," the social contract unraveling, the boat sinking, the earth shaking, his house collapsing—Serres "return[s] to [his] familiar universe, [his] trembling space, the ordinary nudities, [his] essence, precisely to ecstasy" (*NC,* 124). This earthquake, he says, is a permanent relation, it is our home, it is the essence of home. It is a moment when you are here and only here, when your irreplaceability is predicated not on a supposedly unique self but on your identity as that which shakes along with and because of the Other. It is to this space that Serres's turns, his wanderings, lead, from Hermes to the parasite, to the declinations of the Lucretian clinamen.

And here it seems important to remember Serres's horror of critique, of modes of knowledge that amass capital, that are thrifty, that worry about expenditure—but which, in the end, tell only the story that we already know. In contrast, he forges ahead, preferring to "move forward . . . at the risk of falling, skipping over a few weak points" (*C,* 131), preferring "invention with the danger of error to rigorous verification, which is paralleled by the risk of immobility." He avoids philosophies of suspicion, modes of thought which he characterizes as "secondary," "parasitic," whose "ultimate goal is to escape all possible criticism, to be beyond criticism." It is this question of risk, of the dangers involved in moving forward, of courting danger, that returns me to Stuart Hall's characterization of cultural studies as that most dirty of disciplines, as a pursuit of danger, of wagering, of putting everything at risk in order to say something. There is, in the end, for me, a curious affiliation between these two writers, even as their work leads in opposite directions. Hall is correct to be worried about the dangers of institutionalization—and Serres is equally correct in his refusal to speak any longer in terms of the proper, of pollution. On this score, it is important to understand that cultural studies itself aspires to be a type of quasi object, weaving together a new kind of collective, just as Serres's own writings, by their disciplinary crossings and meldings, constitute new kinds of intellectual terrain, offering us road maps for a new collective to wander through.

ERRARE HUMANUM EST

It is human to wander. It is human to stray, to rove, to be in error, to be wrong, to be at fault. The fault is human. "I do not believe I know . . . a better definition of man" (*TK,* 79), writes Serres. I do not believe I know a better definition of Serres's own errant ethic, his wandering, roving course. It may be "impossible," as Latour has said, "to ask what's Serres' ethic"—the ethic is in the turn; it is inherent to the parasitic chain, to the symbiosis that *The Natural Contract* attempts to negotiate. His ethic is his foundation.

At various moments, however, Serres does suggest some rules for "living well," some rules that the wanderer should observe:

> out of regard for the health of life and mind, I had to conceive, for my private use, some rules of ethics or deontology:
>
> After attentive examination, adopt no idea that would contain, on the face of it, any trace of vengeance. Hatred, sometimes, takes the place of thought but also makes it smaller.
>
> Never throw yourself into polemic;
>
> Always avoid all membership; flee not only all pressure groups but also all defined disciplines of knowledge, whether a local and learned campus in the global and societal battle or a sectorial entrenchment in scientific debate. Neither master, then, nor above all disciple.
>
> These rules do not trace a method, but very precisely an exodus, a capricious and seemingly irregular trek constrained only by the obligation to avoid speculative places held by force, generally watched over by guard dogs. (*TK*, 136)

These rules are private, personal, Serres-specific. They are not generalizable to his readers. The lesson that Serres offers those of us working in the spaces that fall between science and the humanities, in postmodern ethics, or in cultural studies, is rather a caution against solidifying our positions, deploying dirt as a means to violence, as a way of policing boundaries. Most of us, of course, will remain within a particular institutional home; we will "interpellate," to use a keyword from the angel with whom Hall wrestled; the point, however, as Donna Haraway remarks, is that the ideological hailing of "interpellation is also an interruption of the body politic that insists that those in power justify their practices, if they can."[33] "It is also best," she adds, "not to forget that 'they' might be 'we.'" If we are interrupted; or, rather, when we are interrupted, will the noise count as a subject? It is in Haraway's own attempts to imagine new kinds of networks and circuits (her "Cyborg Manifesto") and in Latour's imagined "democracy extended to things"[34] and attempts to create "a politics freed from Science"[35] that we can perhaps begin to imagine what such a future might resemble.

Until these radical democratic futures arrive, however (and we are still waiting), following Serres, we might say that the very notion of an "ethical turn" is a misnomer rather than a blind alley or substitute for politics. Ethics, as Derrida will also tell you, is not a place we enter, but a place that, by our turning, we find ourselves already to occupy. It is, for Serres, a question of recognizing that the gift has already been received and ignored—a question of belatedness. And, yes, the end of the *Odyssey* is the "very worst definition" of the home—it is an ethics, albeit of a fascistic kind—but to assert our ownership of that knowledge might prove our best way of dealing with what, a while ago, Deleuze and Guattari observed to be "the material problem" facing us: "knowing whether we have it within our means to make the selection, to distinguish the BwO from its doubles: empty vitreous bodies, cancerous bodies, totalitarian and fascist."[36]

NOTES

1. Simon Critchley, *The Ethics of Deconstruction: Derrida and Levinas* (Oxford: Blackwell, 1992), 1.

2. Lawrence Buell surveys the "ethical turn" in literary studies "In Pursuit of Ethics," *PMLA* 114, no. 1 (1999): 7–19. He sees it as a hopeful but also intensely problematic development—easy prey to charges of political irrelevance from the Left and moral relativism from the Right.

3. Jacques Derrida, *Given Time 1: Counterfeit Money*, trans. Peggy Kamuf (Chicago: University of Chicago Press, 1992), 4.

4. Maria Assad, *Reading with Michel Serres: An Encounter with Time* (State University of New York Press, 1999), 1.

5. Stuart Hall, "Cultural Studies and Its Theoretical Legacies," in *Stuart Hall: Critical Dialogues in Cultural Studies,* ed. David Morley and Kuan-Hsing Chen (London: Routledge, 1966), 262. Subsequent citations are given in the text.

6. Vincent Descombes, *Modern French Philosophy,* trans. L. Scott-Fox and J. M. Harding (Cambridge: Cambridge University Press, 1979), 87.

7. Derrida, *Given Time 1,* 112.

8. Ibid., 113–14.

9. Descombes, *Modern French Philosophy,* cites Serres's essay in *Critique* in his description of Serres's work. Josué Harari and David Bell include the version of this essay included in *Hermès I* in their introduction to Serres's writings, *Hermes: Literature, Science, Philosophy* (1982). And William Paulson offers an engaging commentary on the essay in *The Noise of Culture: Literary Texts in a World of Information* (Ithaca, N.Y.: Cornell University Press, 1988).

10. Derrida, *Given Time 1,* 113n. The last line of the paragraph is withheld by Derrida in the footnote and then delivered as a punch line or knockout blow.

11. Ibid., 113.

12. Paulson, *The Noise of Culture,* 32.

13. Descombes, *Modern French Philosophy,* 85.

14. Ibid., 90.

15. Ibid., 90–91.

16. Bruno Latour, "The Enlightenment without the Critique: A Word on Michel Serres's Philosophy," in *Contemporary French Philosophy,* ed. A. Phillips Griffiths (Cambridge: Cambridge University Press, 1987), 86.

17. Assad, *Reading with Michel Serres,* 6.

18. Critchley, *The Ethics of Deconstruction,* 23.

19. Ibid., 26.

20. Ibid., 31, 23.

21. Ibid., 24.

22. *C,* 48–62, quoted in William Paulson, "Writing That Matters," *SubStance* 83 (1997): 25.

23. On the Copernican counterrevolution see Bruno Latour's *We Have Never Been Modern,* trans. Catherine Porter (Cambridge: Harvard University Press, 1993), and *Pandora's Hope: Essays on the Reality of Science Studies* (Cambridge: Harvard University Press, 1999).

24. Latour, "Enlightenment without the Critique," 89; quoted also in Assad, *Reading with Michel Serres,* 8.

25. Assad, *Reading with Michel Serres,* 67.

26. As the translator of *The Parasite* tells us (*P,* x), in French, the word *parasite* means "static" as well as the full range of meanings operative in English. In.

27. Derrida, *Given Time 1,* 6.

28. Eric White, "Negentropy, Noise, and Emancipatory Thought," in *Chaos and Order: Complex Dynamics in Literature and Science,* ed. Katherine N. Hayles (Chicago: University of Chicago Press, 1991), 275.

29. Derrida, *Given Time 1,* 7.

30. Assad, *Reading with Michel Serres,* 12.

31. Critchley, *The Ethics of Deconstruction,* 109.

32. Jacques Derrida, *The Gift of Death,* trans. David Wills (Chicago: University of Chicago Press, 1995), 53.

33. Donna Haraway, *Modest_Witness@Second_Millennium.FemaleMan_Meets_ OncoMouse^{tm}* (New York: Routledge, 1997), 50.

34. Latour, *Never Been Modern,* 142–45.

35. Latour, *Pandora's Hope.*

36. Gilles Deleuze and Félix Guattari, *A Thousand Plateaus: Capitalism and Schizophrenia,* trans. Brian Massumi (Minneapolis: University of Minnesota Press, 1987).

"BEING FREE TO WRITE FOR A WOMAN"

The Question of Gender in the Work of Michel Serres

MARIA ASSAD

Before raising the question of gender, we should keep in mind that doing so postulates, from the very outset, a binary argument in which gender is introduced as the speculative opposite of a conscious "other" that in this case would be Michel Serres's writings. We must therefore first and foremost raise the *question* of the question of gender. Is it appropriate to raise this issue for a body of work that clearly strives to address the question of human existence per se as an organic part of objective reality, and does so through inquiries that touch all aspects of a new encounter and a hoped-for reconciliation of subject and object? Does not the question of the vital relationship between subject and object surpass and leave far behind—as perhaps irrelevant—the question of gender? Or, to put it in a loosely Hegelian context, is not the latter recuperated by the former in a global and positive fashion? Finally, and more immediate to the enterprise of this writing, is the question of gender necessary as a separate, isolated discourse focusing on a text that hopes to unite the respective discourses of the exact sciences and the humanities?[1]

Serres's unwavering goal has always been the quest for a theory of knowledge that would reconcile the two in an epistemological rebirth that he calls *le nouveau savoir*. It will bring forth a "new human"; it will create the conditions for an educational revolution; it will produce a new way of thinking that will correct or redirect "what convention has rigorously (logically) divided" [was die Mode streng geteilt] (Friedrich Schiller, *Ode to Joy*). And only if we heed this call for epistemological renewal, Serres suggests, do we escape what he often refers to as collective death, which both the exact sciences and the humanities are blindly leading to in their present, often confrontational efforts.[2]

Understanding Serres's "epistemo-critical" work from this global perspective leaves us a long way from the question of gender. And yet, it must
be kept in focus if the inner and local workings of such a unified theory of
knowledge are to be examined under the light of a feminist perspective. In
the context of his universal goal, the question of gender raises the issue of
the discursive means by which Serres arrives at his all-encompassing vision
of the new human. The question of gender is relevant when considered
within this framework. Indeed, feminists may want to open any debate on
Serres's work with the very term new human, which he consistently renders as *le nouvel homme,* meaning "man" or "mankind." However, strictly
linguistically speaking, *le nouvel homme* (as does *mankind*) ignores the fact
that one-half of mankind is female *(les femmes).* The question of the question
of gender may therefore be answered: Gender is an issue to be raised in
regards to Serres's writings, as long as we do not lose sight of the episte-
mologist's overall intent to outline a new knowledge that goes beyond
gender issues, that is, addresses the renewal of the human condition in its
most basic form that, phenomenologically speaking, precedes any division,
including gender orientation. The following arguments aim to clarify in
detail to what degree it is imperative to keep in mind this caveat. Otherwise, the question of gender cannot be integrated into a critical discussion
of Serres's writings. It would fail to connect with the underlying elements
of his global thought. It would produce a discourse unable to find and share
common ground with Serresean discourse; it would thereby become irrelevant to and for the latter.

It is here assumed as unequivocally understood that the question of gender
implies a problematic of "the feminine" in regards to the topic under consideration. Within the scope of feminist writings, one discerns different
approaches, the more conciliatory ones positing the question of the "male"
in opposition, to be resolved dialectically into a synthesis of reconciled
social dynamics between women and men. In a more radical approach, the
question of the "feminine" creates an adversarial forum in which the "male"
appears as the "other," or sometimes more stridently as the excluded one
in a hierarchical reversal, citing historical evidence to justify such a gesture. In the following, however, none of these strategies will be adopted;
elements of each will appear in unexpected circumstances, in order to
crystallize the question of the feminine in Serresean discourse.[3]
For the English-speaking reader of Serres, the question of gender is initially tied up with the question of gendered language on all levels of communication, but in particular in its lexicological ramifications. Second, as
one of the Romance languages, French grammar is marked by the gender
distinction of masculine/feminine substantivizing and its derivation in
adjectives and pronouns. Serres is a masterly craftsman at using his mother

tongue; his linguistic elegance, lyricism, and feats of lexical agility have few peers among contemporary French publications. Finally, what complicates this scenario even more is Serres's outspoken concern for the role of language in general, whenever it becomes the object of his epistemological discourse. *Les Cinq Sens,* where Serres presents language as a kind of screen or filter, placed between the subject and the immediate reality of objects, and underscores the consequences of this filtering of immediate, sensate reality for cognitive knowledge. Being the empiricist he is, Serres regrets the concomitant loss of immediacy for the subject who compensates by producing ever more sophisticated cognitive systems mediated by language. At the same time, Serres laments the marginalization of language in our technologically driven, micro- and soon nano-chip dominated world. The progressive disappearance of poetry and even literature as such from popular culture is a glaring example of this trend.[4]

However, while *Les Cinq Sens* will furnish the conclusive material for the following discussion, the problem of gender in language is completely absent from this work. Only rarely do Serres's other writings touch upon it. One such exception is an interview he granted in his role as a member of the Académie Française, a three-hundred-year-old institution whose task was and remains today the conservation and linguistic integrity of the French language. At one point in the interview the discussion turns to the 1984 proposals, widely debated in France at the time, concerning the "feminization" of names for professions and functions. Although his stance vis-à-vis such efforts is positive, Serres dismisses the notion that gendered language is sexist per se. The English speaker understands this as a cause-and-effect link; she sees, for instance, the indefinite article *a* transposed into either *un* (masc.) or *une* (fem.), and the pronoun *it* into *il* or *elle,* depending on the gender of the French noun referred to, and therefore tends to be more sensitized to the shift toward a pronounced gender-based division.[5]

Recalling that the feminist movement, including the debate on biased language, originated in the English-speaking world (the United States) with its genderless language, Serres points out that French, like other Romance languages, is less sensitive to gender variations and manipulations than English, *because* it is gendered.[6] In other words, a gendered language is basically less sexist in its variations than a genderless language that has no outlet for variations of the type proposed (professions, professionally related functions, etc.) other than those that immediately appear to be sexist.[7] This argument seems to stand on thin ice, and will not convince a feminist who, when everything is said and done, still sees the articulation masculine/feminine attached to gendered linguistic units of speech.

In the interview, Serres acknowledges the weakness of the purely gender-oriented argument and suggests that an overall hierarchical division underpinning the gender bias in language is the real culprit and is inherent in language as such; it produces divisions, between rich and poor, the educated and the uneducated, the metropolitan resident and the peasant in the hinterland, all as pernicious as those between man and woman. Serres places therefore the whole issue of gender-biased language squarely within the more global issue of socially biased language, while simultaneously voicing his conviction that the feminist movement is one of the most positive outcomes of the twentieth century in its efforts to raise the public conscious to all facets of social injustice.[8] In this context, Serres is in close kinship with sociolinguists who are sensitive to feminist critique of gender-biased language, but who also maintain that language will become gender neutral when and only when sex discrimination and injustice per se disappear from real life.[9] At the same time they call for the eradication of disparaging linguistic stereotypes that uphold a general antifeminist tradition in all forms of communication. "It has always been clear that words are valuable, even essential tools in motivating change."[10]

Serres would certainly concur. His writings trace the history and space of injustice whenever he discourses on exclusion and more generally on the problem of evil *(le problème du mal)*. Similarly, the elegant force and poetic beauty of their language testify to the value he places on both the spoken and the written word as a persuasive and powerful tool to effect changes in the "real" world. As Julia Penelope states very concisely in a rather militant treatise, when condemning the "old patriarchal adage" that a good woman is a silent woman, "language is action. . . . When we speak we are acting *in* the world."[11] With the exception of the interview mentioned above, Serres does not directly address the question of gender in, or take issue with, feminist views on language, yet he has a lot to say about the "silent woman," as will be shown in the following.

The feminine as a paradigm enters Serres's writings fairly early on. Woman appears in the *Hermès* texts under the guise of Venus-Aphrodite and of the sorceress. Venus is here the Lucretian version of the goddess-allegorization of a world in creative flux, in contrast to Mars, the god of rigid mastery. Her figure is also woven into the discourse of *La Naissance de la physique,* Serres's seminal text on an epistemology of turbulence and fluids as contrasted to the "sciences of solids." Serres is equally responsive to Jules Michelet's sorceress, the transhistorical woman who is the embodiment of the Other and serves the misogynist Michelet to glorify the "simple people" *(le peuple)* while railing against clerics and all who would corrupt them. The woman-sorceress is Michelet's romantic figure who incarnates the innate naturalness of the simple people.

For Serres, the key ingredient in both Lucretius's goddess and Michelet's sorceress is the "other." In *La Naissance de la physique,* Venus-

Aphrodite is a sort of ontic otherness who is the background for his interpretation of Lucretius's poem as a scientific treatise on a physics of flux,
the "other" physics forgotten by traditional science until the twentieth century rediscovered it. Significantly different in context, Michelet's sorceress is not so much other as "othered," a victim of powerful historical forces
that pushed her and what she represents, namely an innate knowledge of
and about nature and how to reconcile it with the natural intelligence of
the human being, out of all domains of authority. Serres's fascination with
the sorceress lies in Michelet's genius, which creates through her image
the "legend of the sciences," the retelling of which "lays bare the secret
conditions that give birth to (any) science" (*LC,* 222). Serres interprets her
story less as an archaeology of the sciences and more as their "other face,"
less as what lies historically underneath than what is the flip side of science
(*LC,* 223).[12] Since Western thought, informed by the Enlightenment, relegated this dark side to the realms of the imprecise, the arational, the illog-
ical, and even the pathological, Michelet's *Sorceress* is a book about the
"other," which for Serres equals misery, persecution, exclusion, and sub-
servience (*LC,* 230).

Although the feminine is clearly identified as "other" on whom Serres
reimposes—via Michelet and Lucretius—a full measure of a certain kind
of authority and power, neither of these discourses relates in any sense to
the question of gender. Here, woman is Serres's cornerstone, and a very
conventional one at that, for a reinterpretation of Lucretius's work as a
treatise on a physics of fluids, where a long tradition had seen in it (merely)
a lyrical, or at most a didactic, poem. Similarly, in the guise of the sorceress she is the allegorical anchor for Serres's attempts to uncover the secret,
"soft" side of science and to lay the foundation for a discourse that would
embrace as equals the sciences, philosophy, and literature. The feminine is
clearly defined in these passages as the excluded "other," the most important axiomatic condition for Serres's radical attempt at creating a unified
discourse for our epistemologically splintered realm of knowledge. Yet
the feminine appears in either a mythical or a folkloric-romantic form and
so is still relegated to a traditional or canonical element. It is akin to common usages of gender difference in various epistemic discourses, and may
seem incongruous in an otherwise very unconventional and radical new
thought.

In *Hermès IV: La distribution,* Serres extracts once more from Michelet's
writings in order to characterize what he calls two aspects of our episteme:
the father side of knowledge that is compared to light and the sun, and the
mother side that is dark and hidden and is associated with the typical
images of menstrual blood and nourishing milk. In such a traditional
framework, culled this time from Michelet's *La Mer* (which is conventionally aligned in French with *la mère* because of phonemic identity), the blood

and milk, synecdochally replacing the feminine part, become varieties of the elementary, prebiotic "soup" out of which human knowledge arises (*LD,* 1 5 0–54). In turn, this ur-soup is associated with images of chaos, cosmic cyclones, and ur-tempests. The figure of the feminine that crystallizes out of these passages would be identical to long-held convictions that the feminine is the chaotic element sowing disorder in a world shaped by the masculine element of logical clarity and order, were it not for Serres's equally insistent assertion that woman's knowledge lies in empirical detail (*LD,* 1 5 3). The empiricist Serres recognizes as a great advantage her devoted attention to the local, vis-à-vis the masculine inclination to generalize globally: "One needs to be a woman or to become a woman a bit, if one wants to use the microscope" [Il faut être femme ou se faire un peu femme pour réussir au microscope] (*LD,* 1 5 3). It is therefore imperative for his discourse, at least in the *Hermès* texts, to underscore the gender difference in order to focus on what is slowly but persistently emerging in later writings: namely, Serres's quest into chaos and its seminal significance for order, and less concern with what defines order as the elemental epistemological matrix arising from a formless chaos.

As Serres develops his "philosophy of chaos," he recognizes the need to readdress the notion and nature of the *concept* that he understands as a reduction of variabilities and multiplicities to cognitive unity (*G,* 1 7–1 8).[13] Without abandoning the concept as a unit measure of knowledge—after all, the scientist Serres does not allow for such a deconstructive or postmodern betrayal—he traces the very process of conceptualization as a history of exclusion. The result of this archeological endeavor is *Rome: Le livre des fondations* with its thoroughly Girardian interpretation of order (in the form of pax Romana) constructed on a chain of exclusionary gestures that run the gamut of all sorts of murderous deeds.

By the historical example of Rome, Serres demonstrates the absolute exigency of exclusion *(tertium non datur)* not only for conceptual processes of thought but also for an orderly recreation of the world into our Lebenswelt. *Rome: Le livre des fondations* changes the manipulative "excluded third" of *Le Parasite,* who schemes to join a given system and alter it to its/his liking, into the triumphant conqueror who becomes the system itself and its ordered center. However, never forsaking his quest for the excluded, Serres uncovers it in the other hidden side of Rome, where order cedes to the pliable, nonrigid, to the knotty, messy, irregular, nonlogical, in short to the chaotic. The cult of Vesta, but also a sort of Roman Penelope weaving *and* unraveling at her loom, gives Serres enough material to show what the excluded elements contribute to order. Therefore, "I believe it is possible to think without excluding" [Je crois qu'il est possible de penser sans exclure] (*R,* 8 7). This generalization is then elabo-

rated in terms of gender difference: traditional theoretical work is associated with "the masculine, violence, exclusion, and destruction" (R, 87); it
is negative "male" work, whereas knowledge that does not exclude is feminine. Authentic work, in an ontic sense, is feminine, is chaotic, because it
is all-embracing and meanders. Maintaining gender difference is at once a
conventional reliance on the other to define order according to the principle of identity *and* a strategy to arrive at a very unconventional, even controversial reinstatement of the excluded other into a new conceptual construct of the self.

Serres's "new epistemology" is elaborated by implication in a short presentation of the "baker's logic" (R, 87–90). This expression is sometimes
used by chaologists to illustrate nonlinearity, a key concept in chaos theory, and refers to the baker's repeated kneading and folding of his dough.
But Serres offers a gendered version of this figurative expression: the baker
(le boulanger) produces a complex ensemble of regularity; it can be analyzed and dissected (and priced by units, for sale). The woman baker *(la
boulangère,* which can also mean the baker's wife, but not in Serres's text!),
on the other hand, folds and refolds and comes up with, not a regular
product, but a multitude of different things.[14] The woman baker quietly
and privately works a system that harbors deterministic chaos. To introduce this scientific-mathematical theory into his discourse, Serres aligns
the feminine with silence, exclusion, and chaos, but also with nonlinear
logic that includes, implies, folds, mixes, and thereby sets the stage for
what in his writings after *Rome* becomes a philosophy of the Other that
leads eventually into a pedagogical theory of inventive creativity *(le tiers-
instruit).*

In *Rome: Le livre des fondations* Serres stands at the cusp of a discourse that
is conventional in terms of reliance on analytical development, and at the
same time radical in its bold embrace and acceptance of the Other in terms
of the feminine. Having excluded the other, philosophically and epistemologically, Western thought has opted for rational, explanatory clarity and
epistemological linearity and pushed aside the nonsolvable and
nonclarifiable into the realm of the nonscientific, where, incidentally, the
feminine aspects of life are also being housed. Serres reverses this construct through often startling terms and metaphors of which his feminine
version of the baker's logic is only one example. Thus obliquely introduc-
ing complexity and nonlinear systems theory into his discourse, he regrets
our all too linear, rigid thinking in these words: "We have never conceptualized implication, the included, and the fold. . . . We have never seen
nor listened to women" [Nous n'avons pas pensé l'implication, l'inclus, le
pli. . . . Nous n'avons jamais vu ni écouté les femmes] (R, 89). Expressing
in epistemo-historical terms the core concepts of late-twentieth-century
scientific theories on chaos and complexity allows Serres to expose their

roots in ancient thought, although only since Poincaré have they been captured in mathematical equations and today harnessed, so to speak, by simulation on computer screens. They erroneously appear to be new theories,
an illusion that contributed a great deal to the popularity of chaos theory,
especially when augmented by its stunningly beautiful graphic displays of
strange attractors.

On the other hand, opting to present his scientific discourse in a
metaphoric, often allegorical form that favors the feminine, or what tradition and convention perceive to be feminine aspects of our *Lebenswelt,* is a
discursive strategy that has earned Serres the reputation as a maverick
philosopher-scientist who abandoned the rigor of both philosophical and
scientific thinking in favor of a (merely) poetic form of expression. In a
fashion, Serres has become an excluded other for some in the academic
world who are uncomfortable with his meandering discourse that consciously ignores traditional boundaries between the disciplines and
chronological distances, in his search for a nonexclusionary thought system
that globally would represent our entire episteme. Since Serres inge-
niously inserts himself into his own discourse now and then, it is not far-
fetched to assume that he identifies his literary-philosophical self with that
Other he so ardently evokes as the excluded one who would find acceptance in an epistemological discourse open to complex nonlinear systems.
The feminine is the global allegory for this vast undertaking and brings
together the various arguments: "[New] knowledge is feminine; construc-
tive work is marked by the feminine" [La connaissance est féminine, l'oeuvre est au féminin] (*R,* 87).[15] Serres suggests that, in contrast, classical theoretical work is always negative because it relies on violence and
exclusion; he marks it as a masculine effort.

From a strictly feminist perspective, Serres's presentation of the feminine in *Rome: Le livre des fondations* falls short of a satisfactory position on the
gender question, in as much as his text does not reduce the gender difference, but enlarges it by staking out the gap in scientific-philosophic terms:
linear thinking is male, whereas chaotic thought processes bear female
characteristics. Although he clearly takes the feminine side, the fact that he
joins to it the chaotic and the excluded widens and deepens the gap,
because woman and woman's work have always been associated with
nonorderly and nonscientific aspects of human life. In the final analysis, the
fact that Serres puts himself squarely in the camp of feminine, truly nonex-
clusive work does not attenuate the gender difference that separates logical clarity from its dark and ill-defined reverse side.

This is particularly true in *Genèse* and its dominant allegorical figure of
"la belle noiseuse." *Genèse* brings together the themes of the excluded, the
feminine, and complexity in the subject of the "multiple." Chaos as a molecular Brownian movement is the underlying scientific grid on which Ser-

res builds a story of open-ended multiplicity and liberating variability. But the choice of his primary allegorical figure, borrowed from Balzac's novella *The Unknown Masterpiece*, reinforces the image of woman as the bearer of chaotic conditions and fatal disorder. Serres's meandering interpretation of *la belle noiseuse*, with its startling and oddly ingenious associations that go far beyond the Balzacian tale's narrative scope and intent, does not erase the traditional portrait of the feminine as other.[16] On the contrary, Serres's unself-conscious reliance on a conventional "other" echoes Balzac's careful management of any truth value that his story attaches to *la belle noiseuse*. The novelist did, in fact, elide the sobriquet *belle noiseuse* in later revisions of his novella, so that this rather chaotic, disconcerting, even negative surname would not diminish the moral integrity of the woman passionately but chastely adored by the story's central figure, an old master painter. Reinstating the sobriquet allows Serres to give full measure to the chaotic multiple as the harbinger of a true paradigm shift in the full sense that Thomas Kuhn gave to this term. It leads him to discover that *la belle noiseuse* is the simulation of a deterministic system in the process of becoming chaotic. Balzac, of course, expressed this anecdotally, in the portrayal of three artists whose works the narrative introduces as a process culminating—but not ending—in a portrait of chaos. Serres's reading effectively transposes this portrayal into postmodern terms by which his reader may recognize the simulation of a dynamical system's nonlinear behavior over time.

However, this remarkable discovery of nonlinear thinking encoded in a nineteenth-century story is built on the absolute need to preserve gender difference, or more generally on the unalterable otherness that represents all the unpredictable and chaotic aspects of life. In this respect Serres pursues the same conventional divide between masculine clarity and feminine chaos that informs the discourse of most chaologists. Writing on the deeply embedded intertwining of science and culture, Katherine Hayles points to a concomitant ambivalence that confronts nonlinear dynamicists when they "open themselves to the otherness [of chaos]" and do so as scientists for whom chaos is both an immensely promising new direction in scientific research and a threat to classical tenets of scientific rigor and linearity.[17] Hayles sees this paradox as the reason why women are strangely absent from descriptions of the new science and its short history (she uses James Gleick's popular book *Chaos* as an example). "Paradoxically, this exclusion facilitates the incorporation of the feminine principle of chaos into science." The feminine becomes "an abstract principle" and is thus effectively controlled. "As a result, chaos is admitted into the boundaries of scientific discourse, but science remains as monolithically masculine as ever."[18]

By choosing Balzac's novella, Serres handicaps himself in similar fashion, for Balzac had taken precautions to control chaos in his story, making the old master succumb to progressive dementia, thereby rendering his painting of chaos a product of his madness. The chaotic feminine thus remains absolute otherness imprisoned in a "mad" painting, and Serres's reading repeats this linkage. The gender question needs to be addressed elsewhere in Serres's writings.

Les Cinq Sens is not simply a study of and on the five senses. Rather, it presents a demonstration "that our sense of ourselves as 'subjects,' in spite of Socrates' endless words and Descartes' careful *cogito,* is grounded in and cosubstantial with our physical bodies as the seats and receptors of our five senses."[19] It offers an empirical perspective that eschews a purely materialistic point of view and outlines instead a synergic aesthetics that, if adopted in its fullest sense, may redeem language (conceived as an interfering screen between the subjective self and objective reality) and redirect the sciences of the "static" or "thetic" (which are Serresean terms for Cartesian linearity and binary reasoning) to explorations of nonlinear dynamical processes. More than any of Serres's other writings, this text reveals what some critics refer to as Serres's materialistic or scientific mysticism *that denies itself any recourse to transcendence.*

In order to convincingly outline an epistemological thought construct that fluidly passes between empiricism and purely sensate experience, Serres anchors his demonstration in a "system" of implications that is remarkable for two reasons: First, references to nonlinear dynamical systems theory become more and more explicit in a chain of fables, mythological tales, and literary allusions. They culminate in a very novel rendition of Ulysses' "meandering" voyage that is nothing less than a detailed description of a "strange attractor basin" in other—poetic—words. Second, in the absence of any transcendental interpretation or meaning, the "fluid passages" between what is materialistic and what is mystical in Serres's developing philosophy of the sensate acquire a certain quality of *immanence.* This is expressed most succinctly in the subtitle of *Les Cinq Sens, Philosophie des corps mêlés,* and earned Serres the title of "philosopher of the métis." Immanence is put squarely before the reader, sometimes shockingly, as in the opening story of the shipwrecked sailor who experiences his body both as a subjective self and as an object of the world, without however being able to discern the fine line between inner and outer reality. Furthermore, translated by Serres as the "immediate" (*l'immédiat*) or the "immediately given" (*le donné*), the immanent is wedded in this text to the métis who harbors, of course, the nonlinear, chaotic, and unpredictable aspects of life. The key to these global epistemo-critical outlines lies in the linkage between immanence and nonlinearity with its implication of otherness. It is at this juncture that Serres's writings open up wide to the question of the feminine.

Several feminine figures form, as it were, a set of allegorical plumblines that allow Serres to construct his discourse of the five senses. Among them are the painter Bonnard's nudes, the Lady with the Unicorn of the tapestries in the Cluny Museum, and Eurydice of the Orphic myth. From a purely feminist perspective, they are somewhat diaphanous figures that serve an apophantic role for the issues discussed in *Les Cinq Sens*. But for Serres, they are the master key to unlocking the shackles of the excluded middle, so that the latter becomes a liberated other who no longer merely strives to join a given bipolar system in hopes of shedding its parasitic otherness. The other as other, already validated as the chaotic "multiple" in *Genèse,* acquires in *Les Cinq Sens* an aesthetic character that is a *constitutive element* of the authentic self in harmony with immanent reality. The other as other is the seat of "sensate wisdom," a state of grace by which Serres means a state of utter immanence.

Such a state Serres finds it in the figure of Mary, conventionally known as the woman who humbly consented, so that "the Word became flesh." But true to his epistemo-critical vision, Serres does not refer to the traditional icon of the woman-mother-virgin, the woman with child who changed the course of history. Instead of seeing in her the woman "full of grace" through whom the divine Word took on human form, he perceives her as the woman full of grace *before* the divine spirit descended upon her. Serres's unusual perspective on the *immanent gratuitousness* of a woman who, through a long cultural and religious tradition, is celebrated today in all her transcendent power as the Mother of God, comprises a feminist approach that is unique and touches at the core of the question of gender.

In order to recognize the power of Serres's strategy that operates without relying on concepts of transcendence, it is useful to reiterate at this point a particularly profound feminist argument that analyzes the female condition from the standpoint of the Hegelian dichotomy of transcendence and immanence. In a thorough discussion of Simone de Beauvoir's Hegelian critique of the feminine condition, Genevieve Lloyd underscores the renowned feminist's argument that the conceptualization of the self occurs when the human being transcends its biological destiny and becomes a moral, rational, and toolmaking being, who incorporates ethical values, reasoning power, and the rational capacity to control the concrete world of objects.[20] In the process of the appearance of man as such a transcendent being, the purely biological sphere becomes an Other. But since the female human in her maternal being is bound essentially to her biological destiny, she cannot raise herself entirely above her bodily existence. An essential part of her being remains tied to the immanent world that is the other for the male being in transcendence. Nonetheless biologically close and similar to the female, man must therefore take extra care to distance himself from her in order to safeguard his status as an "inalienable

free subject" rising above merely natural existence. It follows that transcendence "is a transcendence *of* the feminine." Lloyd concludes from her
reading of de Beauvoir "that the ideal of transcendence is . . . a male ideal
[and] that it feeds on the exclusion of the feminine."[21] In spite of many similar critical accounts of the Hegelian dualism of the male ideal of transcendence and the feminine destiny whose innate animality binds woman forever to immanent reality, the hegemony of transcendence remains a very
concrete issue for feminists today.

In *Les Cinq Sens,* the passage on Mary is rather short and is soon enlarged
by references to other biblical women. But its brevity, when compared to
other tales in this text, belies its overarching importance. For it is but the
culmination of two hundred pages in which Serres demonstrates that the
subjective self gains its full self-consciousness through the immediate
experience of the senses. A corollary to this tremendous and difficult
project is Serres's reassessment of language as the means by which the subjective self has learned to bypass the immediate experience of sensate
knowledge of reality conceived as potentially dangerous in its raw state.
Mediated through words, the immediate world (the Hegelian "mere life")
is no longer threatening. Language is the screen, says Serres, behind which
the self feels safe in its "higher" being, while the exterior becomes the
other. Language, in the widest Serresean sense, is therefore a save haven;
behind its walls the subject constructs knowledge of the world in a mediated, higher form. In the Serresean discourse, language is the trope that
marks the inner sanctum of the initiated (transcendent) self, what is also
referred to as the sacred ivory towers of science and other domains of
knowledge that exclude the uninitiated.

Serres has thus once again demonstrated the power of the fundamental
principle of identity built on the excluded middle (the other), this time in
terms of the sacred and the laic (the profane).[22] The woman full of grace is
of necessity identical with the laic or uninitiated other, because she lives in
the graceful-ness of immediate reality. Other than humbly consenting, she
does not find words to counter the angel's message. Serres emphasizes her
grace-ful acceptance, in the full gratuitousness of her being, to be the
instrument by which the "Word could become flesh," that is, become
immanence or "mere life." Mary and the other biblical women Serres
recalls share in common their status as silent beings who remain absent and
distant from the sanctum of words (knowledge) and who work patiently
and effectively in the background, without words. They remain outside
the circle of the initiated, for which Serres uses the Last Supper as a founding example. It is the feast of words (language, knowledge) that stands at
the beginning of a long history in the course of which the "Word" grows
into an earth-spanning message, is secularized and a million times multiplied until it has today become the totalizing knowledge of a global tech-

nocracy that leaves behind as other anyone who is not willing or able to follow its dictates.

By going back to the founding hour of Christianity, the Annunciation, and conscious of the full power of the cult of Mary as the instrument by which the divine Word could join human-ness in its biological reality, Serres creates a highly effective scenario for his efforts to rediscover the values of bodily sensate experience. For he sets aside the transcendent significance of the woman, peels away the millennial layers of cultural and religious tradition, and exposes the Other, the authentically laic one, the graceful one, in short, sheer immanence embodied in a woman-as-other. His argument sets out from a starkly different perspective on "transcendence." Instead of understanding it as the formative faculty of a self-conscious being imbued with the ability to create values that supersede mere immersion in biological life, Serres views transcendence as the illusion of a knowledge created by the gesture of exclusion. Transcendence exists when and only when a sanctum has been erected, and a dichotomy of the sacred and the laic has been instituted. For Serres therefore, transcendence is always the harbinger of the fateful separation of the human subject from the objective world "outside"; it cannot and must not play a role in his discourse if the latter is to genuinely pursue the reevaluation of the Other. Seen from Serres's point of view, the feminist argument that Hegelian transcendence is essentially a "transcendence of the Feminine" is flawed, because it implies an intrinsic maleness of transcendence and femaleness as mired in mere biological existence. It does not effectively reduce the dialectic opposition of male and female. Serres, however, relates the immanence of a life experience full of grace through the story of a woman-as-other, whose word-less gratuitousness has the power to tear down the walls of the sanctum erected by words, so that laicism or otherness no longer bears the onus of exclusion.

Serres relates the story of Mary, not of the Annunciation, but of the one "before," full of sensate, immediate experience, the one who is ignorant of the exclusive sanctum of words, the *laic one*. He salutes the woman full of grace in whom he recognizes the chance for a grace-ful birth of the Word, so that language will no longer deluge the world of objects with endless streams of words. Knowledge based on grace-ful language will eventually become the goal for the *tiers-instruit* in Serres's book by the same title. What is of interest here is that the triadic connection between the feminine, the other, and laicism allows Serres to break through the construct of gendered thinking and to arrive at a genuinely nongendered discourse where the other—in any form—evolves into the instructed middle. The dialectic division of maleness and femaleness disappears. Serres's discourse practices in this regard what Alison Wylie expects of a future that will have resolved the question of gender: "My hope is that a genuinely feminist transformation of science and of society will realize a degree of human inclusiveness—intellectually, socially, economically— that will render feminism unnecessary both as a political movement and as a locus of intellectual, scientific engagement."[23] It should not surprise the reader of Serres that there are few feminine references or female figures in his writings that follow *Les Cinq Sens*. Or, stating the same in other words, the feminine is everywhere in *Statues* and *Le Tiers-instruit,* but is there absorbed into a larger, all-embracing dynamical process giving birth to an inventive creativity that does no longer know exclusion. The question of gender finds its answer in the education of the other who grows into an instructed middle. Serres does not hesitate to put himself into *Le Tiers-instruit* as a pupil of such lifelong dynamical learning. One should therefore not take as sheer hyperbole Serres's exclamation: "Je suis féministe convaincu."[24] It is one of the most gender-less statements made by the philosopher of the métis.

NOTES

1. Going well beyond the postmodern critical acceptance of a parallel status for the discourses of science, philosophy, and literature, Serres treats these thought systems as identical, their differences being a matter of historical shifts of perception and metaphorical usage. It is one of the more radical traits of his work that he strives to express this identity in a single global discourse of culture and science. This earns him frequent criticism from scholars, feminists included, who are wary of totalizing tendencies (and their potential political ramifications) inherent in efforts to arrive at a global thought system.

2. For Serres, the sciences have become the agent of collective death by producing tools of global destruction. Similarly, the humanities have boxed themselves into systems that perpetuate linear, repetitive thinking and thereby induce intellectual sterility and a catastrophic paucity of authentic creativity.

3. I feel compelled to offer a caveat at this point. Some feminists may not see the arguments being presented in this essay as valid aspects for a discussion on the question of gender. I would like therefore to clarify that I am not a writer of theoretical feminist critique. Being a woman, I am de facto and in situ a feminist who happens to be immersed in literary and cultural studies, and who is familiar with Serres's work.

4. The recent phenomenon of the "Harry Potter" books with their impact on children who have suddenly (re)discovered the joy of reading seems to contradict this observation. It remains as yet to be seen whether this is genuine literature (of the genre of fairy tales) or simply a media-driven fad. But its very occurrence at a time when computer screens are becoming as fascinating to children as the television screen testifies to the enduring strength of the literary word.

5. Ada Giusti, "L'Académie Française et l'évolution de la langue: Entretien avec Michel Serres," *Contemporary French Civilization* 20, no. 1 (1996): 112–13.

6. Dennis Baron sheds an interesting light on the entire discussion of gendered language by recalling the (almost) forgotten etymological origin of the expression *gender,* meaning a "kind" or "sort," which was used as such in classical Latin writings. No connotation of a sexual division was originally attached to it. The association of grammatical gender with human generation, however, appeared in sixth-century grammars and was reinforced throughout the era of scholastic and patriarchal schooling, to modern times where it is now recognized by many scholars as a linguistic bias based on sexual difference. Dennis Baron, *Grammar and Gender* (New Haven: Yale University Press, 1986), 91.

7. Giusti, "L'Académie Française," 114.

8. Ibid.

9. Baron, *Grammar and Gender,* 217.

10. Ibid., 218.

11. Julia Penelope, *Speaking Freely: Unlearning the Lies of the Fathers' Tongues* (Elmsford, N.Y.: Pergamon Press, 1990), xxix.

12. This is an important interpretative difference and is much later expanded in *Statues,* where Serres draws parallel aspects between ancient sacrificial rites to the gods and supermodern space expeditions.

13. Michel Serres, *Genèse* (Paris: Grasset, 1982), 17–18.

14. This, of course, is the image of the woman in her kitchen preparing dough for her own household, well before the arrival of electric mixers, bread machines, and bread factories. To my knowledge, Serres is the originator of this feminine version of the baker's logic.

15. My translation is deliberately loose, to fit more than one possible meaning of this cited passage. The latter may also allude to the feminine gender of the French nouns for *knowledge* and *work.*

16. For a more detailed analysis of Serres's *la belle noiseuse,* see Maria L. Assad, *Reading with Michel Serres: An Encounter with Time* (Albany: State University of New York Press, 1999), chap. 1.

17. Katherine, N. Hayles, *Chaos Bound: Orderly Disorder in Contemporary Literature and Science* (Ithaca, N.Y.: Cornell University Press, 1990), 173.

18. Ibid., 174.

19. Thomas M. Kavanagh, "Michel Serres, *Les Cinq Sens,*" book discussion, *MLN* 101, no. 4 (1986): 938.

20. Genevieve Lloyd, *The Man of Reason: "Male" and "Female" in Western Philosophy* (Minneapolis: University of Minnesota Press, 1984), 87–102.

21. Ibid., 101.

22. Serres makes exclusive use of the word *laic* to underscore the status of the Other vis-à-vis the sacred space reserved for the initiated. Laicism bears a very precise historical and philosophico-political meaning for French society, since the founding of the Third Republic in the 1870s. Serres plays on this laic" consciousness of the French polity instilled in every French citizen from childhood on, in order to lay bare a much deeper, utter meaning of its othered-ness that radically severs the uninitiated from the "templum" of knowledge. The non-French reader needs to

understand the full extent of Serres's laic perspective if he/she is to follow to its deepest meaning his discourse on the Other who evolves into the instructed middle *(le tiers-instruit).*

23. Wylie, Alison. "Good Science, Bad Science, or Science as Usual?" in *Women in Human Evolution,* ed. Lori D. Hager (London: Routledge, 1997), 51.

24. Giusti, "L'Académie Française," 115.

LOVE, DEATH, AND PARASITES

ISABELLA WINKLER

When Romeo descends into the depths of the Capulet crypt, he does not bother to cover his nose with a handkerchief. He is too distraught by the news of the death of his beloved Juliet to notice that it smells bad down there. It should hardly come as a surprise that crypts stink, in general. Moreover, Tybalt, killed a few days earlier, must certainly have begun to smell under his shroud. But Romeo notices nothing except that his true love is dead, and so he drinks the draft of poison he has brought with him from Mantua. And yet if he had only sniffed at Juliet a little, tragedy might have been averted. Romeo doesn't know how to decrypt what he perceives to be Juliet's dead body as a trick or artifice. He doesn't know that this is a case of the living dead, a "poor living corse, closed in a dead man's tomb."[1] The living dead differ from corpses in that they don't smell as bad since their bodies are still capable of regeneration. Friar Lawrence's potion is a good trick, and it will mimic the effects of death convincingly—Juliet will appear "stiff and stark and cold" (act 4, scene 1); she will look and feel dead, down to the lack of pulse, breath, and rosy cheeks—but she will smell fine because the potion does not go so far as to mimic decay. Perhaps decay marks the difference between the real thing and its imitation, in this case between a real death and a fake one, or between death and the possibility of love.

Today we know that it is bacteria that make things rot and smell. These tiny parasitic creatures become especially active after death, but science tells us they are present on the living organism as well. Indeed, to be rigorously healthy is to be dying a little. Even at Juliet's age, death at the molecular level happens at an alarming rate: stomach, skin, and uterine cells slough off; brain cells expire with no hope of replacement. While one kind of bacteria helpfully ensures proper digestion, another kind is busy eating holes in Juliet's teeth. Regeneration might well be a sign of life, but both the living and the dead organism are subject to decay and odor. God knows the living smell pretty bad sometimes, and go to great lengths to cover it up. Anxiety especially produces sweat, and the recent events of Juliet's life—her secret marriage to Romeo; her cousin's murder; Romeo's subsequent banishment; and the forced engagement to Paris which she can escape only by swallowing some untested, unapproved potion—these ordeals must be the most anxiety-producing of her not-yet-fourteen years. Come to think of it, Juliet probably smells as bad as the dead. It is then not fair to blame a shortcoming of the friar's potion for the tragedy of this love.

In contrast to the organic, the artificial resists decay. This is its problem as well as its benefit. Certainly it is convenient to not have to water the plastic plants, but in the meantime the landfills are overflowing with disposable diapers. It is tempting to designate the nonbiodegradable as a parasite-free zone since it provides nothing for the parasite, who biodegrades for a living, to chew on. But the artificial is where the parasite is most at home. More accurately, making its home at the threshold or on some border, the parasite confounds the difference between the artificial and the real. Unfortunately for the protagonists of our story, the parasite is an excellent mimic. Man-made replicas of the real thing can be so convincing they defy even an expert, especially a lover. Whenever the artificial substitutes for the real, supplanting it so that you can no longer tell one from the other—poison from potion, death from life—the parasite is at work. The artificial may not be susceptible to decay, but inasmuch as it is never far from a certain artifice, it smells overwhelmingly of fish.

As everybody knows, Juliet wakes up to find that Romeo has poisoned himself, and there being insufficient poison on his lips to do her in as well, she plunges his dagger into her own breast. She is eager to join Romeo, as if death was something they could do together, on a date. The problem that results in the tragedy of this story is first of all one of timing and miscommunication. Banished Romeo does not receive the letter from Friar Lawrence cluing him in to the friar's scheme because the messenger could not make it, but another messenger does, this one with the mistaken news that Juliet is dead. The friar finds out that his letter was stopped short in its tracks and hurries to the crypt to explain Juliet's condition to Romeo in person, but Romeo is already dead, really dead since his vial contained the real thing. Timing and miscommunication, but also the proximity between the effects of the potion on the one hand and poison on the other are to blame for the tragic ending of this story. In the case of miscommunication, the problem is that the distance between the friar and Romeo proves not to be successfully traversable. In the second case, the distance between the potion that enables love and the poison that produces death is on the contrary traversable with the utmost of ease. The relation between sender and receiver is too precarious; between poison and potion, death and life, the artifice and the genuine article, not precarious enough. In either case, mishap happens. This problem of distances and relations, no less than that of stench, is a sure sign that the parasite is nearby.

Literally, *parasite* means "to eat next to" (*P, 7*). It comes from beyond the border as a contaminant, compromising the integrity of a host at whose expense it feeds. *Sitos,* Greek for food, can also mean excrement. Already at the level of etymology, the parasite mixes up two things that really ought to be kept separate. In addition, here is a clue as to the source of the smell. To smell something up, to mark it with a scent, is to tag it as your own. The foundation of property, Michel Serres writes in *The Parasite,* is that one's own dung smells good. As he so succinctly puts it: "The first one who, having shit upon a terrain, then decided to say, *this is mine,* immediately found people who were disgusted enough to believe him" (*P,* 144). What is repugnant for another is clean for oneself. One's own is what is clean—the French language helps out by providing the same term for either side of this proposition: *le propre* refers at once to "the clean" and what is owned. The kinship is evident in English as well: property and propriety are only a hair's breadth apart. Property is kept clean and on one's own turf; trash is put out on the curb that is communal. Between dirty and clean, outside and inside, the boundary is permeable; that is why the concept of the disposable works so well. Unlike the real thing—silverware, cloth diapers—the disposable is not really property, and so it does not have to be cleaned. Instead, having first dirtied the item on the inside, you can then put it outside, preferably—since much of what is disposable is made of nonbiodegradable material—as far away as possible. Of course, the door swings both ways, and the porous border also lets the trash and the riffraff slip in without your consent, even without your knowledge. Suddenly the noise of unfamiliar footsteps alerts you to the fact that the pantry is empty, your reserves gone, and the place is a mess. There has been a violation; the inside is no longer sanctified. Serres mentions that burglars sometimes even leave "disgusting trails" in the houses they have robbed, as if the point needed literalizing (*P,* 144). Once the outside has contaminated the inside, the inside is up for grabs. The parasite depends on this for its survival. As the outside and the dirty itself, the parasite befouls someone else's inside(s), and in so doing, appropriates what was not its own to begin with.

The best definition of the parasite, according to Serres, is that it is a "thermal exciter" (*P,* 190). When it infiltrates the body of the host, it causes fever and inflammation. Or, if the parasite is of the human rather than the biological variety, it sickens the host with its saccharine flattery by which it gains access to the tables of the rich, tricking the host into accepting in exchange for food nothing but hot air. The parasite takes over proceedings, making so much noise that no one else can any longer say anything to anyone. "The one who has the strongest and loudest voice," Serres explains, "is always right" (*P*, 141). The parasite infiltrates any system as a surge of energy, stirring things up, causing a disruption. As a thermal exciter it makes noise; this is its most universal characteristic. Serres's native tongue is helpful in this case too: in French *parasite* refers not only to the social and biological kind as in English, but also to static. Serres takes advantage of this to illustrate the parasite's effect on a system; for example, two points related to each other by means of a telephone wire. The conversation is interrupted by a third variable, static, which renders the message cryptic, unintelligible. In a word, parasited. The parasite operates by interrupting the system as static or noise and incapacitating it. Yet as we have seen in the case of Juliet, if things are too quiet, there is just as much cause for alarm. By the same token, even the intact system is only more or less silent. Even a clear channel of communication is not entirely static-free. In every well-functioning system there is always a faint whir, a little hum, some white noise. There is always a bug in the works. That is how it works at all.

> A wire does not have to be heated very much for noise to increase. This excitement stops the message from passing. But sometimes it allows the message to pass, a message that cannot cross an unexcited channel . . . *white noise is the condition for passing* (for meaning, sound, and even noise), and the noise is its prohibitor or its interception. Noise, or again, the parasite, is at the three points of the triangle: sending, reception, transmission. Heat a little, I hear, I send, I pass; heat a little more, everything collapses. (*P*, 194; emphasis added)

We experience static as a nuisance; it interrupts the signal that carries the message. But, Serres suggests, it is perhaps only because of the interruption that we receive the message at all. For a message to pass between two points, say from Friar Lawrence to Romeo, a channel of communication must exist between them. The play of the parasite diverts the message; tragedy ensues. The happy ending in our love story would depend, it seems, on getting rid of the parasite. But this would mean tossing out the message as well. The parasite might interrupt by chance—"and perhaps that is what chance is," Serres writes—but its effects are necessary (*P*, 239). The channel that carries the flow of information necessarily also presents an obstacle to that flow, slowing it down, drowning it out with static, sometimes losing the connection altogether. This presents some cause for anxiety. But take away the channel and you have no possibility of a connection. For a relation to be perfect, it would have to be immediate, which is to say, impossible. The only possible relation is a mediated one that marks itself as parasited with static (*P,* 79). "In order to hear the message alone [without the noise]," Serres writes, "[the receiver] would have to be identical to the sender" (*P,* 70). At the moment there are two terms, sender and receiver, a third one exists between them: a relation that makes the connection, barely. Or from another perspective, a relation that barely manages to keep the terms separated. Static, or the parasite, is this relation, always both uniting and separating. When the message needs to get from point A to point B on the double, the parasite both creates and obstructs the channel of communication. When death should be kept far away from love, the parasite that maintains their distance also brings them fatally close together. The parasitic relation, the only possible relation, thus marks both distance and proximity, attraction and repulsion. It is, as Derrida would say, the condition of possibility of the relation at the same time that it is the condition of its impossibility. In Serres's words:

> The parasite is the essence of relation. It is necessary for the relation and ineluctable by the overturning of the force that tries to exclude it. But this relation is nonrelation. The parasite is being and nonbeing at the same time. Not being and nonbeing that are the names (or the non-names) of stations; but arrow and nonarrow, relation and nonrelation.
> (*P,* 79)

Serres here wants to emphasize that the parasite does not appear as a *coincidentia oppositorum*. It does not contain the two terms that as relation it nevertheless gives rise to while simultaneously depending on them for its existence.[2] Indeed, it does not appear as such at all. Slipping out of the simple alternative of presence/absence, the parasite is, as Derrida would put it, undecidable in its essence. Serres prefers to call it fuzzy. He takes this term from mathematics, where it designates an alternative to a binary logic. Rather than two discrete binary positions, inside and outside, yes and no, zero and one, a fuzzy subset blurs bivalences into a continuum composed of an infinite number of values. Incorporating an infinite number of values amounts to having no value per se. At once being and nonbeing, the parasite is also fuzzy in its effects: it acts at once as potion and poison. Vaccination, Serres reminds us, is based upon this principle: the parasite that enters the body as contaminant then protects it against further contamination. "The parasite gives the host the means to be safe from the parasite," Serres writes (*P,* 193). The inside then lets itself at once be contaminated and fulfilled, supplanted by the parasite without which, as things turns out, it is not complete.[3] Perhaps one could say that the inside is always attracted to the contaminant despite its efforts to distinguish itself, above all, from that very thing. We said earlier that the parasite is an expert mimic;

indeed, that is what Shakespeare's play stakes itself on. In order to "avoid the unavoidable reactions of rejection, exclusion" as if it was a lover, the parasite even mimics the host's tissue. "I don't know if mimicry is entirely parasitic," Serres writes, "but it is a necessary trick for the robber, the stranger, the guest" (*P*, 202). The parasitic foreign body makes a home for itself on the inside, where it is kept in secret as part of the host.

All this has not a little to do with love. In Shakespeare's play, the untimely deaths of Romeo and Juliet are said to have the beneficial effect of reconciling the two feuding families, but from the lovers' point of view, this is no resolution to the tragedy. When Serres writes that "as soon a there are two, there is a medium between us" (*P*, 70), he is talking first of all about love; love is for Serres the parasitic relation par excellence. Always between, "neither dead nor immortal," love is "placed without precision and with rigor in the laws of the logic of the fuzzy area of the threshold, homeless and near the door" (*P*, 242). There is no love without bad timing and miscommunication. Certainly Romeo and Juliet keep waiting for each other and missing each other; the conventional mark of union, marriage doesn't help them one bit. Impossible to be in the same place at the same time, they can't even manage to coordinate their deaths. One might like to explain away their fates as simply a matter of bad luck, but Serres shows that luck or chance goes hand in hand with necessity when the parasite keeps lovers apart.

One lover holds vigil over the other's absence, as if over a dead body. He or she waits for love or the loss of love as one waits for death: with anxiety, in anticipation and already in mourning. Waiting is the lover's condition of possibility: the one waits for an other to arrive with whom he can fall in love, an arrival that always comes unexpectedly despite its being anxiously awaited. Falling in love offers no reprieve: now the lover awaits the other's loss. According to Barthes's encyclopedic fragment *The Lover's Discourse,* this loss is at the very origin of love.[4] Anxious about a rendezvous that never lives up to its name, that is, that never takes place, the lover lives in fear of a mourning that has already occurred.[5] In anticipation of what Derrida writes about Heidegger and death, one might say that the being-possible of the lover is the impossibility of being with the other. Romeo and Juliet never arrive in the same place together because love—like death—names an impossible simultaneity, as we shall see. At the moment the desire for the other is formed, the other is already dead, framed in a memory. Creating a secret but also utterly common language of love, the lover speaks relentlessly about this always already lost other who is at the same time present as the allocutionary, and absent as the referent: "[Y]ou have gone (which I lament), you are here (since I am addressing you)."[6] He or she is like the living dead, buried in a crypt. There is "neither oblivion nor resurrection; simply the exhausting lure of memory."[7] Love is an anamnesis, a memory of, and memorial for, the other, whose return one awaits in anxiety and in vain.

> The inhabitant of a crypt is always a living dead, a dead entity we are perfectly willing to keep alive, but as dead, one we are willing to keep, as long as we keep it, within us, intact in any way save as living.[8]

According to Derrida, a crypt keeps a body safe but at a distance, not entirely dead but excluded from the realm of the living. This resonates with Serres's assessment of what he calls the cistern in his reading of the biblical story of Joseph in the well. In the tale, the enclosure, "an artificial, man-made spot for conservation," functions precisely as the crypt, preserving and expelling the inhabitant who is both included and excluded (*P*, 157). The crypt hides and holds its inhabitant, a loved being, among the parasites. For Derrida, these architectonics determine the space of the crypt itself.

A cleft or fold, the crypt is both interior and exterior to itself. It acts as a safe within space, which makes it also an exception to this space. To this end Derrida plays on the double meaning of *sauf*: safe and save, in the sense of excepting. But there is another level of interiority/exteriority. A safe is sealed, internal to itself, but, placed in a space, it is also external to its interior. In Derrida's words, which it is safest to stick to: "The inner forum is (a) safe, an outcast outside inside the inside."[9] The border is very slippery, if it can even be said that there is a border. Derrida seems to be saying that the crypt is not itself. Or rather, it is itself and is not itself. It is a stranger at home, like the parasite.

The crypt's strange spatial dynamics put a new twist on Rimbaud's formulation of the modern subject's predicament and the basis of its madness: I is an other *and* I am myself. The lover, for Barthes, is mad precisely because he cannot keep himself from becoming himself: "I am not someone else: that is what I realize with horror."[10] The confusion of these two madnesses describes the condition of the Marrano, which, Derrida writes at the end of *Aporias,* is the condition of all of us: inhabiting a space without saying no and without identifying ourselves as belonging to. For Derrida, this bizarre split of identity is the very condition of the self. "[I]dentity . . . can only affirm itself as identity by opening itself to the hospitality of a difference from itself or of a difference with itself."[11] Identity is not constituted simply by a difference from the other, but from the self as well. In a similar move, Serres points out that the Platonic couple of idea and thing can be understood only in terms of a third idea that is still part of the couple. In other words, "[S]upposing he loves, a third Eros is necessary for us to conceive of what Eros participates in when he loves" (*P*, 241).

To open up to the hospitality of a difference from or with the self creates the necessary conditions for the self to keep a secret from itself. This is what the crypt does; that is its name. It keeps something hidden, a body of some sort, and it dissimulates the disguise so the self will not find out. This comes in handy when the self has experienced the loss of a loved one, through that one's death or disenchantment. The incorporation of the lost object by the self—kept safe by the self in the crypt, but kept nevertheless as a stranger—mimes introjection, the process of normal mourning. This mimicry is dependent on secrecy.[12] In introjection, the love object enlarges the ego, expanding the self. For Ferenczi, from whom the term originates, love is only ever directed toward the self; therefore "insofar as he loves an object, [the lover] adopts it as part of his Self" (xvi). Whereas in introjection, the lost object is loved as a living part of the self ("dead *save* in me," as Derrida writes [xvi]), incorporation pretends to keep the object alive only in order to reject it. It is kept "safe" in the self, but as a foreign body, simultaneously included and excluded, safe and save. For this mimicry to work, an "artifice," as Derrida specifies, is necessary: the crypt. The crypt is itself between two: as artifice it is both trick and art, genuine and disingenuous, natural and artificial. It is an artificial consciousness within a divided self, but it is "carved out of nature"; encryption "sometimes mak[es] use of probability or facts" that are already there (xvi). Like the parasite, the crypt is fuzzy or undecidable. Included and excluded by the self, it is constituted by its clandestine mimicry, keeping its secret at the same time that it is kept by it.

Under these conditions, who can be sure of what is properly one's own? The relation to the self is always a relation to the self as other, and reciprocally, no relation to the other as wholly other is possible. Who is the guest and who the host in this scenario of the stranger at home, who the one who arrives, as guest or ghost, revenant, arriving once again? As Derrida points out, the hospitality of the one receiving is in fact preceded by the hospitality of the one who appears to be being received, and who is expected to show gratitude.[13] *Hôte* corresponds to both "guest" and "host": Serres makes much of this in his parasitic system that eats at the walls of the crypt, even if they are made of concrete, as Derrida tells us, and caulked or padded on the inside.[14] For Serres as for Derrida, the parasite, invited in as guest, is sent on his way again, indebted to the host who is suddenly not so hospitable. Within hospitability, hostility begins (*P*, 16). Who knows which one gives and which receives, which one is inviter and which invited? We cannot even much longer speak of the crypt as a receptacle, as that which receives itself and is received by itself, both guest and host. It now becomes clearer why the answer to Derrida's question, "What is a crypt?" is that no crypt presents itself.[15] The problematics of the spatial dynamics of the crypt are constantly crumbling into aporetic rubble. Ruin is the principle of its possibility.

The crumbling does not, however, allow for easy entry, as one might have expected. Despite the acrobatic architectonics of the crypt that would seem somewhere to offer a loophole as passage, the parasited crypt has been sealed off as condemned.[16] We are "incapable even of sheltering ourselves behind what could still protect the interiority of a secret."[17] No border or barrier to hide behind, not even so much as a tombstone. In this space of aporia, there is no longer any problem in the sense of problem.[18] Unfortunately however, this does not mean that a solution has been given or a secret revealed, but simply that there is nothing even to constitute itself as a problem or a secret. This is where we find Serres hoping, since he is near the end of his book, to finally get to the truth. He is at the threshold of the door behind which all the true gods are assembled, engaged in a symposium, with plenty of food and drink and comfortable couches at hand, where the theme of the evening is love—why not? Serres has already tried it from the angle of the *Symposium,* having taken us to the point when Socrates is about to spend the night. Love has been thwarted once earlier that evening: because he was jealous of their love, Alcibiades had put himself between Socrates and Agathon so that they might have quarreled. But now it is late, half the partygoers are asleep, and Socrates, whom Alcibiades has praised as Love himself, is there, as Serres says, in the flesh (*P,* 244). The anticipation is palpable. But all that happens is more talking; Socrates stays up all night philosophizing with the two opposites: Agathon the tragedian and Aristophanes the comedian. Love, it must be remembered, is always between two; neither mortal nor immortal, living nor dead, he waits on the threshold between inside and outside. The son of Penia, goddess of Lack, and Poros the Passage, Eros never acquires the good and the truth for which he longs. He is a strange kind of god, a god of nonidentity if he is a god at all. It is, then, only to be expected that Socrates, who has been identified with Love, consummates nothing despite being amply fed and liquored up. The sun sets on the *Symposium,* but Socrates doesn't make love, preferring to prattle the night away instead. The truth is always supplanted by noise.

There is only one more chance for Serres, who is still in front of the door to the truth: the feast of the gods themselves. He has explained to us earlier in the book that the difference between mortals and immortals is that the gods never get their meals interrupted: "The immortal is the eternal reveller" (*P,* 30). No need to respond to a knock, then. The door simply

opens a bit to leave a passage for Poros. For Poros, a little god, completely drunk on nectar, on nectar, for in those days men had not invented wine. But who is Poros, who comes out of the black box? Alas! he is the passage itself, the path. Poros is the name of the passage. (*P,* 240)

What a letdown! We were almost there with Serres, at the truth, at the god's banquet, where things are unadulteratedly real, "where love is finally love and not punishment, where wine is not drunk for illusions and hangovers, but ambrosia finally gives the invariability of what is" (*P,* 240). In the end, we have arrived at another beginning. We found out that what goes through the door is the nothing but the door itself. "The only thing that passes in the channel is the name of the channel" (*P,* 240). Serres is so disappointed that he hurries up and finishes his book. There is no beating the parasite. We have gotten to the limits of truth and found out that at this limit is a trick with a name. (The name of the trick is the name itself, and the trick is to make the name appear as it disappears. But this is not just a "language or logic game," Derrida is right to issue the caveat.)[19] The flow of traffic through the channel has ebbed, now that it is clear that nothing but the name of the channel passes through the channel. The parasite is itself parasited. When the channel passes itself, the channel collapses. All that is left is the name. Under this condition, there is no relation: "[T]he coming or the future advent of the event [has] no relation to the passage of what happens or comes to pass."[20] Poros, drunk as he is, has passed out in the doorway.

We have arrived at the aporia; we have, in truth, never been anywhere else. We have known for a while that the parasite as relation is nonrelation. Here we have come to the possibility of the impossible, an unmediated mediation. Not relation as nonrelation but nonrelation as such. For Derrida there are borders that are blocked, disallowing passage, and those that are so porous that no path is necessary, and then there are nonpassages due to the lack of the topological condition that would support an aporia. In this case, the impasse itself is impossible; the aporia parasites itself. No more step, no more *pas,* as Derrida puts it. The aporia is "the event of a coming or a future advent, which no longer has the form of the movement that consists in passing, traversing, or transiting."[21] Or transmitting, we could add. When the channel collapses, the impossibility of an unmediated relation becomes possible. It is a coming without a step, without *pas.* This nonstep is illustrated in the third possibility of meaning of the untranslatable sentence Derrida posits: *il y va d'un certain pas* [it involves a certain step/not; he goes along at a certain pace]. We understand several different things in this sentence: first that someone is walking with a certain gait. Derrida provides us with an example that includes—what good fortune for this paper—a bed in which to love or to die: "[H]e is going there (to town, to work, to combat, to bed—that is to say, to dream, to love, to die) with a certain gait [pas]."[22] The second meaning of *il y va d'un certain pas* is more concerned with the gait itself; it is a question of a certain step, a particular passage. The third possibility, at which Derrida arrives by no path, having started off with the intention to "limit myself to just two possibilities" is one where one can secretly, quietly, "in inaudible quotation marks . . . mention a mark of negation"; the *pas* as "not."[23] In all modalities of the sentence, the "not" is always there with the *pas*. The passage to bed, in order to love or to die, is always, as Derrida says, a nonpassage.

Derrida inserts as a clause in the middle of a sentence the unfathomable aside that the nonpassage "can in fact be something else."[24] This clause reckons with that measure of the incalculable which approaches the limits of truth. The nonpassage can allow for the arrival of something completely other, unappropriable and inappropriate, a future coming that is awaited but unexpected, a matter of chance and necessity. Along the nonpassage, absolute singularity arrives. Perhaps this is why Serres does not get to his secret by telling stories; he never gets to the end of the passage where he wants to find the black box that hides the workings of the parasite. If there is box at the end of the passage, one can no more get to it than the pot of gold at the end of the rainbow. In Serres's words:

> The story doesn't yet tell of the banquet, but of another story that tells, not yet of the banquet, but of another story that, again . . . And what is spoken of is what it is a question of: bifurcations and branchings. That is to say, parasites. The story indefinitely chases in front of itself what it speaks of. (*P*, 241)

It is no longer possible to take refuge in dissimulation. Enough empty prattling, spewing of hot air, enough *Gerede*. We must look death squarely in the face and await it in anxiety; only that way can we approach truth. Why death? According to Derrida, death is the name that is left over in the collapsed channel, the name of the nonpassage that is characterized by the anxious anticipation that accompanies the passage of time, which will always have been too short, in any case. Death is the name of the aporia. Perhaps it is more serious than we thought and Poros passed on rather than out when he fell, having arrived at his ownmost potentiality-for-being as A-poros. For if Poros is like Dasein, and he doesn't seem too godlike, then death is his most proper possibility, the possibility par excellence of the kind of being proper to Dasein, that of being-possible (*Seinkönnen*, in contrast to the being, *Zuhandenheit* or *Vorhandenheit*, of things that are not Dasein). As being-possible, Dasein is always ahead of itself. In this being-toward-the-end, Dasein is its not-yet as long as it is. Thus, Dasein does not fulfill itself until it is dead; it is complete at the same time that it is no longer at all. Always split, Dasein waits for death and misses itself, like the lover. Indeed as Derrida has discovered, Dasein in some translations "has a rendezvous" with itself when it "stands before" (also translated as "precedes") itself in this manner.

When Dasein stands before (precedes, has a rendezvous with) itself in its ownmost potentiality for being, "all its relations to any other Dasein have been undone."[25] Death is absolutely nonrelational. It is for Dasein the possibility of no-longer-being-able-to-be-there (or being-able-to no-longer-be-there, as Derrida suggests, emphasizing the possibility): its unique and uncontestable truth and its ownmost possibility. As Heidegger writes, famously: "Death is the possibility of the absolute impossibility of Dasein."[26] This possibility of impossibility becomes understood, Derrida shows, "as the possibility of the impossibility of any existence at all."[27] Death is then the most proper possibility of Dasein and the most proper possibility *as* impossibility. The enigma of the *as* "keeps in reserve the most unthinkable";[28] it approaches the limits of truth beyond all calculability and measure. The aporia, for Dasein alone as *Seiendes,* is that the impossible nevertheless appear as possible and as such, "an impossibility that one can await and expect, an impossibility the limits of which one can await or expect or at whose limits one can wait, these limits of the *as such* being, as we have seen, the limits of truth but also the possibility of truth."[29]

What does one await at these limits? "With death, Dasein awaits itself in its ownmost potentiality-for-being" [Mit dem Tod steht sich Dasein selbst in seinem eigensten Seinkönnen bevor].[30] This awaiting (or preceding, standing before, having a rendezvous with) itself conveys the anxious anticipation that is required of Dasein to be authentic in the face of its most proper possibility. The anticipation is that of one whose arrival is imminent, awaited, but who comes as a surprise. Derrida's analysis of Heidegger's untranslatable expression makes the multiple meanings of "awaiting itself" visible. First of all, one can simply await oneself and "nothing else."[31] The other two possibilities entail a relation to an other. On the one hand, one awaits oneself as other, "outside myself in myself,"[32] the other that constitutes the self in an act of originary mourning, resulting forever in a "bereaved apprehension."[33] On the other hand, the reflexive *s'attendre* means to wait for another outside of oneself, to wait for someone to love. About this third meaning of "awaiting oneself" Derrida writes:

This reference is more heterological than ever—others would say as close as ever to the limits of truth—when waiting for *each other* is related to death, to the borders of death, where we wait for each other knowing *a priori,* and absolutely undeniably that life always being too short, the one is waiting for the other there, for the one and the other never arrive there together, at this rendezvous (death is ultimately the name of impossible simultaneity and of an impossibility that we know simultaneously, at which we await each other, at the same time, *ama* as one says in Greek: at the same time, simultaneously, we are expecting this anachronism and this contretemps).[34]

Ama, one might also say, about the anachronism of waiting for each other and this contretemps of mourning, as if it came from Latin roots, from *amare,* to love. Remember *Romeo and Juliet* and the figure of the lover who waits. Love and death are both names of impossible simultaneity, where the one and the other never arrive together. Naming is some of what is at stake because it distinguishes Dasein from animals that can neither speak nor die properly. Only Dasein can say, "my death." This phrase is irreplaceably singular since my death is my own; no one can experience my death but me. But this completely unsubstitutable syntagm *my death* is at the same time completely substitutable: anyone who can speak can say it. Death is an utterly private and an utterly public name, a shibboleth, the "common name of a secret"[35] always on the border between two, like the discourse of the lover, the space of the crypt, or the figure of the parasite.

The question Derrida asks about the possibility of the impossible appearing as such is whether it can appear "without immediately disappearing, without the 'as such' already sinking beforehand and without its essential disappearance making *Dasein* lose everything that distinguished it . . . [a]nd without its *properly-dying* being originarily contaminated and parasited by the *perishing* and the *demising.*"[36] For if the possibility for Dasein is that the impossibility of the "as such" can appear as such, then the appearance of the as such is impossible; it immediately disappears, just as for animals, or for inauthentic Dasein. This is the end of properly dying. A relation to death, as to the other (and it is the same, says Derrida), is not guaranteed by an ability to name death. "The death of the other, this death of the other in 'me,' is fundamentally the only death that is named in the syntagm 'my death.'" In this it is like the experience of originary mourning that institutes the relation to the self. Thus the ultimate aporia is that no aporia can exist as such (78). The *as such*

> marks and erases the borders which only happen by erasing themselves, which only succeed in erasing themselves [*n'arrivent qu'à s'effacer*], [by tracing] them[selves] as still possible while also introducing the very principle of their impossibility, the principle of ruin, which is also their chance and which promises the line while compromising it in parasitism, grafting, and indivisibility. (73)

This is the secret to which Derrida penetrates in Heidegger, which is already in Heidegger as a "secret that cannot be kept and that presents itself cryptically" (74). Derrida comes to the same conclusion as Serres: there is no access to the truth that is not already parasited, and this is the possibility of any truth at all.

Ravaged by the parasites that make it possible, the crypt is the resting place, the place that rests, that remains, the place of the rest. Here Derrida finds the Marrano, whose culture has been declared finished by the Spanish courts in 1992, who is the figure of that which lives without a name, who stays faithful to a secret he has not chosen, which "keeps the Marrano even before the Marrano keeps it."[37] Living in the home of the occupant, staying "without saying no but without identifying himself as belonging to," the Marrano, like the parasite, is the anachronistic figure of the included and the excluded that regularly change places, the mark of identity itself.

There is a way into the crypt, to the secret, but it requires a little effort, a trick or two, as both Juliet and Romeo demonstrate. There isn't simply a path that leads to a door. Juliet's trick is more refined; Romeo rather inelegantly slays those in his way. Getting out, however, is a different story, and both Juliet and Romeo end up as fodder for the parasites. Something like the predicament faced by many legendary heroes, no one can gain access to the secret and live. Or more accurately, the secret doesn't make itself accessible in the first place, and death is in any case your lot. In fact, death is the possibility of this impossible access, and this is the unveiling of the secret as well. That "the aporia can never be endured as such" is not to be construed as a challenge.[38] The aporia, like the relation, like the name *death,* like love, only ever appears insofar as it disappears. Awaiting (one another at) the limits of truth, death is the possibility of the impossible as such. As such it is the figure of the aporia that allows for a remarkable substitution: the name *death* can replace all that is possible only as impossible. Derrida's list does not fail to include love. Because of the play of the parasite, death, the absolute nonrelation, has the same structure as love, the relation par excellence. Names matter, Derrida says early on, but in the figure of the aporia we arrive at the limits of nomination, so that names like that of the Marrano and the parasite can be added, in memory of, and according to, the figure of that which lives without a name. Although there is no escaping the parasite, there is no need to fear it, better just to be a little anxious and to remember next time you're in a crypt to bring a handkerchief.[39] Smell your beloved before doing anything rash; she may just be dreaming.

> Victory to the parasites, those who eat and drink and who have hidden so well that we no longer know their names, their number, or their presence, shadows, victory to the parasites on the chain that erase the very chain itself, victory to the parasites who erase their own footprints as they go by, victory to the parasites who have disappeared, named, appearing to substitute themselves for others, drinking and drunk, eating, eaten, snapping up the bread and snapped up by history. (*P,* 236–37)

NOTES

1. William Shakespeare, *Romeo and Juliet* (New York: Washington Square Press, 1959), act 5, scene 3.

2. The parasite thus functions like the chora, Plato's figure in the *Timaeus* for the place that confounds binaries: that is neither sensible nor intelligible but belongs to a "third genus" and that gives rise to oppositions without itself belonging to them. *Timaeus,* trans. Benjamin Jowett, *The Collected Dialogues of Plato,* ed. Edith Hamilton and Huntington Cairns (Princeton: Princeton University Press, 1961), 48a. Plato describes the chora using several figures including that of "imprint bearer." For Serres this resonates with the "black box," the place that hides the parasite's secret operation and "relative to which inclusion and exclusion are thinkable" at all (*P,* 216).

3. The parasite behaves as a pharmakon as elucidated by Jacques Derrida in "Plato's Pharmacy," in *Disseminations,* trans. Barbara Johnson (Chicago: University of Chicago Press, 1981). There Derrida writes: "The pharmakon is that dangerous supplement which breaks into the very thing that would have liked to do without it yet lets itself at once be breached, roughed up, fulfilled, and replaced, completed by the very trace through which the present increases itself in the very act of disappearing" (110; translation modified).

4. Roland Barthes, *A Lover's Discourse,* trans. Richard Howard (New York: Hill and Wang, 1987), 30.

5. Ibid.

6. Ibid., 15.

7. Ibid.

8. Jacques Derrida, "Fors," trans. Barbara Johnson, in *The Wolfman's Magic Word: A Cryptonomy,* by Nicolas Abraham and Maria Torok, trans. Nicholas Rand (Minneapolis: University of Minnesota Press, 1986), xxi.

9. Ibid., xiv.

10. Barthes, *A Lover's Discourse,* 121.

11. Jacques Derrida, *Aporias,* trans. Thomas Dutoit (Stanford: Stanford University Press, 1993), 10.

12. Derrida, "Fors," xvii.

13. Derrida, *Aporias,* 10.

14. Derrida, "Fors," xiv.

15. Ibid.

16. Ibid., xvii.

17. Derrida, *Aporias,* 12.

18. For Derrida, "problem" resonates in its derivation from the Greek *problema,* which signifies projection or protection: a border that one poses in front of oneself or "we put forth in order to represent, replace, shelter or dissimulate ourselves, or so as to hide something unavowable" (ibid.).

19. Derrida, *Aporias,* 72.

20. Ibid., 21.

21. Ibid., 8.

22. Ibid., 9.

23. Ibid.

24. Ibid., 8.

25. Martin Heidegger, *Being and Time,* trans. John MacQuarrie and Edward Robinson (New York: Harper and Row, 1962), 294.

26. Ibid., 250.

27. Ibid., 262.

28. Derrida, *Aporias,* 71.

29. Ibid., 73.

30. Heidegger, *Being and Time,* 250.

31. Derrida, *Aporias,* 64.

32. Ibid., 61.

33. Ibid.

34. Ibid., 65.

35. Ibid., 74.

36. Ibid., 71.

37. Ibid., 81.

38. Ibid., 78.

39. In the section named "How This Book Is Constructed," Barthes brings up a handkerchief as a sort of marker in a game of substitution and supplementation by which the encyclopedic entries of the lover's discourse can be filled according to each individual reader's and lover's history. According to Barthes, his text is open, exemplary rather than definitive; the figures of the discourse are to be "made free with, to be added to, subtracted from, and passed on to others" (*A Lover's Discourse,* 5). He writes, "[A]round the figure, the players pass the handkerchief which sometimes, by a final parenthesis, is held a second longer before passing it on" (5). The handkerchief is, then, important for those who love and die, not just to recognize the presence of the parasite by its smell, or to wipe away tears, but to mark while erasing all that is possible only as impossibility.

WORKS CITED

Adams, Henry. *The Education of Henry Adams.* Ed. Jean Gooder. London: Penguin, 1995.

————. "A Letter to American Teachers of History." In *The Degradation of the American Dogma.* New York: Capricorn, 1958.

Adams, Percy G. *Travel Literature and the Evolution of the Novel.* Lexington: University Press of Kentucky, 1983.

Aristotle. *Physics.* In *The Works of Aristotle,* ed. W. D. Ross. Vol. 2. Oxford: Clarendon Press, 1930.

Arnheim, Rudolf. *Art and Visual Perception.* Berkeley and Los Angeles: University of California Press, 1964.

Assad, Maria L. "Michel Serres: In Search of a Tropography." In *Chaos and Order: Complex Dynamics in Literature and Science,* ed. Katherine N. Hayles. Chicago: University of Chicago Press, 1991.

————. *Reading with Michel Serres: An Encounter with Time.* Albany: State University of New York Press, 1999.

Assmann, Aleida. "The Curse and Blessing of Babel; or, Looking Back on Universalisms." In *The Translatability of Cultures: Figurations of the Space Between,* ed. Sanford Budick and Wolfgang Iser. Stanford: Stanford University Press, 1996.

Banta, Martha. "Being a 'Begonia' in a Man's World." In *New Essays on "The Education of Henry Adams,"* ed. John Carlos Rowe. Cambridge: Cambridge University Press, 1996.

Baron, Dennis. *Grammar and Gender.* New Haven: Yale University Press, 1986.

Barthes, Roland. *A Lover's Discourse: Fragments.* Trans. Richard Howard. New York: Hill and Wang, 1978.

————. *S\Z.* Paris: Éditions de Seuil, 1970.

Bataille, Georges. *Les Larmes d'Éros.* Paris: Jacques Pauvert, 1961. Trans. Peter Connor as *The Tears of Eros* (San Francisco: City Lights Books, 1989).

Baudrillard, Jean. *L'Échange symbolique et la mort.* Paris: Gallimard, 1976.

Beckett, Samuel. *Collected Dramatic Works.* London: Faber and Faber, 1986.

————. *The Unnamable.* Trans. by the author. London: Calder and Boyars, 1975.

Bell, Lawrence. "In Pursuit of Ethics." *PMLA* 114, no. 1 (1999): 7–19.

Bernstein, Charles. *Content's Dream: Essays, 1975–1984.* Los Angeles: Sun and Moon Press, 1986.

Berressem, Hanjo. "Matter That Bodies." *Gender Forum: Mediating Gender,* June 2002. http://www.genderforum.uni-koeln.de.

———. *Dark City.* Los Angeles: Sun and Moon Press, 1994.

Blanshard, Brand. *The Nature of Thought.* London, 1948.

Bloom, Harold. *The Anxiety of Influence: A Theory of Poetry.* New York: Oxford University Press, 1973.

Blumenberg, Hans. *Schiffbruch mit Zuschauer. Paradigma einer Daseinsmetapher.* Frankfurt am Main: Suhrkamp, 1979. Trans. Robert M. Wallace as *Shipwreck with Onlooker* (Cambridge: MIT Press, 1997).

Brockden-Brown, Charles. *Edgar Huntly, or, Memoirs of a Sleep-Walker.* Ed. Sydney J. Krause and S. W. Reid. Kent, Ohio: Kent State University Press, 1984.

Brodkey, Harold. *The Runaway Soul.* New York: Farrar, Straus and Giroux, 1991.

Brown, Norman O. *Hermes the Thief.* Great Barrington, Mass.: Lindisfarne, 1990.

Budick, Sanford, and Wolfgang Iser, eds. *The Translatability of Cultures: Figurations of the Space Between.* Stanford: Stanford University Press, 1996.

Bunyan, John. *The Pilgrim's Progress.* Ed. Roger Sharrock. Harmondsworth: Penguin, 1965.

Cage, John. *Silence.* Middletown, Conn.: Wesleyan University Press, 1976.

Castells, Manuel. *The Rise of the Network Society.* Oxford: Blackwell, 1996.

Cervantes Saavedra, Miguel de. *Don Quixote.* Trans. John Ormsby. Revised and ed. Joseph R. Jones and Kenneth Douglas. New York: Norton, 1981.

Chalfant, Edward. "Lies, Silence, and Truth in the Writings of Henry Adams." In *Henry Adams and His World,* ed. David R. Contosta and Robert Muccigrosso. Philadelphia: American Philosophical Society, 1993.

Clayton, Jay. *The Pleasures of Babel: Contemporary American Literature and Theory.* New York: Oxford University Press, 1993.

Contosta, David R., and Robert Muccigrosso, eds. *Henry Adams and His World.* Philadelphia: American Philosophical Society, 1993.

Cosgrove, Dennis. *Mapping.* London: Reaktion Books, 1999.

Cowley, Abraham. "To the Royal Society." In *Poems of Abraham Cowley.* Ed. A. R. Waller. Cambridge: Cambridge University Press, 1905.

Critchley, Simon. *The Ethics of Deconstruction: Derrida and Levinas.* Oxford: Blackwell, 1992.

Daniel, Jean. "Notre XXe siècle." *Le Nouvel Observateur,* December 23–29, 1999.

Davis, Erik. *Techgnosis.* New York: Harmony Press, 1998.

Decker, William Merrill. *The Literary Vocation of Henry Adams.* Chapel Hill: University of North Carolina Press, 1990.

Deleuze, Gilles. *The Fold: Leibniz and the Baroque.* Trans. Tom Conley. Minneapolis: University of Minnesota Press, 1993.

———. *The Logic of Sense.* Trans. Mark Lester with Charles Stivale. Ed. Constantin V. Boundas. New York: Columbia University Press, 1990.

Deleuze, Gilles, and Guattari Félix. *Anti-Oedipus.* Vol. 1 of *Capitalism and Schizophrenia.* Trans. Robert Hurley, Mark Seem, and Helen R. Lane. Minneapolis: University of Minnesota Press, 1983.

————. "From Chaos to Brain." In *What Is Philosophy?* Trans. Hugh Tomlinson and Graham Burchell. New York: Columbia University Press, 1994.

————. *A Thousand Plateaus.* Vol. 2 of *Capitalism and Schizophrenia.* Minneapolis: University of Minnesota Press, 1993.

de Man, Paul. "The Resistance to Theory." *Yale French Studies* 63 (1982): 3–20.

Derrida, Jacques. *Aporias.* Trans. Thomas Dutoit. Stanford: Stanford University Press, 1993.

————. "Fors." Trans. Barbara Johnson in *The Wolfman's Magic Word: A Cryptonomy,* by Nicolas Abraham and Maria Torok. Trans. Nicholas Rand. Minneapolis: University of Minnesota Press, 1986.

————. *The Gift of Death.* Trans. David Wills. Chicago: University of Chicago Press, 1995.

————. *Given Time 1: Counterfeit Money.* Trans. Peggy Kamuf. Chicago: University of Chicago Press, 1992.

————. "My Chances/Mes Chances: A Rendezvous with Some Epicurean Stereophonies." In *Taking Chances: Derrida, Pyschonanalysis and Literature,* ed. Joseph H. Smith and William Kerrigan. Baltimore: Johns Hopkins University Press, 1984.

————. *Of Grammatology.* Trans. Gayatri C. Spivak. Baltimore: Johns Hopkins University Press, 1974.

————. "Plato's Pharmacy." In *Disseminations,* trans. Barbara Johnson. Chicago: University of Chicago Press, 1981.

Descartes, René. *Discourse on Method.* Trans. J. Lafleur. New York: Macmillan, 1989.

Descombes, Vincent. *Modern French Philosophy.* Trans. L. Scott-Fox and J. M. Harding. Cambridge: Cambridge University Press, 1979.

Dreiser, Theodore. *Sister Carrie.* Ed. James L. W. West III and Alfred Kazin. London: Penguin, 1995.

Egan, Kieran. *The Educated Mind: How Cognitive Tools Shape Our Understanding.* Chicago: University of Chicago Press, 1997.

Ermarth, Elizabeth Deeds. *Realism and Consensus in the English Novel: Time, Space, and Narrative.* 2d ed. Edinburgh: Edinburgh University Press, 1998.

Foucault, Michel. "The Discourse on Language." In *The Archaeology of Knowledge,* trans. A. M. Sheridan-Smith. New York: Pantheon, 1972.

————. *The Order of Things: An Archaeology of the Human Sciences.* London: Tavistock, 1980.

Freeland, Cynthia A. "Accidental Causes and Real Explanations." In *Aristotle's Physics: A Collection of Essays,* ed. Lindsay Judson. Oxford: Clarendon Press, 1991.

Freese, Peter. *From Apocalypse to Entropy and Beyond: The Second Law of Thermodynamics in Post-war American Fiction.* Essen: Die Blaue Eule, 1997.

Gale, Monica. *Myth and Poetry in Lucretius.* Cambridge: Cambridge University Press, 1994.

Gellert, W., et al., eds. *VNR Concise Encyclopedia of Mathematics.* 1975; reprint, New York: Van Nostrand Reinhold, 1989.

Gibson, Andrew. *Towards a Postmodern Theory of Narrative.* Edinburgh: Edinburgh University Press, 1996.

Girard, René. *Le Bouc émissaire.* Paris: Bernard Grasset, 1982.

————. *Deceit, Desire, and the Novel.* Trans. Yvonne Freccero. Baltimore: Johns Hopkins University Press, 1965.

————. *Des choses cachées depuis la fondation du monde.* Paris: Bernard Grasset, 1978. Trans. Stephen Bann and Michael Metter, with revisions by the author, as *Things Hidden since the Foundation of the World* (Stanford: Stanford University Press, 1987).

————. *Je vois Satan tomber comme l'éclair.* Paris: Bernard Grasset, 1999.

————. *Mensonge romantique et vérité romanesque.* Paris: Bernard Grasset, 1961.

————. *Quand ces choses commenceront.* Interviews by Michel Terguer. Paris: Arléa, 1994.

————. *Le Violence et la sacré.* Paris: Bernard Grasset, 1972. Trans. Patrick Gregory as *Violence and the Sacred* (Baltimore: Johns Hopkins University Press, 1978).

Giusti, Ada. "L'Académie Française et l'évolution de la langue: Entretien avec Michel Serres." *Contemporary French Civilization* 20, no. 1 (1996).

Gollub, Jerry, and Harry L. Swinney. "Onset of Turbulence in a Rotating Fluid." *Physical Review Letters* 48 (1975): 927–30.

Gombrowicz, Witold. *Cosmos.* Trans. Eric Mosbacher. New York: Grove, 1970.

Greenberg, Mark L., and Lance Schachterle, eds. *Literature and Technology.* London: Associated University Press, 1992.

Griffiths, Phillips A., ed. *Contemporary French Philosophy.* Cambridge: Cambridge University Press, 1987.

Guattari, Félix. *Chaosmosis: An Ethico-aesthetic Paradigm.* Trans. Paul Bains and Julian Pefanis. Bloomington: Indiana University Press, 1995.

Hager, Lori D., ed. *Women in Human Evolution.* London: Routledge, 1997.

Hall, Stuart. "Cultural Studies and Its Theoretical Legacies." In *Stuart Hall: Critical Dialogues in Cultural Studies,* ed. David Morley and Kuan-Hsing Chen. London: Routledge, 1996.

Haraway, Donna. *Modest_Witness@Second_Millennium.FemaleMan_Meets_Onco-Mouse^{tm}.* London: Routledge, 1997.

————. *Simians, Cyborgs, and Women: The Reinvention of Nature.* London: Routledge, 1991.

Hardy, Thomas. *Far from the Madding Crowd.* Harmondsworth: Penguin, 1981.

Harris, Paul A. "The Itinerant Theorist: Nature and Knowledge/Ecology and Topology in Michel Serres." *SubStance* 83 (fall 1997): 37–58.

Hartveit, Lars. *Workings of the Picaresque in the British Novel.* Oslo: Solum Forlag, 1987.

Hayles, Katherine N. *Chaos Bound: Orderly Disorder in Contemporary Literature and Science.* Ithaca, N.Y.: Cornell University Press, 1990.

Heidegger, Martin. *Being and Time.* Trans. John MacQuarrie and Edward Robinson. New York: Harper and Row, 1962.

Hertz, Robert. *Sociologie religieuse et folklore.* Paris: Presses Universitaires de France, 1970.

Hinman, Robert B. *Abraham Cowley's World of Order.* Cambridge: Harvard University Press, 1960.

Hugo, Victor. *La Fin de Satan.* Paris: Gallimard, 1984.

Irwin, John T. *The Mystery to a Solution: Poe, Borges, and the Analytic Detective Story.* Baltimore: Johns Hopkins University Press, 1994.

Jakobson, Roman. "Closing Statement: Linguistics and Poetics." In *Style and Language,* ed. Thomas Sebeok. Cambridge: MIT Press, 1960.

Jenkins, Philip. *A History of the United States.* London: Macmillan, 1997.

Judson, Lindsay. "Chance and 'Always for the Most Part' in Aristotle." In *Aristotle's Physics: A Collection of Essays,* ed. Lindsay Judson. Oxford: Clarendon Press, 1991.

Kavanagh, Thomas M. "Michel Serres, *Les Cinq Sens.*" Book discussion. *MLN* 101, no. 4 (1986): 937–41.

Kerényi, Karl. *Hermes: Guide of Souls.* Trans. Murray Stein. Dallas: Spring Publications, 1976.

Kline, Morris. *Mathematical Thought: From Ancient to Modern Times.* Vol. 3. New York: Oxford University Press, 1972.

Lacan, Jacques. Appendix to "The Purloined Letter." Trans. Jeffrey Mehlman in *The Purloined Poe: Lacan, Derrida, and Psychoanalytic Reading,* ed. J. P. Muller and W. J. Richardson. Baltimore: Johns Hopkins University Press, 1988.

———. *The Four Fundamental Concepts of Psycho-analysis.* Trans. Alan Sheridan. New York: Norton, 1978.

Laplace, Pierre Simon, marquis de. *A Philosophical Essay on Probabilities.* Trans. Frederick William Truscott and Frederick Lincoln Emory. New York: Dover, 1951.

Latour, Bruno. "The Enlightenment without the Critique: A Word on Michel Serres' Philosophy." In *Contemporary French Philosophy,* ed. A. Phillips Griffiths. Cambridge: Cambridge University Press, 1987.

———. *Pandora's Hope: Essays on the Reality of Science Studies.* Cambridge: Harvard University Press, 1999.

———. "The Politics of Explanation: An Alternative." In *Knowledge and Reflexivity: New Frontiers in the Sociology of Knowledge,* ed. Steve Woolgar. London: Sage, 1988.

———. *We Have Never Been Modern.* Trans. Catherine Porter. Cambridge: Harvard University Press, 1993.

Lévi-Strauss, Claude. *L'Homme nu.* Paris: Librarie Plon, 1971. Trans. John Wrightman and Doreen Wrightman as *The Naked Man* (New York: Harper and Row, 1981).

Lietzmann, W. *Visual Topology.* Trans. M. Bruckheimer. New York: American Elsevier, 1965.

Livesey, Steven J. "*Metabasis:* The Interrelationship of the Sciences in Antiquity and the Middle Ages." Ph.D. diss., University of California at Los Angeles, 1982.

Lloyd, Genevieve. *The Man of Reason: "Male" and "Female" in Western Philosophy.* Minneapolis: University of Minnesota Press, 1984.

Lorenz, Edward. "Deterministic Aperiodic Flow." *Journal of Atmospheric Science* 20 (1963): 130–41.

———. "Predictability: Does the Flap of a Butterfly's Wings Set Off a Tornado in Texas?" In *The Essence of Chaos.* Seattle: University of Washington Press, 1993.

Lucretius, T. Cari. *About Reality (De Rerum Natura).* Trans. Philip F. Wooby. New York: Philosophical Library, 1973.

————. *De rerum natura.* Ed. William Augustus Merrill. New York: American Book Company, 1907.

————. *On The Nature of the Universe.* Trans. Sir Ronald Melville. With introduction and explanatory notes by Don Fowler and Peta Fowler. Oxford: Clarendon Press, 1997.

Marx, Karl, and Frederick Engels. *Collected Works.* Vol. 1. New York: International Publishers, 1975.

Maupassant, Guy de. *Selected Tales of Guy de Maupassant.* New York: Random House, 1945.

Mauss, Marcel. *The Gift.* Trans. W. D. Halls. New York: Norton, 1990.

Morley, Raoul. *French Philosophers in Conversation.* London: Routledge, 1991.

Motte, Warren F., Jr. "Clinamen Redux." *Comparative Literature Studies* 23, no. 4 (1986): 263–81.

Nethercot, Arthur H. *Abraham Cowley: The Muse's Hannibal.* London: Oxford University Press, 1931.

Norris, Frank. *McTeague: A Story of San Francisco.* London: Penguin, 1994.

Patin, M. "L'Anti-Lucrèce chez Lucrèce." In *Études sur la poésie latine.* Vol. 1. Paris: Librairie Hachette, 1868.

Paulhan, Jean. "Alain ou la preuve par l'étymologie." In *Oeuvres completes.* Paris: Cercle du livre précieux, 1966.

Paulson, William. "Le Cousin Parasite: Balzac, Serres et le démon de Maxwell." *Stanford French Review* 9 (1985): 397–414.

————. "Writing That Matters." *SubStance* 83 (fall 1997): 22–36.

————. *The Noise of Culture: Literary Texts in a World of Information.* Ithaca, N.Y.: Cornell University Press, 1988.

Pecora, Vincent. *Households of the Soul.* Baltimore: Johns Hopkins University Press, 1997.

Penelope, Julia. *Speaking Freely: Unlearning the Lies of the Fathers' Tongues.* Elmsford, N.Y.: Pergamon Press, 1990.

Perloff, Marjorie. *Radical Artifice: Writing Poetry in the Age of Media.* Chicago: University of Chicago Press, 1992.

Piaget, Jean, and Rolando Garcia. *Psychogenesis and the History of Science.* Trans. Helga Feider. New York: Columbia University Press, 1989.

Plato. *Timaeus.* Trans. Frances Cornford. New York: Liberal Arts Press, 1959.

Porush, David. "Literature as Dissipative Structure: Prigogine's Theory and the Postmodern 'Chaos' Machine." In *Literature and Technology,* ed. Mark L. Greenberg and Lance Schachterle. London: Associated University Press, 1992.

Prigogine, Ilya, and Isabelle Stengers. *La Nouvelle Alliance. Métamorphose de la science.* Paris: Éditions Gallimard, 1979.

————. *Order Out of Chaos: Man's New Dialogue with Nature.* London: Heinemann, 1984.

Prigogine, Ilya, and G. Nicolis. *Self-Organization in Non-equilibrium Systems: From Dissipative Structures to Order through Fluctuations.* New York: Wiley, 1977.

Pynchon, Thomas. *Mason and Dixon.* New York: Holt, 1997.

Ramachandran, V. S., and Sandra Blakeslee. *Phantoms of the Brain: Human Nature and the Architecture of the Mind.* London: Fourth Estate, 1999.

Robbe-Grillet, Alain. *The Voyeur.* Trans. Richard Howard. London: John Calder, 1965.

Robinson, Arthur H., and Barbara Bartz Petchenik. *The Nature of Maps: Essays toward Understanding Maps and Mapping.* Chicago: University of Chicago Press, 1976.

Rowe, John Carlos. *Henry Adams and Henry James: The Emergence of a Modern Consciousness.* Ithaca: Cornell University Press, 1976.

————. "Henry Adams's *Education* in the Age of Imperialism." In *New Essays on "The Education of Henry Adams,"* ed. John Carlos Rowe. Cambridge: Cambridge University Press, 1996.

Ruelle, David, and F. Takens. "On the Nature of Turbulence." *Communications in Mathematical Physics* 20 (1971): 167–92.

Samuels, Ernest. *Henry Adams.* Cambridge: Harvard University Press, 1989.

Schlesinger, Arthur M., Jr. *The Disuniting of America: Reflections on a Multicultural Society.* Knoxville: Whittle Direct Books, 1991.

Serres, Michel. *Angels: A Modern Myth.* Trans. Francis Cowper. Paris: Flammarion, 1994.

————. *Atlas.* Paris: Éditions Juillard, 1994.

————. *Les Cinq Sens.* Paris: Grasset et Fasquelle, 1985.

————. "Le Don de Dom Juan Ou La Naissance de la Comédie." *Critique* 250 (March 1968): 251–63.

————. *Éclaircissements: Entretiens avec Bruno Latour.* Paris: Éditions François Bourin, 1992. Trans. Roxanne Lapidus as *Conversations on Science, Culture, and Time* (Ann Arbor: University of Michigan Press, 1995).

————. *Eloge de la philosophie en langue française.* Paris, Fayard, 1996.

————. *Feux et Signaux de Brume: Zola.* Paris: Grasset, 1975.

————. *Genèse.* Paris: Grasset, 1982. Trans. Geneviève James and James Nielson as *Genesis* (Ann Arbor: University of Michigan Press, 1995).

————. *L'Hermaphrodite: Sarrasine sculpteur.* Paris: Flammarion, 1987.

————. *Hermes: Literature, Science, Philosophy.* Ed. Josué V. Harari and David Bell. Baltimore: Johns Hopkins University Press, 1982.

————. *Hermès I: La Communication.* Paris: Editions de Minuit, 1969.

————. *Hermès II: L'Interférence.* Paris: Minuit, 1972.

————. *Hermès III: La Traduction.* Paris, Minuit, 1974.

————. *Hermès IV. La Distribution.* Paris: Minuit, 1977.

————. *Hermès V: Le Passage du nord-ouest.* Paris: Minuit, 1980.

————. "Interferences et Turbulences." *Critique* 30 (January 1979): 380.

————. *Jouvences sur Jules Verne.* Paris: Éditions de Minuit, 1974.

————. "Literature and the Exact Sciences." *SubStance* 18, no. 2 (1989): 3–34.

————. *La Naissance de la physique dans le texte de Lucrèce: Fleuves et turbulences.* Paris: Minuit, 1977. Trans. Jack Hawkes as *The Birth of Physics,* ed. David Webb (Manchester: Clinamen Press, 2000).

————. *The Natural Contract.* Trans. Elizabeth MacArthur and William Paulson. Ann Arbor: University of Michigan Press, 1995.

————. *Les Origines de la géométrie.* Paris: Flammarion, 1993.

————. *The Parasite.* Trans. Lawrence R. Schehr. Baltimore: Johns Hopkins University Press, 1982.

————. *Rome, le livre des fondations.* Paris: Grasset, 1983. Trans. Felicia McCarren as *Rome: The Book of Foundations* (Stanford: Stanford University Press, 1991).

————. *Le Tiers-instruit.* Paris: François Bourin, 1991. Trans. Sheila Faria Glaser with William Paulson as *The Troubadour of Knowledge* (Ann Arbor: University of Michigan Press, 1997).

————. "Voyages extraordinaires au pays des parasites." *Libération,* March 8–9, 1980.

————. *Nouvelles du monde.* Paris: Editions J'ai Lu, 1999.

Serres, Michel, with Bruno Latour. *Conversations on Science, Culture, and Time.* Trans. Roxanne Lapidus. Ann Arbor: University of Michigan Press, 1995.

Shakespeare, William. *Romeo and Juliet.* New York: Washington Square Press, 1959.

Shestov, Lev. *Athens and Jerusalem.* Trans. Bernard Martin. Athens: Ohio University Press, 1966.

Smith, Bruce R. *The Acoustic World of Early Modern England: Attending to the O-Factor.* Chicago: University of Chicago Press, 1999.

Sokal, Alan, and Jean Bricmont. *Impostures intellectuelles.* Paris: Odile Jacob, 1997.

Sophocles. *Oedipus Rex.* In *The Theban Plays,* trans. E. F. Watling. Harmondsworth: Penguin, 1947.

Storr, Robert, ed. *Mapping.* New York: Museum of Modern Art, 1994.

Strugnell, A. R. "Diderot's *Neveu de Rameau:* Portrait of a Rogue in the French Enlightenment." In *Knaves and Swindlers: Essays on the Picaresque Novel in Europe,* ed. Christine J. Whitbourn. Oxford: Oxford University Press, 1974.

Toynbee, Arnold. *Cities on the Move.* Oxford: Oxford University Press, 1970.

Trollope, Anthony. *The Prime Minister.* Vol. 2. Oxford: Oxford University Press, 1974.

Varey, Simon. *Space and the Eighteenth-Century Novel.* Cambridge: Cambridge University Press, 1990.

Verlaine, Paul. *Oeuvres poétiques complètes.* Ed. Y.-G. Le Dantec, completed by Jacques Borel. Paris: Bibliothèque de la Pléiade, Gallimard, 1962.

Waldrop, Rosmarie. *Split Infinites.* Philadelphia: Singing Horse Press, 1998.

White, Eric. "Negentropy, Noise, and Emancipatory Thought." In *Chaos and Order: Complex Dynamics in Literature and Science.* Chicago: University of Chicago Press, 1991.

White, R. J., ed. *Political Tracts of Wordsworth, Coleridge, and Shelley.* Cambridge: Cambridge University Press, 1953.

Woolgar, Steve, ed. *Knowledge and Reflexivity: New Frontiers in the Sociology of Knowledge.* London: Sage, 1988.

Wylie, Alison. "Good Science, Bad Science, or Science as Usual?" In *Women in Human Evolution,* ed. Lori D. Hager. London: Routledge, 1997.

CONTRIBUTORS

NIRAN ABBAS is a lecturer at Kingston University. She is the editor of *Thomas Pynchon: Reading from the Margins* (Fairleigh Dickinson University Press, 2002). She has published on new technologies, theory, and literature, and her current work is on the history of automata and the posthuman.

MARIA ASSAD is professor of French language and literature at the State University of New York, Buffalo. She is the author of *Reading with Michel Serres: An Encounter with Time* (SUNY Press, 1999) and *La Fiction et la mort dans oeuvre de Stephane Mallarmé* (Peter Lang, 1987). She is translator of Raymund Schwager's *Must There Be Scapegoats* (Harper and Row, 1987) and wrote the introductory essay for *Encyclopedia of Literature and Science,* edited by Pamela Gossin (Greenwood, 2002).

HANJO BERRESSEM teaches American literature and culture at the University of Cologne. He is the author of *Pynchon's Poetics: Interfacing Theory and Text* (University of Illinois Press, 1992) and *Lines of Desire: Reading Gombrowicz's Fiction with Lacan* (Northwestern University Press, 1998). He has published numerous articles in the fields of postmodern literature, poststructuralism, psychoanalysis, cultural studies, and the relation between the hard and the soft sciences.

STEPHEN CLUCAS is senior lecturer in English and humanities at Birkbeck College. He works primarily in the fields of early modern intellectual history and history of science. His recent publications include a translation of Paolo Rossi's *Clavis Universalis* entitled *Logic and the Art of Memory* (University of Chicago Press, 2000).

STEVEN CONNOR is professor of modern literature and theory at Birkbeck College. His publications include *Charles Dickens* (Blackwell, 1985), *Samuel Beckett: Repetition, Theory, and Text* (Blackwell, 1988), *Postmodernist Culture: An Introduction to Theories of the Contemporary* (Blackwell, 1989), *Theory and Cultural Value* (Blackwell, 1992), *The English*

Novel in History, 1950 to 1995 (Routledge, 1995), *James Joyce* (Northcote House, 1996), *Dumbstruck: A Cultural History of Ventriloquism* (Oxford University Press, 2000), and *The Book of Skin* (Cornell University Press, 2003). His website at www.bbk.ac.uk/eh/skc/ makes available over fifty unpublished essays, lectures, and broadcasts.

ANDREW GIBSON is professor of modern literature and theory, and director of the masters program in Postmodernism, Literature and Contemporary Culture at Royal Holloway, University of London. His publications include *Reading Narrative Discourse: Studies in the Novel from Cervantes to Beckett* (Macmillan, 1990), *Towards a Postmodern Theory of Narrative* (Edinburgh University Press, 1996), *Postmodernity, Ethics, and the Novel* (Routledge, 1999), and *Joyce's Revenge: History, Politics, Aesthetics* (Oxford University Press, 2002). He has also edited and coedited various volumes of essays, including *Pound in Multiple Perspective* (Macmillan, 1993), *Reading Joyce's "Circe"* (European Joyce Studies, 1994), and *Joyce's "Ithaca"* (European Joyce Studies, 1996). He is currently a Leverhulme Research Fellow.

RENÉ GIRARD is Andrew B. Hammond Professor of French Language, Literature and Civilization at Stanford University and is regarded as one of the most important contemporary thinkers. His books, all of which have been translated in several languages, include *Deceit, Desire, and the Novel; Violence and the Sacred; Things Hidden since the Foundation of the World;* and *The Scapegoat*. His most recent publication is *Je vois Satan tomber comme l'éclair* (Grasset, 1999).

PAUL HARRIS is professor of English at Loyola Marymount University. He has published essays on literature and science, interdisciplinary study of time, Oulipo, and literary theory, and he is coeditor of *SubStance.*

MARCEL HÉNAFF is a distinguished philosopher and anthropologist, as well as a professor of literature at the University of California, San Diego. He is the author of *Sade, the Invention of the Libertine Body* (1978; translation published by University of Minnesota Press, 1999), *Claude Lévi-Strauss and the Making of Structural Anthropology* (1991; translation published by University of Minnesota Press, 1998), and *Le Prix de la vérité. Le don, l'argent, la philosophie* (Editions du Seuil, 2002); and coeditor with Tracy Strong of *Public Space and Democracy* (University of Minnesota Press, 2001).

WILLIAM JOHNSEN is professor of English at Michigan State University. He is the author of *Violence and Modernism: Ibsen, Joyce, Woolf* (University Press of Florida, 2003) and has published articles on transatlantic poetry, Joseph Conrad, W. B. Yeats, Henry James, modernism and postmodernism, René Girard, Northrop Frye, Flaubert, and Djuna Barnes.

WILLIAM PAULSON is professor of Romance languages and literatures at the University of Michigan. He is the author of *Enlightenment, Romanticism, and the Blind in France* (Princeton University Press, 1987), *The Noise of Culture: Literary Texts in a World of Information* (Cornell University Press, 1988), *Sentimental Education: The Complexity of Disenchantment* (Twayne, 1992), and *Literary Culture in a World Transformed: A Future for the Humanities* (Cornell University Press, 2001). He is cotranslator of two books by Michael Serres: *The Natural Contract,* with Elizabeth MacArthur (University of Michigan Press, 1995) and *The Troubadour of Knowledge,* with Sheila Glaser (University of Michigan Press, 1997).

MARJORIE PERLOFF is Sadie Dernham Patek Professor in the Humanities emerita at Stanford University and a member of the American Academy of Arts and Sciences. She is the author of *Twenty-first Century Modernism: The "New" Poetics* (Blackwell Manifesto series, 2002), *Radical Artifice: Writing in the Age of Media* (University of Chicago Press, 1991), *Wittgenstein's Ladder: Poetic Language and the Strangeness of the Ordinary* (University of Chicago Press, 1996), and *Poetry On and Off the Page: Essays for Emergent Occasions* (Northwestern University Press, 1998).

PHILIPP SCHWEIGHAUSER is currently teaching at the University of Berne. He has published on Nabokov and American realism and masculinities, and has recently completed his Ph.D. dissertation, "The Noises of American Literature: Toward a History of Literary Acoustics, 1860–1980."

ISABELLA WINKLER is a Ph.D. candidate in comparative literature, State University of New York at Buffalo. Her specialties include film theory and criticism. She is currently working on a project on Irigaray, Deleuze, Derrida, and dream interpretation.

JULIAN YATES is associate professor of English, University of Delaware. He is the author of *Error, Misuse, Failure: Object Lessons from the English Renaissance* (University of Minnesota Press, 2003).

INDEX